Navigating Interracial Borders

Navigating Interracial Borders

BLACK-WHITE COUPLES AND THEIR SOCIAL WORLDS

ERICA CHITO CHILDS

Rutgers University Press
New Brunswick, New Jersey, and London

Library of Congress Cataloging-in-Publication Data

Childs, Erica Chito, 1971–
    Navigating interracial borders : black-white couples and their social worlds / Erica
    Chito Childs.
        p. cm.
    Includes bibliographical references and index.
    ISBN 0–8135–3585–9 (hardcover : alk. paper)
    ISBN 0–8135–3586–7 (pbk. : alk. paper)
  1. Interracial marriage—United States. 2. Interracial marriage—United States—Public
opinion. 3. Interracial dating—United States. 4. Race awareness—United States. 5.
Racism—United States. 6. Race relations in motion pictures. 7. United States—Race
relations. I. Title.
  HQ1031.C485 2005
  306.84'6—dc22   2004021377

A British Cataloging-in-Publication record for this book is available from the British
Library.

Manufactured in the United States of America

To my two loves, Christopher and Jada

CONTENTS

ACKNOWLEDGMENTS

In many ways, this book really began as my own journey to understand how and why people react the way they do to seeing interracial couples. Knowing the questions and scrutiny one often goes through as part of a multiracial family, I want to give my deepest thanks to the wonderful couples who opened up to me about their lives, their families, and their experiences. Also, I am indebted to the individuals who participated in the focus groups I conducted and who discussed their views on interracial couples, because there were many who refused to even engage in a dialogue about these issues. While not all of those interviewed will agree with the arguments I put forth, please know that this is not meant to be a critique of any individual or couple, but an examination of racial attitudes, beliefs, and behaviors that are sometimes only visible through responses to interracial relationships.

I conducted most of the research for the book as a doctoral student at Fordham University, and I want to thank all of the faculty, administrators, and others there who were extremely supportive of my project, including Rosemary Cooney, Mark Chapman, Mark Naison, Rosa Giglio, and Mark Warren. I would also like to thank Clara Rodriguez, for challenging me to think about race in different ways, including my own position; Lynn Chancer, for helping me better conceptualize and organize my ideas through engaged and enthusiastic critiques; and my mentor, E. Doyle McCarthy, for her theoretical insight, serious and careful critiques of many drafts, and emotional support. Eastern Connecticut State University, in particular the sociology department and administration, was also particularly supportive as I made final revisions and navigated the publication process. Numerous colleagues have contributed to this book through their critiques, readings of drafts, comments on presentations, and support, such as Joane Nagel, Kerry Ann

Rockquemore, Abby Ferber, Elijah Anderson, Marlese Durr, Ronald Taylor, Charles Gallagher, Tyrone Forman, Alex Lyon, and Jeane Flavin. In particular, I want to thank Eduardo Bonilla-Silva and Heather Dalmage for their in-depth comments and questions on earlier drafts, which helped transform the work. Also my editor, Kristi Long, has been continually supportive and helpful.

Since this research comes out of my own experiences, I need to acknowledge and thank everyone I have encountered who influenced me through our experiences, both good and bad. I want to acknowledge my school friends and community members in Rhode Island who taught me about white privilege and still provide subtle reminders of how opposition to interracial relationships works both knowingly and unknowingly. My undergraduate experiences at San Jose State University and, most notably, my relationship with my former partner Derrick Childs also provided me with insight. As an undergraduate, I routinely wrote papers on interracial marriage but was always left wanting more from the research that existed, which mainly looked to explain the couples through an analysis of their characteristics, motives, and relationships. While being biased myself, since I was involved in an interracial relationship and surely didn't want to focus on our motives and characteristics, I still knew that the way others responded to individuals like us was as important, or probably even more important, than the couples themselves. This is what inspired me to interview other couples, to see what their experiences were, and to talk to other communities to see if the opposition I observed was individual or prevalent throughout society.

Finally, this book would not have been completed without my parents, Joan and Charles Chito, and my sister, Sandra Chito, who have always provided me with support in many ways, financial, emotional, and, most of all, the care of my two children; my late brother, Christopher, who always challenged me to think and believe that I can and will; and my children, Christopher and Jada, who made me believe that challenging interracial borders is not only important but also essential.

Navigating Interracial Borders

Introduction

THE INTERRACIAL CANARY

As for you two and the problems you're going to have, they seem
almost unimaginable. . . . I'm sure you know what you are up
against. There will be 100 million people right here in this country who will be shocked, offended, and appalled at the two of you.

*T*he 1967 Academy Award–winning
movie *Guess Who's Coming to Dinner* concluded with this warning from a
white father to his daughter and her "Negro" fiancé. That same year, the Supreme Court overturned any laws against interracial marriage as unconstitutional. Yet how does the contemporary U.S. racial landscape compare? In this
ever-changing world of race and color, where do black-white couples fit, and
has this unimaginable opposition disappeared?

While significant changes have occurred in the realm of race relations
largely from the civil rights struggle of the 1960s, U.S. society still has racial borders. Most citizens live, work, and socialize with others of the same
race—as if living within borders, so to speak—even though there are no
longer legal barriers such as separate facilities or laws against intermarriage.
Yet if these largely separate racial worlds exist, what social world(s) do black-
white couples live in and how do they navigate these racial borders? Even
more important, how do white communities and black communities view and
respond to black-white couples? In other words, do they navigate the racial
borders by enforcing, ignoring, or actively trying to dismantle them? My goal
is to explore these issues to better understand the contemporary beliefs and
practices surrounding black-white couples. This book takes an ethnographic
look at interracial couples. Unlike most ethnographies, however, it is not geo-
graphically located but rather an exploration of the social worlds of interracial couples. My data comes from varied sources, including Web sites,

black-white couples, Hollywood films, white communities, and black communities.

Black-white couples are often heralded as a sign that racial borders or barriers no longer exist. For example, in *Interracial Intimacies: Sex, Marriage, Identity, and Adoption,* Harvard law professor Randall Kennedy argues: "Americans are becoming increasingly multiracial in their tastes, affections and identities. The rates of interracial dating, marriage and adoption are inching, and in some places rocketing, upward. This trend is, in my view, a positive good. It signals that formal and informal racial boundaries are fading."[1] Furthermore, the idea that American society is "color-blind," or at least steadily moving in that direction, has become extremely popular and widely heard. The notion that not acknowledging race or refusing to "see" color is desirable has generated wide acceptance. In two major news magazines, *Time* and *Newsweek,* there have been articles on "color-blind love" and interracial couples, a phenomenon that has spread across the country.[2]

This color-blind discourse, or color-blindness, has been identified by various scholars as the dominant ideology based on a belief that refusing to see or acknowledge race is politically correct and humanistic.[3] Color-blindness is based on the belief that "if we were to make people aware of racial differences, simply by noticing we would reintroduce the illusion of race and thus inevitably polarize and divide, or perhaps even worse, stigmatize." By not acknowledging race or racial difference, the problem of race disappears—somewhat of a see no evil, hear no evil, speak no evil mentality.[4] In her work on whiteness, Ruth Frankenberg identifies color-blindness as "color-power evasiveness," where race is viewed as increasingly less significant, emphasizing the importance of the individual. The growing visibility of interracial couples is often cited as an example of how "color-blind" society is, even in matters of the heart. Yet this color-blind ideology or color-power evasiveness is problematic because it ignores, even disguises, the power and privilege that still characterizes race relations in this country.[5] Can anyone—even interracial couples—really be color-blind in a "color-conscious" society like ours?

Despite the color-blind discourse, there is also an emphasis on multiculturalism—celebrating, or at least recognizing, the role race plays in individuals' lives as members of racial and ethnic groups. Interracial couples are also seen as a symbol of this multicultural world and an example of how race and racial difference can be recognized and celebrated. Frankenberg defines this alternate discourse of race consciousness as an insistence on the importance of recognizing race and difference, understood in historical, political, social, or cultural terms rather than essentialist ones. Unlike color-blind ideologies, this way of thinking emphasizes the need to be race conscious. Yet, these ambivalent and contradictory discourses on race tell us that race is at once all and nothing, where the message is that "things" (race relations) are getting better, yet the boundaries between black and white somehow persist.

Nowhere is this complex intersection of racialized views more prominent than with the issue of black-white unions. A 2003 *Time* magazine piece on "Color-Blind Love" argues that individuals' choices in partners is increasingly becoming color-blind, but then details stories of racist white families, black women picketing an interracial couple's home, and a white woman who married a black man but forbids her white daughter (from an earlier relationship) to date black boys.[6] In the 2000 *Newsweek* article "Love without Borders," the author argues that "Americans are intermarrying like never before, and they're reshaping life couple by couple."[7] The piece also reports as a side note that one interethnic Asian couple "are spared the obvious stares that white and black mixed couples sometimes face."[8] If love erases racial borders and racial borders are eroding, then why are black-white couples capable of eliciting stares and still so uncommon?[9] I argue that black-white interracial couples, rather than being a sign of the breaking down of racial borders, enable us to see how racial borders still exist. Society is stratified by race, and black-white couples exist on this racial divide. Opposition to black-white relationships still exists, yet like contemporary racism it is more subtle and harder to see. Therefore, it is important to consider the various discourses of color-blindness, race consciousness, and those in between that are drawn upon by black and white communities, within media and popular culture, and even by black-white couples themselves when discussing the meaning and acceptance of interracial relationships.

Based on the low rates of black-white intermarriage and the obvious differences between these unions and other interracial relationships, the issue of black-white relationships and the views of whites and blacks on these relationships needs to be studied separately from other racial combinations of interracial couples.[10] Opposition to relationships between blacks and whites is still based on the belief that these unions violate one of the greatest taboos.[11] In the United States, the concept of race is not based simply on skin color or ancestry; it also has social, political, and economic meanings and consequences specific to different racial groups. The strong emotions, such as fear and loathing and negative visual images, associated with blacks fuel antiblack attitudes and contribute to the emotional opposition of most whites toward interracial relationships between blacks and whites.[12] Many studies have found that whites, especially, consider an interracial relationship involving a black person to be much less acceptable than one involving a Latino or Asian person.[13] This points to the fact that black-white intermarriages represent far greater racial transgressions than those between other ethnic and "racial" groups. These marriages may be small in number, but their significance is socially and politically great, serving as an indicator of the state of relations between blacks and whites in society.

While all these issues are reasons why I believe this book and research is important, my own story also brought me to this research. The social world of black-white couples is the world I navigate. From my own experiences, I have seen the ways most whites respond to an interracial relationship. Growing up white, second-generation Portuguese in a predominantly white Rhode Island suburb, race never was an issue, or at least not one I heard about.[14] After moving to Los Angeles during high school and beginning college, I entered into a relationship with an African American man (who I eventually married), never imagining what it would bring. My family did not disown me or hurl racial slurs. Still, in many ways I learned what it meant to be an "interracial couple" and how this was not what my family, community, or countless unknown individuals had scripted for me. Not many whites ever said outright that they were opposed to the relationship, yet their words and actions signaled otherwise.

One of the most telling examples occurred a few years into our relationship. An issue arose when my oldest sister's daughter wanted to attend her prom with an African American schoolmate she was dating. My sister and her husband refused to let him in the house the night of the prom or any other time because, they said, he was "not right" for her. It was clear to everyone, however, that skin color was the problem. To this day, my niece will tell you that her parents would never have accepted her with a black man. Yet my sister and her family never expressed any opposition to my relationship and even seemed supportive, in terms of inviting us over to their house, giving wedding and holiday gifts, and so forth. Although my sister never openly objected to my relationship, she drew the line with her daughter— quite literally enforcing a racial boundary to protect her daughter and family from blackness. For me, this personal story and the countless stories of other interracial couples point to the necessity of examining societal attitudes, beliefs, images, and practices regarding race and, more specifically, black-white relations. Interracial couples—because of their location on the line between white and black—often witness or bring forth racialized responses from both whites and blacks. As with my sister, opposition may exist yet is not visible until a close family member or friend becomes involved or wants to become involved interracially.

Looking at the social worlds of black-white couples allows the exploration of many stories. The stories of interracial couples, the stories white and black communities tell about interracial relationships, and the stories we see in films about interracial couples can all be looked at collectively. They share many parts although the individuals and their circumstances are much different. What is similar are the surrounding images, discourses, and communities' responses. While I argue that there is no one type of individual who dates and marries interracially, there are certain collective images and beliefs about interracial couples that exist, regardless of the individual characteristics of the couple. This book is about those images and beliefs, or, in other words, the societal responses and understandings of interracial couples—assumptions, expectations, and perceived realities. It is not only explicit opposition that is critiqued but also the surprise, confusion, and inability of others to recognize or understand the relationship that contributes to the marginalization of black-white couples, somewhere beyond the borders between black and white. The racial boundaries that persist become clearer when we take a closer look at whites' and blacks' beliefs about who belongs with whom or who is imagined as partners. I notice this process often. Most recently, I was at an academic conference where a well-known black scholar was speaking, and he referred to his wife in the audience. After the talk, a white scholar in the same field asked if the speaker's wife was there. I answered yes and pointed to her, a white woman sitting a few rows in front of where we were standing. The white scholar appeared confused and said, "Where is she?" looking directly at the back of the white woman I was pointing to. Again I pointed, this time saying, "The white woman with blond hair." He looked at me confused, "Really . . . hmm." I did not interpret his expression and confusion as opposition. He just clearly had not expected, assumed, or even imagined his black colleague would have a white wife.

Interracial Relationships as a Miner's Canary

It is these community and societal responses, as well as the images and beliefs produced and reproduced about these unions that provide the framework within which to understand the issue of interracial couplings. Underlying these responses and images is a racial ideology, or, in other words, a dominant discourse, that posits interracial couples and relationships as deviant.

Still, the significance of these discourses and what exactly they reveal about race in society can be hard to see. For some of us the effects of race are all too clear, while for others race—and the accompanying advantages and disadvantages—remain invisible. As a white woman, it was only through my relationship, and raising my two children, that I came to see how race permeates everything in society. Being white yet now part of a multiracial family, I experienced, heard, and even thought things much differently than before, primarily because whites and blacks responded to me differently than before.[15] I think of the metaphor of the "miner's canary"—the canaries miners use to alert them to a poisonous atmosphere. In *The Miner's Canary: Enlisting Race, Resisting Power, Transforming Power*, Lani Guinier and Gerald Torres argue that the experiences of racial minorities, like the miner's canary, can expose the underlying problems in society that ultimately affect everyone, not just minorities. In many ways, the experiences of black-white couples are a miner's canary, revealing problems of race that otherwise can remain hidden, especially to whites. The issues surrounding interracial couples—racialized/sexualized stereotypes, perceptions of difference, familial opposition, lack of community acceptance—should not be looked at as individual problems, but rather as a reflection of the larger racial issues that divide the races. Since interracial couples exist on the color-line in society—a "borderland" between white and black—their experiences and the ways communities respond to these relationships can be used as a lens through which we can understand contemporary race relations.[16] Their experiences are a reflection of how individuals and groups in society respond to interracial couples; through these responses, we see how the interracial couples' relationships and everyday experiences are "racialized," meaning that the relationship takes on or is given a racial meaning within the context of American society.[17] Therefore, these relationships need to be examined not only by looking at the couples themselves but also by the ways that interracial couples and their children are received and understood by their relatives, neighbors, communities, and the larger society. In essence, the ways that interracial couples are socially constructed within society mirrors the social construction of race and racial groups.

Studying Interracial Couples: Past, Present, and Future

Like race, interracial relationships between blacks and whites have been given various meanings, symbolizing many things over the history of this country. From an assimilationist perspective, interracial marriage has been heralded as the way to erase racial difference and the ultimate step for a racial group in blending with the dominant white society. Yet, simultaneously, black-white marriage has been viewed as the ultimate problem of race relations, a symbol of racial impurity among whites or an internalization of racism among blacks. Though there has been a small increase in black-white marriages, the opposition to these relationships has not necessarily disappeared. No matter how black-white relationships are viewed, what is intriguing about them are the responses they bring forth from the white and black communities. While the ability of two individuals of different races to love each other (even in growing numbers) cannot change the social structure of race in this country, the societal responses to these relationships—the images produced, the discourses used, the meanings attached—does give us insight into the social and political hierarchy of race. To understand the dominant images and beliefs about black-white couplings and just how interracial couples are socially constructed through group responses, theories of symbolic interaction, social construction, and critical race theory are central. It is only in a society where race is "a fundamental dimension of social organization and cultural meaning" that the idea of an *interracial couple* acquires its social meaning.[18]

There is a significant body of literature that addresses the issue of interracial marriage and relationships specifically, yet there is little research on the ways interracial couples are socially constructed and the societal responses to interracial relationships. One of the major critiques of most existing research on interracial couplings is that they reify race and neglect to examine it as a changing sociohistorical concept and construct. Put differently, much of the research is rooted in "essentialist" thinking about race, thereby reproducing uncritical conceptions of interracial couples. When researchers study interracial relationships without first acknowledging race and racial groups as socially constructed and subject to conflict and change, they reproduce the idea of racial difference as a *real* and *natural* phenomenon: "discrete racial and ethnic groups are assumed to exist and engage in intermarriage."[19] Rather than challenging the racialized ways that groups in American society respond to these unions, researchers have tended to approach the issue of interracial relationships as an isolated phenomenon that can be explained through a study of the couples themselves.

Much of the research relies on the assimilationist framework, using intermarriage as an indicator of assimilation of the minority group or a site of comparison with same-race couples.[20] This framework has a number of shortcomings, especially when discussing black-white interracial marriage: it tends to use an immigrant analogy for racial groups, reduces race to ethnicity, and does not take into consideration the different ways racial groups are constructed and conceptualized within society.[21] Also, in an assimilationist framework that focuses on the couple, interracial marriage is seen as the final stage of assimilation, a sign of improving race relations that masks the overwhelming opposition that may exist toward the couple.

Furthermore, a large number of the studies that look at interracial relationships objectify the couple by looking to explain or understand the relationship and the reasons for coming together rather than explain or understand how (and why) interracial relationships are viewed and treated differently than same-race unions within our society. Even the studies that do explore issues involving interracial couples from a social constructionist perspective and address societal responses lack any research on community or group attitudes and beliefs. The research tends to be based simply on the experiences and interpretations of the interracial couples without exploring the attitudes and views of the couples' communities. Traditionally, works within the social sciences on interracial marriage have sought to identify the characteristics of individuals in interracial relationships to account for the occurrence of interracial marriage, or to compare these unions to same-race unions. Many of the studies that directly address the issue of interracial couples have tended to focus on the couple as a relatively isolated phenomenon, using either psychological[22] and/or sociological theories to explain how or why they came together,[23] or evaluating the characteristics of the couple, looking at their demographic similarities and differences.[24] These various works on interracial couples all express or imply that interracial couples are inherently different from same-race couples, therefore making it necessary to explain, account for, and/or describe their relationships.[25] By comparing interracial couples to same-race couples, same-race couples are established as the standard or the norm. It is only within a society such as America's, which places such emphasis on race and racial groups, that the idea of an interracial couple has meaning. In particular, studying interracial couples for their motives, their characteristics, or their similarity/difference to same-race couples comes out of a belief or assumption that interracial couples are different.[26] Also problematic are a number of recent works that offer qualitative accounts that promote a multicultural understanding of interracial relationships yet do not fully analyze these relationships' significance or critique societal responses.[27]

Interracial sex and marriage remains a hotly debated topic. A number of recent works explore the larger implications of interracial relationships. These studies take a variety of different approaches, such as Abby Ferber's

White Man Falling: Race, Gender, and White Supremacy, which emphasizes the connection between white supremacist discourse and the fear of interracial sexuality, arguing that the white supremacist's obsession with preventing interracial sexuality is based on mainstream white American views on interracial relationships. Heather Dalmage's *Tripping on the Color-Line: Black-White Multiracial Families in a Racially Divided World* explores "the ways in which multiracial family members' identities, politics, and communities both shape and are shaped by the color line," drawing from in-depth interviews with interracial couples and families.[28] Dalmage's work takes the focus off the couples and instead looks at the issue of interracial families within a discussion of other issues such as census categories, transracial adoption, and housing segregation. Three other works—Renee C. Romano's *Race Mixing: Black-White Marriage in Postwar America*, Rachel Moran's *Interracial Intimacy: The Regulation of Race and Romance*, and Randall Kennedy's *Interracial Intimacies*—provide extensive documentation of legal, political, and social barriers to interracial marriage and parenting. Romano documents the history of interracial relationships and uses the experiences of interracial couples to show how far we have come as a society and how far we still need to go. Both Kennedy and Moran also provide historical and legal analyses of the issue of interracial intimacy, exploring how racial intimacy has shaped and in turn been affected by laws and customs in the United States. While the works of Moran and Romano emphasize the opposition to interracial relationships that still exists, Kennedy's work takes a different approach, describing the use of race in choosing or accepting relationships as a form of racial discrimination, and his work targets what he describes as state-supported discouragements of interracial intimacy in marriage and parenting:

> As I seek to persuade readers to eschew state-supported racial separatism in its various manifestations, I also urge that we all embrace a positive ideal: a cosmopolitan ethos that welcomes the prospect of genuine, loving interracial intimacy. . . . The prominence of race in our society does not mean that individuals must or should continue to use race as a factor in choosing their intimate affiliations. We are free to restructure and improve the society we have inherited, and we should do so. For now, one way to accomplish that is to view racial discrimination of *any* sort, even in the most intimate spheres of our lives, as a cause for concern, a matter worthy of worry, something that requires careful justification.[29]

Kennedy's focus is on illustrating how these attempts to prevent interracial marriage and parenting are problematic on a number of levels, arguing that "against the tragic backdrop of American history, the flowering of multiracial intimacy is a profoundly moving and encouraging development."[30]

While all of these studies have provided important perspectives on understanding interracial relationships, my study is different because it places societal responses to interracial relationships at the center and seeks to understand the relationships through these societal responses and the voices of both white and black communities. To look at the social worlds of black-white couples, I draw from research within black and white communities, cultural images, and interviews with couples themselves, which is significantly different than previous studies. Any study of interracial couples needs to begin with the framework that race is a social, cultural, and political construction. Drawing from critical race theory, it is "human interaction rather than natural differentiation [that] must be seen as the source and continued basis for racial categorization."[31] Just as race is a social construction, interracial couples, or rather the idea of couples being interracial (different from the norm of same-race couples) are also a social construction.

The Social Construction of Interracial Couples

The idea of race has been produced and reproduced through the construction of racial groups and social interaction, having real consequences in beliefs and practices.[32] As F. James Davis argues, "the black population in the United States is a socially constructed category backed by law, not a grouping established by physical anthropologists or biologists. Both the definition and the treatment of the group are based on publicly held beliefs about race and racial mixing, not on scientific conclusions." Therefore, the images and meanings attached to black-white relationships are not simply produced by the couples themselves but rather are constructed—socially, culturally, politically—in the various realms of society and by the varying social groups. The couples' own understandings of their identities and relationships are undoubtedly shaped by the responses of others and the images of interracial couples that exist. Therefore the couples' experiences and narratives need to be examined within the context of an analysis of community responses and beliefs as well as the larger social structure and social institutions. The study of interracial unions should not be reduced to a study of the individuals but rather should focus on "the beliefs, tendencies and practices of the group taken collectively."[33]

In my research, interracial relationships are significant—culturally, socially, and politically—not because of the characteristics of the individual couples, but rather because of the larger sociopolitical meaning that these couplings have for the white and black cultural communities within which they occur. As Omi and Winant argue, our images and ideas about race, and in this case interracial couples, "testify to the way a racialized social structure shapes racial experience and conditions meaning." Though interracial relationships and marriage have traditionally been seen as an important measure of group assimilation and evidence of progress toward a multicultural society, black-white couples (or even the possibility of a relationship) can often invoke racialized retreats into separate black and white spaces. I use the term *interracial borders* because within the social worlds of interracial couples borders certainly exist—borders between black and white and between race and sexuality. Throughout this work, I also add stories of my own border crossing—as part of an interracial family and as a researcher traveling the racial landscape of black-white couples, white communities, and black communities.

Studying the Social Worlds of Interracial Couples

This book is about interracial relationships—the experiences of black-white couples, the attitudes and beliefs of white and black communities, and popular culture and media depictions. It is a story about the images and discourses that have been constructed about interracial relationships and how these images and discourses contribute to the construction and maintenance of racial borders. I approach the study of black-white couplings, understanding these interracial unions as socially constructed through not only the couples' experiences but also the larger society—family, neighborhoods, communities, churches, schools, workplace, and other social institutions. This will not be a nationwide representative study of attitudes, beliefs, or occurrences that can be generalized. That is neither feasible nor desirable. Rather, this book provides an ethnographic look at the social worlds of interracial couples through in-depth interviews, focus groups, film analysis, media examples, and Internet research, as well as some use of census and survey data where needed.[34] The goal is to illustrate the cultural and collective stories that are told by and about interracial couples.[35] Using the critical race theory strategy of storytelling as a methodological tool, the stories of interracial couples, and of white and black communities, as told by individuals, the media, filmmakers, and the Internet are understood not as singular accounts or examples, but as "social events that instruct us about social processes, social structures, and social situations."[36] Narrative in this context is important, since I will pay particular attention to the words used to discuss, describe, and explain interracial relationships and how those words compare to the choices the narrators have made in their lives. For instance, what does it mean when a white person says she is completely supportive of others marrying interracially, even though she never would because she has nothing in common with black people. Would you say that individual is supportive, negative, or somewhere in between?

Analyzing such statements is an integral part of my research. Discursive strategies are important because they are used to construct attitudes and experiences in very particular ways. As critical race theorists argue, "our social world, with its rules, practices and assignments of prestige and power, is not fixed; rather, we construct it with words, stories and silence."[37] In this research, it is noteworthy not only what the respondents say but also how they say it and what they leave out. When studying the issues of race, it is essential to critically examine what people say, particularly since the ways individuals respond to interracial couples may have changed, with opposition becoming more subtle and coded within a "color-blind discourse." As Eduardo Bonilla-Silva argues, "the language of color blindness is slippery, apparently contradictory, and often subtle. . . . the rhetorical maze of confusing, ambivalent answers to straight questions; of answers speckled with disclaimers such as 'I don't know, but . . . ' or 'Yes and no.'"[38] The discourse that an individual or group employs can be studied to reveal the meanings attached to the issue being discussed. Michel Foucault argues it is necessary to question what is the meaning or significance of the discourse against sexuality—in this case, interracial sexuality—"what reciprocal effects of power and knowledge they ensure . . . and what conjunction and what force relationships make their utilization necessary."[39] In other words, if interracial sexuality is constructed as deviant, or viewed as undesirable, it is important to consider why, what purpose it serves, and whom it benefits.

Life on the Border: Narratives of Black-White Couples

From 1999 to 2001, I interviewed fifteen black-white heterosexual couples who were referred to me through personal and professional contacts, and some of whom I encountered randomly in public.[40] They ranged in age from twenty to sixty-nine and all were in committed relationships of two to twenty-five years. Nine were married. The couples' education levels varied. All respondents had finished high school or its equivalent; twenty-one respondents had attended some college and/or had received a bachelor's degree; and four respondents had advanced degrees. The socioeconomic status of the couples ranged from working class to upper middle class. The respondents included a college student, waitress, manager, factory worker, university professor, social worker, salesperson, and postal worker. All couples lived in the northeastern United States, from Maine to Pennsylvania, yet many of the couples had traveled extensively and had lived in other parts of the country, including California, Florida, and the South.

I interviewed the couples together, since I was interested in their experiences, accounts, narratives, and the ways they construct their lives and create their "selves" and their identities as "interracial couples."[41] The interviews lasted for two to three hours, and I ended up with more than forty hours of interview data.[42] As mentioned earlier, I analyzed the couples' narratives for indications of larger social processes, since the narratives reveal "the social world" the narrator shares with others.[43] These accounts are seen not only as "descriptions, opinions, images, or attitudes about race relations but also as 'systems of knowledge' and 'systems of values' in their own right, used for the discovery and organization of reality."[44]

The Separate Worlds of Whites and Blacks

To explore the larger cultural and sociopolitical meanings that black-white couplings have for both the white and black communities in which they occur, a significant portion of this work is based on original qualitative research in white communities and black communities about their ideas, beliefs, and views on interracial sexuality and marriage. Community research was conducted to further explore the responses to interracial couples that are found in social groups and communities—family, friends, neighbors, religious groups, schools, etc.[45] The ways that these couples provide the occasion for groups to express and play out their ideas and prejudices about race and sex are integral to understanding the social construction of interracial couples. There were numerous social realms, such as the workplace, recreation centers, and neighborhoods, where this research could have been conducted, but I chose churches and universities as community sites because the black-white couples interviewed all had very strong views and often significant experiences in these two social institutions.[46] In particular, the couples indicated that certain churches were more or less accepting of interracial couples based on their own experiences or beliefs, yet the couple's beliefs were often in direct contrast to each other. Similarly, the couples all discussed their college campus and/or college experience as one that either encouraged or discouraged interracial dating. Using grounded theory, I draw from the black-white couples' narratives and experiences to conduct community research that can be analyzed in context with these couples' responses.

Based on these views and experiences, I selected three different denominations of churches that couples either attended or avoided: a predominantly white Catholic church, a predominantly black Baptist church, and a racially diverse Unitarian Universalist church. All the churches were middle- to upper-middle class and located in the Northeast.[47] Three different universities were selected that reflected the couples' experiences, including an elite Ivy League university, a private university, and a state university.[48] The idea was to choose churches and student groups on the college campuses that identified or could be classified as white or black, in order to explore the attitudes and beliefs in the context of a racial community. Church communities, like the neighborhoods they draw from, are often racially segregated. College campuses, even if they have a racially diverse student population, are also often racially divided. The only exception was the Unitarian Universalist church; yet even in its diversity of people and views, it still reinforced the ideas that were heard among the white and black groups.

I used similar research methodology at the churches and the universities. At the churches, I conducted an initial interview with the priest, minister, or reverend, and then I arranged group meetings with parishioners. At the universities, I conducted an initial interview with an administrator (or administrators) familiar with issues of race relations and student life, and then I scheduled meetings with a predominantly black and a predominantly white student organization on campus. In the interviews with the church officials and university administrators, I asked them about race relations in their institutions, their perceptions on the issue of interracial unions and student/church member experiences, as well as any other relevant incidents that may have occurred. Since the goal was to explore community responses rather than individual beliefs, I conducted focus-group interviews with the church members and student groups. "A focus group allows the researcher to collect data in a social context, where participants share their views in the context of others' views."[49] At the churches, the focus groups were conducted at a weekly or monthly meeting of church members, and at the universities, the focus groups were conducted at the student organizations' weekly meetings. In all focus groups, I asked the respondents to discuss their views on race relations in general and their views and perceptions of interracial dating and marriage. The focus groups at the churches and universities consisted of both men and women, averaging eighteen to twenty people for the church groups and fifteen to thirty people for the university student groups. For these focus groups, emphasis was placed on their perceptions of group and societal views, though many participants also offered personal perspectives and experiences. I also visited the churches and universities on at least three separate occasions before and after the focus groups.

Imagining the Social World: Media and Popular Culture Depiction

Since the couples' experiences and the communities' views are undoubtedly shaped by the ideas, images, and beliefs that exist within contemporary discourse and culture, I also integrate a discussion and critical analysis of media, popular culture (focusing on mainstream American film), and Web sites.[50] Popular culture images and depictions are particularly important because community responses are not individual; rather, they are often based in these larger images and discourses that exist in society.[51] "Media culture also provides the materials out of which any people construct their sense of class, of ethnicity and race, of nationality, of sexuality, of 'us' and 'them.'"[52] Using content analysis—like the transcript of an interview—I read and reviewed language and images in print or on Web sites for content and meaning as "social products in their own right, as well as what they claim to represent."[53]

I integrate the discussion of mainstream films that contain depictions or storylines with black-white couples throughout the chapters. Given the multilayered dynamics operating in most films (Web sites) and the varied social locations of the viewers, there are multiple readings on any given text: people invest very different meanings in the images they see.[54] While it is impossible to know how the varied audience "sees" or receives the film, there is a dominant ideology or "dominant gaze" that is produced; in other words, there is a "subtle (or not so subtle) invitation to the viewer to empathize and identify with its viewpoint as natural, universal, and beyond challenge."[55] In particular, I explore the role of these mediums in the production and reproduction of certain ideas and discourses about interracial unions. I also discuss the relative lack of depictions of interracial couples, as well as the dominant images that tend to reproduce the idea of interracial couples as deviant. Drawing on recent works within the realm of cultural studies and film theory,[56] the images of black-white couples in the selected films are discussed and understood through the concept of the "gaze." The idea of a "dominant gaze" is used to show how American popular film has a tendency to replicate through narrative and imagery the racial inequalities and biases that exist in society.[57] In this work, I use the concept of the "dominant gaze" to understand the way interracial relations are made to be marginal and deviant within an intraracial perspective or worldview that seeks to bolster its own legitimacy. Through the racial images that are created—positive or negative, real or imagined— there is a "power to define difference, to reinforce boundaries, and to reproduce an ideology that maintains a certain status quo."[58]

I argue that the infrequent yet growing interest in portraying interracial intimacy does not signal acceptance; rather, mainstream film (even in the depictions of black-white couples) and Web sites still reveal a social structure that privileges intraracial unions. The images in these films socially construct interracial couples as deviant, and these films provide certain ways of thinking about or understanding interracial relationships that serve to reproduce racial boundaries, even when attempting to challenge the existing racial hierarchy. By looking at film depictions and Internet sites of black-white couples, with the responses of black and white community members and the experiences of interracial couples, I argue that certain images and ideas about black-white couples exist and are expressed or articulated not only in film but also by whites and blacks in society. These images and depictions of black-white couples reveal the underlying beliefs about interracial unions that are prevalent within both white and black communities—and are understood as not only a reflection of dominant beliefs but also a powerful influence on what people believe.[59]

Drawing from this varied research data, I integrate the common threads to talk about the social worlds of black-white couples and, more important, collective societal responses. I draw from different sources, including media, to show that certain patterns exist in the experiences, words, and actions of interracial relationships. At many points in the book, I offer critical analysis of the research, pointing out what is "culturally problematic" about participants' stories and what may produce narrative difficulties, complexities, or inconsistencies.[60] Identifying these inconsistencies or complexities is important not just for validity but also to place the couples' experiences within the larger contextual framework of society.[61] The process of analysis and interpretation can be difficult, especially when interviewees discuss an event or conversation that is explicitly racial yet do not identify it in racial terms. A number of researchers have grappled with these types of contradictions by contrasting the participant's statement or interpretation against the actual words used or actions taken, to illustrate that what the respondent reports may not reflect or be consistent with what they do or experience.[62] "Relying mainly on words or actors' narratives, for example, can clarify a perspective on the lifeworld, but unless a context is clearly articulated, the definition of the situation may be lost."[63] The shared rather than individual reconstructions of experiences and interpretations of social reality provide a connection to the larger structural component of race relations and, more specifically in this case, interracial unions.[64] By emphasizing the discourses used and the practices described by the interviewees, I identify shared interpretations and patterns. While this research is qualitative and not generalizable to all interracial couples and communities, the experiences and narratives discussed here raise issues that allow the impact of racial discourses, racialized images, and the lingering racism of contemporary society to be examined. While the couples' experiences are used as a framework to begin the discussion, the responses of society—in the form of families, communities, and media—are most relevant to understanding the issue of black-white relationships and why these unions are still perceived in certain ways. Therefore, the experiences of black-white couples and the ways they discuss these experiences and the responses of others will be explored for the meanings interracial relationships have for the communities in which they occur.

The Plan of the Book

In chapter 1 I look at the ways black-white couples navigate racial borders, through a discussion of their perceptions of their own identities, their relationships, and the larger societal responses. I also lay the framework for the argument that opposition to black-white relationships still exists, yet it often takes keen eyes and ears to detect it. In chapters 2 and 3, I explore the collective views of racial communities and the ways whites and blacks respond to black-white unions. Drawing from focus-group interviews with white and black church communities, popular culture images, and couples' experiences, I emphasize the relevance of the ways whites and blacks discuss their views on interracial couples in relation to their lifestyles and practices. Drawing on the symbolic interactionist tradition, certain meanings are attached to interracial couplings that are not intrinsic but arise from how the individual or group acts toward the interracial couple.[65] In chapters 4 and 5, I explore the experiences of black-white couples and the societal responses of white and blacks in two distinct social institutions: the family and the college campus. In chapter 6, I explore the dominant images and discourses about interracial couples on the Internet. I identify the three main categories of Web sites that feature images or discussion of interracial couples and discuss their significance, meaning, and relevance to societal views. In the conclusion, I briefly summarize the main arguments of this book—that racial borders exist and that when crossed by interracial couples certain responses are elicited—and provide some thoughts about the future of research in this area. Throughout each chapter, I attempt to connect these various elements to illustrate how interracial unions have social and political implications that can be studied from the individual experiences of couples through the community responses and beliefs about these unions.

CHAPTER 1

Loving across the Border

THROUGH THE LENS OF BLACK-WHITE COUPLES

A black person and a white person coming together has been given many names—miscegenation, amalgamation, race mixing, and jungle fever—conjuring up multiple images of sex, race, and taboo. Black-white relationships and marriages have long been viewed as a sign of improving race relations and assimilation, yet these unions have also been met with opposition from both white and black communities. Overall, there is an inherent assumption that interracial couples are somehow different from same-race couples. Within the United States, the responses to black-white couplings have ranged from disgust to curiosity to endorsement, with the couples being portrayed as many things—among them, deviant, unnatural, pathological, exotic, but always sexual. Even the way that couples are labeled or defined as "interracial" tells us something about societal expectations. We name what is different. For example, a male couple is more likely to be called a "gay couple" than a gender-mixed couple is to be called a "heterosexual couple."

Encompassed by the history of race relations and existing interracial images, how do black-white couples view themselves, their relationships, and the responses of their families and communities? And how do they interpret these familial and community responses? Black-white couples, like all of us, make meaning out of their experiences in the available interpretive frameworks and often inescapable rules of race relations in this country.[1] Individuals have the ability to construct multiple identities and views, yet we still operate within social groups and a social structure that provide available "scripts" to follow.[2]

Though the fifteen couples I interviewed for this study varied in many aspects—education, income, religion, geographical location—there were similarities in the discussions of their experiences.[3] Despite these similarities, the couples' narratives were often divided between those couples who minimized the racial aspects of their identities, their experiences, and others' responses, and those couples who emphasized race and the role it played in their experiences and the ways others treated them. The different discursive strategies that the couples used mirror the competing discourses of color-blindness and race consciousness that are found in society. Using this framework of competing discursive strategies, I will explore the couples' experiences and the ways in which they describe them.

Black, White, and Interracial

The framework of this study is based on the concept of looking at how groups in society construct certain ideas about black and white individuals who come together, in essence creating "interracial couples" since only in a society that invests meaning in race is the term (or practice) even significant.[4] I gave couples an opportunity to define who they are and how they see themselves by beginning each interview with questions about identity, being that racial identity is central to the construction of interracial couples (without the use of race as an identity we would not have "interracial" couples). Certain patterns emerged in the individuals' identification choices and in the way they discussed their experiences. Racial identity is a complex issue within society, and not surprisingly those in interracial relationships often struggle with their racial identity. The ways couples articulated their racial identities differed. They either emphasized or deemphasized their racial identity and continued to do so while discussing their relationships and societal responses.

Among the black partners, ten individuals clearly stated that they were black or African American. They emphasized that their racial identity, affiliation, and "blackness" was integral to how they saw themselves and how others viewed them. Lee, a thirty-three-year-old retail salesperson living in Massachusetts with his white partner, Jill, a twenty-eight-year-old office manager, and their three-year-old daughter, India, described his identity in a typical way:

> LEE: I just call myself black. I'm just a black man. That's it. And I am a black man before anything else. Before my relationship I was a black man and by myself I still get treated the same way.

Lee described his racial identity as something that is always there and inescapable. The way others treat him is based on his race, according to his statements.

In contrast, the five other black individuals (Victor, David, Frank, Sharon, and Nancy) were more ambivalent, acknowledging that they were black but that they preferred not to think in racial terms. For example, Sharon, a forty-seven-year-old office worker married to Kevin, a forty-nine-year-old musician, identified herself as "African American" but added that she often replies that she is simply part of the "human race." Similarly, Victor, a thirty-five-year-old middle school teacher (married to Lisa, a thirty-three-year-old middle school teacher) identified as "obviously black but (I'm) human not a color." To further illustrate how he thinks about his racial identity, his remarks on growing up in the South and being one of the first black kids to integrate previously white establishments such as grade school and Boy Scouts, are noteworthy:

> VICTOR: I can remember being one of the first black kids to integrate. I always found myself . . . even the school I teach in today, I'm the only black teacher. I have to admit I like being the only one, or the first one [black person]. But I always got treated well . . . however, I have seen the ugly side, like being yelled at by white adults as a child, that I didn't belong at the school with the white kids . . . but my mom refused to let it bother us, she always said you are no better than white people, you are no worse than they are, you are all people. . . . I can remember going to school with white kids and thinking they're just like me. You know, they don't like homework, they're afraid of this, they like to dance, they like to party, they swear . . . I always made friends. Well, I always felt like I didn't want to be treated like a color and I'm not going to let them think of themselves as a color. We're people. You're human, I'm human . . . I refuse to look at color. I want to see your character. I want to see your integrity. I don't care what color you are.

Through Victor's narrative, the way he negotiates his social environment reflects how he conceptualizes his (and others') identity. In the face of obviously overwhelming prejudice as a child integrating white places where the whites did not want him, he downplayed the role of race. So, when he went to school with white kids, he focused on his realization that the white kids were the same as him. In his narrative, he discussed these issues as an individual who has control over how he is viewed and how he views others. Victor deemphasized his membership in a racial group that others effectively use to categorize and exclude him. He stated that he enjoys being the only black teacher in his school and does not see this as a lack of diversity or as a reflection of the inequality between blacks and whites.

Among the white partners, all fifteen reported little or no attachment to their racial identity, either stating that race was not meaningful or did not play a significant role in how they thought of themselves. Kim, a fifty-five-year-old nurse who lives in Boston and is married to Stanley, a sixty-three-year-old anesthesiologist, gave a typical response: "I am quote/unquote white [*gesturing quotation marks with her fingers*] . . . but I'm just a happy person . . . it's hard for me to think about race since it just isn't my reality." For some of the white partners, their ethnic identities played a more salient role in defining who they are, acknowledging they are white but also identifying with their ethnicity. For example, Jill identified herself as "a white Irish woman but I wouldn't say I describe myself as white . . . I like to be around different people . . . I have very diverse beliefs."

These responses can be understood in a number of ways: "white privilege" allows whites to ignore their own racial identifications; whiteness is believed to be a nonracialized standard. Yet ignoring race can also be due to people's relationships and memberships in an interracial family. Many times their attachment to their racial or ethnic heritage has lessened, especially when there is a heightened awareness of the existence of racism and inequality perpetuated by whites on blacks. Bill, a white high-school teacher in his fifties, discussed this issue in relation to his wife, Gwen, a college professor in her forties:

> BILL: Gwen answered [about] her sense . . . having a very strong sense of herself as a black woman . . . my experience was different being a white man. My sense of my own racial identity, obviously, is very low on my threshold. Usually for white people they don't think about race and I think that being in an interracial relationship and marriage that I have become more aware of my whiteness . . . especially aware of the fact that I'm white . . . I'm sensitive to the fact that I'm a white male.

Five of the white partners distanced themselves from their "whiteness" because of how white racism and prejudice has negatively impacted their black partner and community. Consider the way Kevin discussed his racial identity or "whiteness":

KEVIN: I am white, and I realize all bad behavior is not necessarily white, you know all whites aren't racist . . . yet it is difficult, I actually had sort of an identity crisis . . . hung out with all black guys, I was the only white, [others] even said I acted black . . . and many blacks feel so comfortable around me, you know they talk about whites but say, "not you, you're not white."

Through these white individuals' comments regarding their racial identity or racial consciousness, one can see how negotiating a white racial identity is difficult and seems to be even more complex when one is involved in an interracial relationship. Responses range from denying that "being" white is a salient piece of their identity, to expressing difficulty with understanding whiteness or race, to struggling with being white yet feeling more comfortable with blacks, or the transformation in *recognizing* their whiteness as a result of the relationship. In *Tripping on the Color Line*, Heather Dalmage argues that the articulations of identity for white individuals in interracial relationships may shift but still are trapped in essentialist thinking: for example, some whites become aware of the discrimination faced by African Americans through their relationships and therefore try to distance themselves from whiteness, viewing all whites as "bad" and all blacks as "good." One of the main critical arguments Dalmage makes involves the language that we have to talk about race, a language that leaves little room for renaming our racial identities.

The way the black partner identified racially seemed to influence not only the way the white partner conceptualized race and interracial relations but also the way the couple discussed their relationship. For example, Frank, a black fifty-five-year-old retired police officer adopted a color-blind approach to race and raising their two children, which his wife, Olivia, a forty-eight-year-old office manager follows.

FRANK: Well, we're all human beings and that's what I tell my sons . . . we breathe air and we bleed. You demonstrate everything else to your ability, to achieve.

OLIVIA: . . . and if he had been very strong in wanting them to have a more traditionally black upbringing, I would have been supportive of that. . . . every single application I have ever filled out . . . has always been "Other" [for son's racial identity] . . . I'm going to raise them as human beings.

Similarly, Gwen's strong sense of racial identity and commitment to racial issues is articulated by Bill:

GWEN: I'm a black woman who happens to be married to a white male. I identify as a black woman. I think it's important that I have a racial identity. It's important for my son that he knows what my racial identity is.

BILL: . . . so what we attempt to do is to expose [our son] as much to black experience and culture as possible, whenever there's some event or something going on in town or anywhere. There was an African . . . not African dance troupe, but a dance troupe from Harlem that was up . . . and we took [him] there.

Kim, who stated she has trouble even thinking about race, especially in terms of her own racial identity, has always supported and followed Stanley's race-conscious approach to their relationship and raising their son, which includes living in a predominantly black neighborhood and sending their son to racially diverse schools and social gatherings.

Naming one's racial and/or ethnic identity is part of a process of group identification and reflects the way the individuals think about the self: "racial and ethnic labels are rooted in historical eras and the prevailing self-definitions and self-images of groups."[5] As we move into the couples' narratives on their relationship, the ways that individuals define themselves racially or ethnically plays a role in how they perceive their relationship and the responses of others.

Becoming Interracial

How these individuals became involved interracially if black-white relationships are not the norm is an important piece of this complex issue to explore. Those who get involved interracially form a relationship across existing racial borders and often encounter obstacles. The couples in this study met in various ways, such as at college, at work, or through acquaintances and community networks.[6] Often this meant that one of the individuals was already hanging out in a different racial environment. For example, David, who is black, had mostly white friends when he met Sandra at college, and Jill, a white woman, met Lee at a predominantly black dance club. While no couple explicitly stated that being of different races motivated their decision to become involved, the couples did discuss different views they had entering into their relationship, which was often influenced by their exposure while growing up to other cultures and whether or not they had previous interracial relationships. In general, the black partners were more aware of the potential problems of being in an interracial relationship. The responses varied from those who felt that entering into the relationship would be a challenge to those who did not even consider it an issue personally or from a societal perspective.

Some couples discussed their initial decision to date in color-blind terms, describing race as unimportant and not a potential source of difference or problems, as illustrated in Sharon and Kevin's discussion.

> SHARON: Being involved with a white man wasn't a big deal to me . . . I grew up in a mostly white school . . . and basically men are men. I've dated black, whites, Hispanics.

> KEVIN: For me, it's more about character than color . . . never really thought about *race* . . . I mean the first girl I kissed was black.

For Sharon and Kevin, becoming involved interracially was not a concern because their earliest dating experiences were interracial. Another example is Jennifer, a white twenty-year-old college senior, and her twenty-year-old boyfriend, Lance, who have been dating for two years. They describe how they did not consider any issues of race before entering into their relationship.

> JENNIFER: I mean, I dated [interracially] in high school. Most of the guys I am attracted to have been black, so it wasn't an issue for me . . . it's the weirdest thing. When I see him I just see Lance. Like I don't say think of him as a black man, like I don't notice.

> LANCE: You know, I didn't have a problem with [dating a white woman] so when I met her I really didn't consider it. For me it's not an issue, but me, I'm not really concerned with what others think.

The complex ways that race is negotiated is evident within Jennifer's statement that she is primarily attracted to black men, yet she does not "see race." Also, she and Lance, later in the interview, clearly discussed the problems they have with family, friends, and other places in racial terms, though she deemphasized the role of race when discussing her own views or reasons for entering into the relationship. While both couples argue that racial difference did not present a problem for them in their decision to date, they are less clear on whether they were attracted, at least initially, to each other because they were of different races.

Two other partners, Frank and Victor also discussed their decision to date white women in color-blind terms. Frank described his dating choices in the following way:

> FRANK: I've always dated interracial . . . they were just females. If I like you, I mean you can say yes or you can say no—no problem . . . it was not that I had to date one particular race, because I don't understand that concept. Human being . . . I like you . . . a lot of black women I wouldn't actually date if my life depended on it.

Victor has also primarily only dated white women, and both of his marriages have been to white women, but he stated race has never played a role in his choice of a romantic partner.

> VICTOR: I truly feel that if I had met . . . I don't think it would have mattered what nationality or what ethnic background the woman was, if we had connected and connected on inter-lateral and spiritual and mental levels, that would have been a match . . . but, let's face it, if I really wanted to marry a black woman, I would. I could have gone out of my way . . . I could have gone there and done that, but that wasn't my priority. You know my priority is more . . . love, but you know love has no color so then there's the intellect and the spiritual and then there's a belief system about how I deal with the world. That's what important to me.

Victor's response is often incoherent and contradictory. He discussed his thoughts about entering into an interracial relationship by stating that race does not matter; what matters is how he "connects" with the woman. He explained that finding a black woman was not "his priority" without saying that finding a white woman was. While he denies that he prefers white women, he also implies that he did not want to be with a black woman. Victor downplayed the issue of race and maintained that love is color-blind, emphasizing the importance of individual and personal characteristics.

The role that race played in these couples coming together cannot be determined, yet other studies have offered "racial motivation" theories about black-white couples such as rebellion, guilt, low self-esteem, and self-hatred. Whites are viewed as motivated by curiosity, racialized sexual attraction, or other reasons such as rebellion, rejection, or neurosis.[7] The choice of blacks, especially black men, to date and marry only interracially has often been attributed to a self-internalization of racism.[8] As Frantz Fanon argued, blacks who become involved with whites seek to "whiten the race, save the race, but not in the sense that one might think: not 'preserve the uniqueness . . . in which they grew up,' but make sure that it will be white."[9] In the narratives of some of the couples, statements were made that could be read in terms of racial motivation, such as Victor's statements describing himself as being exclusively attracted to white women because they treat him better,[10] or Kayla's description of having an intense physical attraction to black men.[11] Yet the purpose of this study is not to draw conclusions about why the couples came together;[12] rather, the ways these individuals/couples describe their decisions to become involved interracially is acknowledged and highlighted to emphasize how color-blindness permeates couples' narratives, even when they are specifically identifying a racial preference in dating.

On the other end of the spectrum, some of the partners—especially those who had never been involved interracially before—acknowledged that they had thought about the implications of being interracially involved and the ways that race (or at least others' views on race) could impact their relationships. White partners, like Kayla, a twenty-eight-year-old supervisor, and Sara, a twenty-one-year-old college senior, discussed that they had some hesitation about the relationship at first for a number of reasons—in particular, the expectation that their family and others in society might have a problem if they got involved interracially.

> KAYLA: I did think about it [race] . . . I did because I actually . . . I had to explain it to my parents . . . more like what will everyone say . . . I got the feeling at the time that I'm really attracted to black men a lot more . . . I think their skin is beautiful and I envy it, and I just think they are beautiful . . . I've always been into their culture—Adidas, hip-hop urban wear, the music.

> SARA: I thought about it . . . I knew presenting myself and my relationship with Andre was going to be . . . I knew it was going to be a challenge with my family. . . . well, I remember saying this when I was little—well you can't stop me if I come home with someone who's black. . . . but I knew that I never wanted to be like [my father, who uses racial slurs] and I wanted to understand why he was like that.

Both white women's comments come from the knowledge that their relationships could be a problem for their family or friends. Sara credits her strong beliefs about accepting all people as the reason she didn't let the potential opposition of others deter her. Kayla describes her reasons for choosing to enter an interracial relationship despite potential opposition as based in her preference for black men and attraction to hip-hop culture, which she narrowly defines as black culture.

Black men like Chris, a twenty-eight-year-old business executive who is married to Victoria, a twenty-eight-year-old social worker, and Mark, a thirty-two-year-old construction worker who lives with Brittney, a twenty-six-year-old waitress, didn't have any hesitation on entering into an interracial relationship, but they did describe their views on how race mattered to them when they met. Neither man had ever been in a relationship with a white woman before, and they discussed their initial views, emphasizing the significance of race.

> MARK: I never have [been with a white woman]. The reason being because, really, I mean, there wasn't a lot of white women around me . . . it's like when I was in high school, okay, we saw other white women . . . we didn't even bother. It was just like you knew. It was something that was already preprogrammed. You already knew— don't talk to them. They ain't talking to you. Don't waste your time . . . when my sister had me come down to meet Brittney, I didn't know she was white.

> CHRIS: She was the first white girl that I got involved with . . . I mean I had talked to white girls, "Hey, what's up!" But not relationships . . . and I think when I met her I didn't really think about what it meant because we were in college and I wasn't thinking long term, but then I guess she was different.

Chris and Mark both discussed similar experiences of never thinking that dating interracially was a possibility, even though they had distinctly different backgrounds. Chris grew up in what he described as a racially mixed upper-middle-class suburb and Mark grew up in what he described as a predominantly black lower-income urban area.

Gwen also discussed her difficulty as a black woman deciding to become involved with Bill, yet she described it as much different than a previous relationship with a white guy during college.

> GWEN: Bill wasn't the first person I had dated, I had dated a [white] guy when I was in graduate school for about three or four years . . . but in that relationship had difficulty. I don't even think I ever admitted to anyone that we were actually dating . . . I mean there were people who suspected it. I never told them we were dating. . . . I had always said I would never date someone who's white. Never, ever, and I thought that to do that, it was betraying your race . . . that

I could never love someone who was from a different racial background because they wouldn't understand me, my culture. . . . I was
always self-conscious about doing things with him, and I think it
was because I hadn't come to terms with our relationship, but I
wasn't so sure he didn't see me as a novelty. He had never dated
anyone black and I had never dated anyone white. We were both
coming to this as naive people.

When asked what changed her mind, she said it was a number of factors.

GWEN: I did remember that [in this first relationship] being in the
mall, places like that, with him and going up the escalator one day
and there were these black girls behind us and they were insulting
to me and I got angry. I think what they also did was toughen me
up a little bit and decide that I could do what I wanted to do and
didn't feel that I had to conform to anyone . . . and with Bill there
was probably a different combination, since we weren't in school
together or in the same field, there wasn't the issue of him having
breakfast with our white colleagues and having to come back and
tell me what happened.

Gwen's narrative reveals how initially she let her perception of black opposition to interracial dating (and her own opposition) affect her dating choices,
but with Bill she had grown "stronger" from the way she had been treated
previously and she felt more comfortable being in an interracial relationship.
Some of the other black partners also expressed these type of initial feelings. Lee discussed how when he first met Jill he was "experimenting," but
as a relationship developed, he asked himself, "Do I want to put myself
through this? Is it worth it?" and he decided it was "somewhat of a problem," but now any initial hesitation or doubt is gone.

The black partner in the relationship often expressed initial hesitation,
primarily because they were concerned about whether the white partner understood the implications of getting involved. Stanley and Kim started dating in the mid-1970s, so he was initially worried about Kim because "she
was naïve," and he wanted to make sure that she understood how people may
perceive her in a negative way because of their relationship. Furthermore, it
is not only the black partner's belief that race may affect the relationship; it
is also the white partner's lack of thought on the issue. (This pattern will
emerge again within the community research, where most white respondents
report never having thought about interracial relationships, while the black

respondents interviewed all had extensive views on the issue.) For example, Aisha, a twenty-four-year-old computer analyst, described how initially she was "really conscious of having a relationship with a white guy," citing that she was "afraid" of what people would say, particularly her family and friends. Her hesitation also revolved around the motives of her partner, Michael, a forty-year-old computer analyst. Before she "let him into her world, " she asked him why he wanted to be with a black woman and made sure he knew "how people would react." Michael described his initial feelings that he didn't even "think about her as black" and didn't see race as an issue. Over time he has come to realize what Aisha was referring to, through their relationship as well as through classes on race, which he has taken in his pursuit of a bachelor's degree. Michael's response seems to be common among white individuals who are completely unaware of the potential issues involved with dating or marrying interracially, especially those who have had limited contact with other racial groups.

Victoria described how little she knew and how, as a white woman, she had no idea that being in an interracial relationship would be a problem for others:

> VICTORIA: I have to say, I was so clueless . . . I guess I was really ignorant to racism, because I didn't even think about it when I met Chris . . . I mean I had just started college and was really into certain music, and parties, or things that there were definitely a lot of black people at . . . so I don't think Chris knew that I didn't get it . . . looking back I realize now how many times I saw, knew things that would have let me know, "oh, being with a black guy is not kosher," but at those times, I just didn't even think about it.

For some whites such as Victoria, Michael, and Bill, the relationship opened their eyes to issues of race and racism that previously they could not or would not see.

These stories of how the couples came together reveal the different ways race is viewed among them. Five of the couples stated that race played no role in their relationships and emphasized the idea that love is color-blind, that they didn't see their partners in racial terms, even initially. The individuals who discussed their first meeting and initial attraction in color-blind terms were also the ones who acknowledged that they were primarily attracted to or had dated outside their race previously, a theme that will be discussed later. Beyond the differences in acknowledging the role of race, the differences between the white and black partners' awareness of what entering an interracial relationship meant is also important.

Being Interracial: The Private/Public Dichotomy

Despite different views on becoming an interracial couple, all of the couples responded that when alone their interracial status was not a salient piece of their relationship. Racial differences did not exist, did not affect their treatment of each other, or were simply a source of diversity to celebrate, not to dwell on. The couples' narratives of how others viewed their relationships, however, were often dramatically different, ranging from couples who asserted that being in an interracial relationship had no effect on how they were received or treated to couples who felt their life choices were significantly altered because of societal perceptions and responses to their relationship. This illustrates the ways that Americans construct the public and private as separate, which has always been fundamentally shaped by race and gender.[13] Many of the couples described their relationships quite differently when discussing how they view their relationships and interact with one another, as opposed to how others view their relationships, which will be discussed in greater depth through their narratives.

The couples differed in their perspectives on whether any aspect of their lives or treatment from others had changed as a result of their relationship. Four of the couples—Lisa/Victor, Olivia/Frank, Sandra/David, and Nancy/Robert—adopted a color-blind approach, emphasizing the ordinariness of their relationship and stating that they did not experience any racism or opposition. In contrast, five of the couples—Kim/Stanley, Chris/Victoria, Danielle/Keith, Gwen/Bill, and Aisha/Michael—emphasized that they were continually made aware of others' views of them as an interracial couple. With the other six couples—Brittney/Mark, Jill/Lee, Kayla/Hank, Jennifer/Lance, Sharon/Kevin, and Sara/Andre—their stories were ambivalent, at times acknowledging being perceived differently, other times emphasizing the normalcy of their relationship.

Among those who deemphasized the importance of race were Nancy, a forty-two-year-old financial consultant, and her husband, Robert, a forty-seven-year-old postal worker. They described themselves as an "ordinary couple," which was a typical response among the couples. Although Nancy described having experiences with racism and discrimination when she was a child, she and Robert both stated that now it is "the media which makes race a problem . . . or people who play the race card."

ROBERT: Race isn't a big deal . . . I personally am oblivious to race. As far as I was raised there is good and bad in everyone . . . hey, I mean we all bleed the same.

NANCY: Exactly. Just treat me like a human being . . . I don't understand to identify with others just because they are the same color.

These sentiments are echoed in popular culture, especially the media, who often discusses race as a problem only when it is made into a problem, something that does not necessarily exist but can be "played."[14] Similarly, Sharon and Kevin deemphasized race when discussing their relationship.

KEVIN: [It's] just different pigmentation, and it's society's problem not ours . . . with more and more [interracial] couples it is becoming mainstream besides.

SHARON: To me, it's not a big deal . . . people are going to talk no matter who you are with.

Mark and his partner, Brittney, a white twenty-six-year-old waitress, discussed their resentment at being labeled an interracial couple and having people place emphasis on their racial differences.

BRITTNEY: We look it as like we're a team. We're partners.

MARK: I think [being thought of as interracial] sucks. We're a couple. Never mind the interracial stuff . . . just labeling . . . I don't like that stuff. It doesn't matter what you are, you know what I mean. What you are is living. So just be that . . . we're a couple and we have a son and as a result of us that's our son [*pointing to their infant son in his swing*].

Couples who took a color-blind approach of deemphasizing race when discussing their relationship stated that others did not treat them differently or they did not notice how others responded, which may be a means of dealing with racism and the discourse against interracial relationships.

SANDRA: I don't notice what others may think or say . . . if they stare like there is a problem, I've never been aware, I guess. . . . I may be in denial about [interracial] couples, but what is the point of thinking otherwise?

DAVID (*adding to Sandra's statement*): . . . but we never really encountered negative views . . . it's [interracial couples] all over the place. They have to know this race thing is getting to be ridiculous.

We're human beings. None of us are supposed to have a color. Give
me a break. We're people, not a color.

According to these couples, race plays no role in their lives or choices. For
example, when asked if being an interracial couple factored in to their decision on where to live, some couples answered that race played no role:

SANDRA: To be honest, I don't think race, definitely not being interracial even came up when we were looking for a house. It's not diverse here, but we wanted to be located convenient for both me and
David [he works at a firm in Manhattan and she teaches at a college
in New Jersey]. Of course, schools were important.

FRANK: Olivia and I were both working in [the same city]. I did a
radius . . . being twenty-five miles limit because we had to commute.
We had the boys, so I was bringing the fact in, had an associate friend
of mine told me about [town they live in]. The only thing about it,
it's all white.

Both couples stated that proximity to jobs and schools was important, but
the racial makeup of the area was not viewed as a consideration in their
choice, and there is no discussion or acknowledgment of white racism. Other
couples expressed ambivalence about race as a factor in their lives.

KAYLA: With [Jay, my ex-husband] I think I focused on race, and it
was hard because I didn't want people to be like, "Oh, see, he is a
bad black guy" . . . but with Hank, he's everything in a man, black
or white, that I've ever wanted . . . so I don't notice [people look-
ing], not really as much as I did before, and I think it's because I'm
not looking as much. I'm just so happy, and I'm so happy with my
children that I'm looking beyond [opposition].

Kayla struggles with the issue of how others view interracial relationships,
stating that with her ex-husband she felt people had a problem with the relationship, but with her boyfriend, Hank, she feels his positive qualities over-
shadow any opposition that may exist. Other individuals are also ambivalent
about the impact of race. For example, Jennifer shifts between stating that
she does not see Lance as a black man to discussing how everywhere they
go she feels that people, black and white, look at them differently. This brings
us back to the issue of the public versus the private realm, where couples
may not "see" race within their personal relationship, yet others may
"racialize" the relationship—that is, they may view the couple differently

because of race or racial difference, thereby making it difficult for the couples to explain what role race plays in their relationship.

Ten of the fifteen couples discussed things they don't do or places they won't go because they are aware that they would not be accepted, which is one way that being an "interracial" couple impacts them.

> AISHA: Being married to a black man would be easier . . . I go to dance clubs [predominantly black] without him because it would be uncomfortable . . . or when he came to the West Indian Day Parade, it was a problem, everyone was like, "Who's this? How dare you bring a white guy to this."

> LISA: When he was [working as a disk jockey] at an all black club . . . and the first night . . . he didn't want me to go and I wanted to go, but I don't think it was that he was afraid, I think it was because he wanted to [do a good job], so if I was there . . . the presence of me, maybe the black women . . . it might make them unfriendly? I don't know . . . because of my reception of the black women there.
> VICTOR: And that's exactly what it was . . . now I wouldn't worry about bringing her there. I still know if I bring you there, there's a certain percentage of black women that are going to give you and me dirty looks.

Illustrating the complexity of interracial relationships, these two couples also stated that their lives are not "different" because they are interracial couples, even though they discussed how there are certain places they don't go.

Some couples explicitly described how others' responses have impacted their relationship, and they critiqued the color-blind discourse of other couples:

> DANIELLE: I couldn't say that I don't even notice that Keith is black, because that is who he is and part of why I'm with him, I mean his ways of doing things, or just everything comes from how he grew up . . . but you know I also think about him being black because I know what other [white] people say, and it makes me pissed, like you don't know him but you look at him like he's a piece of shit.

> KEITH: I didn't marry her because she's white, but, yeah, she's white [*laughing*] . . . we laugh all the time because some things she does or I do and we both just joke, "Oh, that's because you're white," I

mean just stupid things like the way I iron my jeans or the way she makes scrambled eggs. I don't know, but I think it's funny when people look at us. She gets more upset sometimes, but I say, hey, if people, black or white, want to be ignorant, then let them get worked up about us, but don't let it bother you, you know.

Gwen and Bill also clearly state the role that they see race plays:

GWEN: I am a black woman. I see Bill as a white man . . . I'm a black woman who's married, who happens to be married to a white male. . . . I don't think love is color-blind, if it were they'd have more interracial mixing. People tend to choose people to fit an image to what is desirable to them. I can't say when Bill and I started dating that I didn't notice the second we'd met that he is white, but when we got together I could love him regardless of what he looks like.

BILL: Saying you don't see race or you're just human is sort of a convention. It's more a belief that you want to have—a kind of idealized sense of themselves . . . so it is in a sense a belief statement, not actual life . . . but of course as love becomes more complex, one doesn't see the racial identity of the other partner, at the same time one becomes more acutely aware of it, not in a negative way . . . especially aware that I'm a white male and that's factored into the relationship in a way that I'm sensitive to.

These couples dismiss the idea that people no longer see race or that love is color-blind, but again there is a distinction between private and public. Bill acknowledged how in their private time together Gwen's race is not a factor, or, as Gwen stated, when he forgets to put his dirty socks in the hamper, he is just her husband, not "her white husband." Yet in their experiences with others, even close family and friends, they feel their "racial differences" are central. For Bill, in some aspects race has become even more important because he sees the many ways that his whiteness affects not only the way he is treated but also the way Gwen and their relationship is understood.

Among the couples who consistently emphasized the role race played in the responses of others to their relationship, white partners revealed a heightened sense of awareness about issues of race and the existence of racism as a result of their relationships. Oftentimes the relationship brings the white partner to experience different things or to find a commitment to issues of diversity. For Victoria, her relationship with Chris has affected her choices and her awareness of race:

VICTORIA: A lot of the reason I became a social worker had to do with Chris, in a weird way, because after we met I became real aware of inequality, racially and just in general, poverty, abuse, now I think I just really feel comfortable in diverse environments and I like that Chris and I talk about issues and are committed to something [their work in inner-city communities and membership in organizations like the NAACP], a lot of people don't have that.

CHRIS: It definitely makes a difference that I know she feels like I do, and I think that even makes me respect her more because it's like she didn't have to do this. I mean, I'm black, this is about improving my community, my people, but for her she could have married a nice white guy and lived in white suburbia [*laughing*] and not even thought about it, that's why if someone even tries to disrespect her [because she's white] I'm not having it.

Sara, who navigates between color-blindness and race consciousness, discussed the way her relationship with Andre has changed her:

SARA: I've become more aware of what it must be like for the one African American man in my class and we went on an interview to a job together and how I realized immediately that he was the only person of color there and stuff like . . . I think I've become more aware of other people's situations on a more personal level as opposed to just, "Oh, you know, they're the black kids that like to hang out together. Why are they being so exclusive?" I think I've begun a little more to understand maybe why people are like that and situationally and things like that, but sometimes I wonder if, you know, Andre would be better off with someone . . . better off with someone who could, was bi-racial or black or something like that. I felt inadequate myself. Could I not understand him because I'm different?

Sara's response reveals not only how she has become more aware of race but also how this awareness has made her more self-conscious of whether her whiteness makes her unable to be an acceptable partner for Andre.

In some cases, the white individuals were already involved in culturally diverse organizations or groups and that is how they entered into their relationships. For example, Kevin enjoys a number of activities involving different cultures and different races/ethnicities. He is a Latin percussionist studying to be an ethnomusicologist, and he is very involved in Santeria. All of these affiliations, as well as his diverse group of friends make his relationship with Sharon easier.

Other couples reported that they do face opposition when they go out, but they do not avoid certain places or leave their partners at home because of potential opposition. Opposition occurred in both predominantly black and predominantly white social environments:

> LANCE: We go to parties, especially in my neighborhood [predominantly black] and there is usually a problem, but you just deal.
> JENNIFER: Well, sometimes he is like, "Maybe we shouldn't go," but I say screw that. I'm not gonna stay home like I did something wrong, we have nothing to hide, and I feel the same about bringing him to [white] parties on campus.

> GWEN: We've never excluded each other. I go to a lot of public functions and he was always there with me, I'm sure that people say things. The fact that we are together is an issue, but they haven't said it to us publicly.
> BILL: The only observation I can make is the kind of awareness you have when you enter into a social situation where you end up and people don't know who I am. So it became a sort of, became humorous for us, I think, to register people's expressions on their face, so we walk in places and she introduces me and we see them looking back and forth.

Not letting opposition deter them from activities or functions is a source of empowerment for these couples.

The Larger Picture in Black and White

When asked to think about the overall acceptance of black-white relationships in society today, all of the couples agreed that interracial couples have an easier time today than thirty years ago. Yet the couples differed in their views on what role race still played in others' responses to their relationships. Some couples stated that society is accepting of interracial couples, arguing that things have gotten so much better that it is no longer an issue, while other couples stated that there is still a significant amount of opposition, but, as with contemporary racism, contemporary opposition is often expressed in more subtle forms. Eight of the couples stated they did not feel that any opposition existed against interracial unions, or if it did it was small and isolated in certain areas such as the Deep South. Lisa and Victor's response is typical of the color-blind strategy that couples employed when discussing the responses of society to interracial couples: they minimize or deemphasize the role of race.

> VICTOR: I think it has changed, I've seen it change . . . we've seen that [the opposition] change because we've seen it so much [referring to interracial couples]. I mean, when you walk places that's what you see. I can remember we went to Boston, and, I mean, they were all over the place, very interracial . . . it's not going to be a big deal . . . but there's probably places down there [South] that still, it's not to be done . . . but we're quite fond actually of spotting interracial couples wherever we go. We call them IRCs . . . "Did you see the table behind you? Oh, yeah, cool," course she's always checking out the kids . . . to see what the mix looks like. Honestly, it's going to be the wave of the future. There'll be more of it and people will think less of a taboo about the whole thing.

> LISA: Your father said the browning of America.

> VICTOR: No, that was my cousin. I think it's changing, more popular. I know that interracial marriages last longer as a whole, as a general rule, than regular, the other marriages. I think people are waking up and definitely paying attention to that . . . but, like I said, we have friends who don't think it's a big deal.

> LISA: I don't think it's ever been a problem with us.

Lisa and Victor addressed the issue of societal opposition by stating all the reasons they think there is none. Victor draws on different things, such as seeing more interracial couples, the idea of the browning of America, his belief that interracial marriages last longer, and the assertion that interracial marriage and biracial children are the future. Other couples also expressed these sentiments.

> ROBERT: It's just not a problem anymore, you used to see black men with white women, now you see more and more women of color with white men . . . it's just more acceptable these days.

> NANCY: I mean, nobody looks at us and says, "Oh, My God" . . . it's just more accepted.

MARK: We really don't have much problems, I think most people have accepted the fact that they can't change what's going to be . . . when people start raising their children to be more open-minded to the world—that everything isn't white or everything isn't black—but everything is black and white and everything in between, I think they'll have a better perception of everything.

Couples who deemphasized race in terms of their own identities or experiences were most likely to say that others in society also didn't care that they were an interracial couple, drawing on common phrases such as "love sees no color" or the "browning of America." Though all of the couples had some experiences where others in society responded negatively to the relationship, these couples simply did not discuss the opposition in racial terms. Some couples explained it in terms of a personal choice "not to see opposition." Sandra's comments are typical: "I don't notice what others may think or say. . . . if they stare like there is a problem, I've never been aware, I guess. . . . I may be in denial about [interracial] couples, but what is the point of thinking otherwise." For these couples, opposition does not exist because they do not acknowledge it—similar to the ideology of color-blindness.

Those couples who emphasized the role of race in their own identities as individuals and couples characterized others in society as still harboring negative views of interracial relationships. These couples cited how others often refuse to acknowledge that the two are a couple or make it known through words and actions that they are different. For example, Sharon and Kevin mentioned the stares they receive "all the time" in restaurants, in the park, or just walking down the street. Aisha and Michael stated that opposition exists because they get "tons of comments and looks, plenty of problems," citing numerous examples of waitresses "being nasty," encountering problems while skiing in Vermont, and blacks and whites looking at them on the subway. Jill and Lee recounted incidents of people staring at them, from a white woman who became disgusted when she saw them embrace in a retail store to a black man who taunted them while they ate at an outdoor restaurant in New York City.

The couples—across class statuses and social locations—maintained that many people have a problem with interracial relationships, because they are continually being treated differently when they go out in public. This occurred among couples of varying socioeconomic positions and educational levels. For example, Keith and Danielle are both working-class, high school graduates who live in a predominantly black area:

KEITH: It doesn't matter if we're at the car wash, the market, the club, somebody is going to look or make a comment under their breath.

DANIELLE: You just get used to it . . . even expect it now, depending on our mood we say certain things when they don't think we're together, like at K-mart or if the waitress gives bad service.

On the other side of the class spectrum, Gwen and Bill both have doctorates and work in academia. Within their highly educated upper-class social circles, they have experienced opposition at balls and fund-raisers sponsored by black and white civil and public organizations.

BILL: People look at black and white couples. They're always looking back and forth between them. There's almost an involuntary look. They're trying to figure us out.

GWEN: When we dance people look, a lot they look . . . we know we are on display. . . . they're interested because who we are [interracial]. They don't look at other couples unless they are really unique dancers, but we certainly aren't.

Despite social location, there seems to be a sense that being an interracial couple will bring forth a response.

One recurring example of opposition—or at least an acknowledgment that they are not the norm—that these couples reported is the common inability of people to recognize them as a couple or as a family:

BILL: Even at restaurants or other places, I could be standing right in back of her and somebody will look and ask me what I want or whether I've been waited on . . . it happens all the time.

GWEN: Yeah, we get that all the time . . . that's a common thing, that people make the assumption that we're not together.

Even for couples with children, the assumption is often that they are not together, or at least that the kids are not related biologically.

KAYLA: I was in a supermarket with my two girls, and Hank was down another aisle, and this [white] woman came up to me smiling and said, "I just had to say hi, because my husband and I are thinking of adopting also," and before she could continue, I said, "these are mine," and then she saw [Hank] coming walking down the aisle and she had this look of disgust on her face and walked away. I couldn't believe it. She looked at me like I had two heads.

Kayla described how the woman was friendly and supportive when she believed that the children were adopted, but Kayla read her response as one of disgust when she realized that these children were a result of her relationship with a black man. While it is impossible to know for sure how this woman felt, Kayla's interpretation of the event illustrates that, at the very least, this woman did not expect that the children were Kayla's biologically.

Through the couples' narratives, the different ways they understand and interpret their identities, their relationships, and others' responses emerged. Based on the stories they told to accompany their views, it seems that the couples' experiences are very similar, but their interpretations and choice of discursive strategies are different. Gwen and Bill emphasized race in all areas of their narrative, while Lisa and Victor deemphasized the role race plays throughout their narrative. Still other couples fluctuate back and forth, sometimes emphasizing race and sometimes deemphasizing it. Their interpretations are tied to the discourses they have invested in, as well as the complexities of family, community, and group responses to their couplings, which I will explore in the next few chapters.

An important aspect of the couples' narratives is the difference between the private and the public, especially concerning how the couples view their relationships. All of the couples have come together despite any opposition that may exist, thereby minimizing the importance of race or racial boundaries. Within their intimate and everyday lives, the couples all stated that their race, or more specifically their racial differences, were not an issue or source of problems between each other. It was only when others outside the relationship highlighted or emphasized race that it became an issue. Andre's statements summarize the complex negotiations necessary to be in an interracial relationship and reflect the divide between personal and political.

> ANDRE: Being in an interracial relationship kind of teaches people that race is . . . it's everything and it's nothing. It's a very, race is a big paradox that people have to negotiate themselves through . . . but . . . it's not the . . . it shouldn't be the most important thing that decides how you relate to people and if it is . . . if someone is in this relationship and all they can think about is how the other person is different, or if there's a difference . . . if you see a difference, then you probably shouldn't be in a relationship with the person.

Beyond this public/private dichotomy there also exists some key similarities and differences among the couples' narratives. The couples share a common bond through the societal perception of them as "interracial couples," yet their interpretations or understandings of what that means to them and to others differs. What begins to emerge is the importance of racial discourse. Within their articulation of identity and interpretations of societal responses, each couple has its own unique way of understanding their experiences. Yet two distinct and opposite strategies were used that tie their narratives to the larger social structure through dominant discourses that exist.

Using color-blind language, couples chose to *deemphasize* the importance of race when discussing their individual identity and identity as a couple. Couples who deemphasized race tended to ignore, avoid, or state that opposition does not exist, yet the couples' decision to deemphasize race may be a result of a number of factors. These couples seem to minimize opposition in order to maintain a positive identity and outlook. Couples who stated that race did not play a prominent role in their identities or the way they were treated seem to be empowered by this strategy, possibly because it allows them to "avoid" or prevent opposition against interracial unions from "touching" them. Also, emphasizing race or allowing oneself to be categorized primarily by race was viewed as a constraint on their individualism and ability to be successful or happy. By de-emphasizing race, some couples may have been transcending race and in essence objecting to the very categories of race that have been constructed to separate different groups.

Couples who emphasized the role of race employed a race/color conscious approach. These couples (four consistently, six sporadically) tended to acknowledge, confront, and/or challenge societal opposition, but they may have other reasons for placing an emphasis on race and their "interracial" relationship, such as having faced different forms of opposition or experiences that led them to adopt this strategy. Understanding their identity, their relationship, and others' responses in terms of race may be empowering, and placing the emphasis on race may allow them to confront or challenge what they perceive as opposition or differential treatment.

The ways the couples choose to interpret or understand their relationship and experiences is complex. These two strategies are not exhaustive or mutually exclusive, but they represent two distinct types with many variations. These can be understood as discursive strategies or even defense mechanisms that the couples use to negotiate their relationships and others' responses to them in order to make sense of the contradictory and conflicting racial narratives. Either way, these strategies seem to allow the couples to maintain their relationship, and relationships with those close to them.[15] While my aim is not to depict the couples as right or wrong for the strategies they have chosen, I am arguing that color-blind language is problematic because it "disguises (sometimes deliberately) or normalizes (sometimes unwittingly) relationships of privilege and subordination."[16] Deemphasizing race in identity, relationships, and others' perceptions does not acknowledge or challenge the central and undeniable role that race plays. If individuals and communities in society were color-blind, approximately 98 percent of today's spouses would not be matched by race and color and couples would not be labeled interracial.

CHAPTER 2

Constructing Racial Boundaries and White Communities

*I*nterracial couples can be understood as social products in that they are formed and transformed by the defining process that takes place in social interaction, the ways in which others act toward them, and, just as important, the ways in which others produce images and ideas about them and their relationship.[1] The experiences of black-white couples and the meanings their families, communities, and even popular culture attach to black-white unions are not individual but based on one's group. "Human beings act toward things on the basis of the meanings that the things have for them," and these meanings are often shared among groups and communities.[2] In particular, racial groups are *primary groups*, primary in the sense that they give the individual their "earliest and completest experience of social unity."[3] An individual is born into a group of people, where all the potential experiences and general types of situations have already been defined and the appropriate group responses long developed.[4] There is a "social stock of knowledge . . . which is transmitted from generation to generation and which is available to the individual in everyday life" and through interaction with others and participation in communities. As Michael Omi and Howard Winant suggest, "Everybody learns some combination, some version, of the rules of racial classification, and of her own racial identity, often without obvious teaching or conscious inculcation. Thus are we inserted in a comprehensively racialized social structure. Race becomes 'common sense'—a way of comprehending, explaining and acting in the world."[5]

Furthermore, recent census and survey data illustrate commonsense ways among white groups of experiencing the world. While recent surveys on racial attitudes, such as the Gallup Poll, report that increasing percentages of whites (and blacks) express support for interracial relationships, their life choices remain remarkably monoracial. According to the 2000 Census, only 1 percent of whites are married to an African American. It is this question of interracial support, segregated lives, and opposition that I will explore more closely, looking critically at the idea that whites are accepting of interracial relationships, as the media and surveys often report. Like manifestations of contemporary racism, white opposition to interracial unions is often subtle and not readily apparent or revealed because it is articulated as part of a color-blind ideology in individual or nonracial terms.[6] Rather than rely simply on survey data, which rarely tells the whole story and allows respondents' views to remain hidden within politically correct check boxes, I will use narratives, stories, and dialogues to explore the nuances of white opposition.

It can be difficult to engage white communities in race dialogues, however, since discussions of race often serve to silence most whites. Many whites have difficulty discussing race, racial identity, and particularly interracial intimacy: even those whites involved in black-white relationships can have trouble articulating racial issues or identifying the role race plays in their experiences.[7] In this chapter, it is precisely these "difficulties of race" among whites and the ways whites navigate interracial relationships that I will explore, through the experiences of the couples with white families and communities, the statements of the white communities interviewed, and images in popular culture. A major piece of my analysis involves the language whites use when discussing their views on interracial relationships, especially the way color is described as insignificant. Any issues concerning black-white unions that whites may have are often articulated in a color-blind discourse that deemphasizes race—though the very reason people make these statements is because skin color and race do matter, often most to those who espouse this color-blind discourse.[8] Interracial relationships in particular and blacks in general are outside white groups' social worlds. And for those white partners of black-white couples, the responses of their families and communities illustrate just how problematic these relationships still are when they occur within one's family or community. Media and film images also promote a color-blind world where race does not matter, even though simultaneously certain racial images are emphasized. By looking at film depictions of black-white couples, with the responses of white community members and white partners in interracial relationships, one can see how certain images and ideas about black-white couples exist and are expressed or articulated not only in film but also by whites in society. The popular culture images discussed, like the community responses, construct black-white couples in certain ways by privileging same-race unions and establishing them as the standard by which

interracial unions are compared. Based on the common meanings whites attach to black-white unions, certain patterns of responses are evident and mirrored in the couples' experiences, the community's responses, and certain film
images.

Interracial Relations and White Communities
in Historical Context

Historically, interracial unions have played an integral role in the construction of racial categories and boundary maintenance among whites. Interracial sex and marriage became deviant within the construction of a white
identity that was in opposition to blacks—the underlying basis for interracial sexuality as deviant being the claim that blacks and whites are biologically and culturally different.[9] An integral part of the concept of race and
racial boundaries is based upon how whites often experience and perceive
blacks as threats to a kind of racial purity, as well as to the category of whiteness itself. The issue of interracial sex and marriage is an integral part of the
construction of race and racial groups, with the opposition to and the fear of
interracial sexuality often used as a means to implement and justify racist
ideologies and practices. The long-standing rule of racial classification—the
"one drop" rule—referred to sexual encounters, since the only way that individuals received this "one drop" of black blood was through sexual intercourse: "if, as the laws and conventions dealing with the matter commonly
declared it to be, a person having 'any Negro blood whatever is, with all his
descendants, a member of the Negro race,' then race in America is not a state
of being; it is a matter of speculation about American sexual history."[10]

The central role that white fear of interracial sex and relationships
played in the construction of racial boundaries cannot be overstated.[11] Among
whites, interracial sex was constructed as deviant within the institution of
slavery of black Africans, and from the beginning this notion of deviancy
was primarily aimed at preventing black male slaves from engaging in sexual
relations with white women. Numerous historical incidents have been documented where those who engaged in interracial relations were formally and
informally punished through fines, whippings, banishment, and/or imprison-
ment.[12] Racial boundaries are created and enforced by placing interracial intimate relations outside the realm of acceptable behavior for whites.

From the very beginning, the responses of white communities to black-
white intimacies were politicized and intertwined with the social, legal, and
political realms of society. For example, within this long and complex history

of "race relations," marriage rules and laws (informal and formal) can be seen as extensions of the white construction of race and political supremacy. As Max Weber argued, the legal prohibitions against intermarriage and "the sense of horror at any kind of sexual relationships between the two races . . . are socially determined" and "result from the tendency . . . to monopolise social power and status" based on racial differences.[13] Interracial sex and marriage could blur the line between black and white, thereby challenging whites and the whole racial hierarchy. In order to ensure that sexual relations between the races did not occur, laws were passed and racist belief systems were institutionalized that constructed black bodies as physical and dangerous in contrast to civilized white bodies.[14] Throughout American history, white preoccupation with preventing interracial unions existed, and the "fear of miscegenation continued to rise as a response to changing racial relations," especially in periods such as black emancipation: "whenever pressure to produce secure racial classifications increased, public outcry over interracial sexuality also increased. . . . Regulations prohibiting interracial sexual relationships actually serve to produce and consolidate racial identities."[15]

For example, there are numerous incidents where the *fear* of interracial sexuality has influenced the response of whites to interracial relationships and blacks in general. Even in the mid-twentieth century, "every form of political and economic equality for blacks was depicted as a threat to white racial purity, responded to with fears of interracial sexuality, and argued against on this basis."[16] Throughout the struggle for black freedom and equality, whites were more frightened by the possibility of interracial sex and marriage if blacks were given equality than by blacks gaining political power through voting rights or better education through desegregated schools. Gunner Myrdal, in his landmark study, *An American Dilemma*, argued that whites are more concerned about preventing interracial marriage and maintaining racial purity than they are about competing with blacks. Myrdal illustrates this by asking white Southerners to list in order of importance what they thought blacks wanted and comprising their answers into a "rank order of discrimination." Intermarriage and sexual intercourse with whites came first, and political, legal, and economic opportunities came last.[17] This opposition to interracial marriage was echoed throughout the political and social realms of society. In 1954 President Dwight D. Eisenhower told U.S. Supreme Court Chief Justice Earl Warren that white Southerners opposed to school desegregation were "not bad people. . . . All they are concerned about is to see that their sweet little girls are not required to sit in school alongside some big overgrown Negroes."[18] After the 1954 *Brown v. Board of Education,* many whites, including Mississippi Circuit Court Judge Thomas Brady, stated their fierce opposition to race mixing and warned that this would bring forth the "tragedy of miscegenation."[19]

During the civil rights movement, for whites the word "integration" construed images of race mixing, with special emphasis on black men desiring equal access to white women, while for blacks integration meant equal access to social, legal, economic, and political institutions.[20] An example of this contradiction occurred in the summer of 1961 when Robert Kennedy called a meeting with two civil rights organizations, CORE (Congress on Racial Equality) and SNCC (Student Non-Violent Coordinating Committee), who were working on improving their everyday conditions of life by desegregating public facilities and modes of public transportation. Kennedy offered a tax exemption if they would concentrate on voter education rather than stage interracial Freedom Rides and sit-ins: "Negro voting did not incite social and sexual anxieties and white Southerners could not argue against suffrage for their Negro fellow citizens with quite the same moral fervor they applied to the mingling of races in schools."[21] Many whites believed that desegregation and racial integration was the equivalent of promoting interracial sexual relations and marriage. These incidents reveal how sexuality, and even the potential for interracial sex to occur, influenced not only social interaction between blacks and whites but also the economic and political realms.

These historical incidents are mentioned to establish how opposition to black-white relationships was institutionalized into the fabric of white American society. One's attachment or perceived membership in a racial group "presumptively sets apart group members and groups, treating them stereotypically as alike and different from those perceived not to belong to the group, thus reducing individuals and their racial group to a fixed and devalued understanding of possibility, propriety, and acceptability."[22] Relations between whites and blacks also need to be understood in terms of these power relations, "the racialized thinking and emotions of the white-racist system are much more than a matter of how whites view people of color. They are also about—and perhaps principally about—how whites see *themselves* as individuals and a racial group."[23] Whites as members of the dominant racial group are expected to act toward blacks in a manner that is representative of the subordinate position of blacks in society; intimate associations and intermarriage are not generally included in the defined situations that are available to whites within their group.

Interracial Relationships and White Communities in Contemporary Society

When it comes to asking whites about their views on black-white relationships, they are often silent or hesitant to speak on issues of race and race relations in society. I think of my own family, whom I do not remember making racial comments or ever talking about race growing up. When I became involved with a black man, many within my family raised "concerns," never expressing them in explicitly racial terms. My family still prefers not to discuss "racial issues," especially in terms of my children's identity. Instead, they say, "They're just Christopher and Jada. We don't see them as a color, no different than their cousins" (who are all white). In many ways, what they are saying when they don't see race is that they are choosing not to see their blackness. These types of subtle expressions of racial beliefs, attitudes, and racism in nonracial terms is common in contemporary society and makes it necessary to closely examine not only what is said but also the underlying implications and meanings.[24]

As the couples' narratives illustrated in chapter 1, the couples' discussions and interpretations of their experiences were markedly different, generally either emphasizing the role of race or deemphasizing its significance. The actual experiences they recount are not markedly different, even though the ways the couples chose to frame them was. The importance of language is clear with the use of color-blind versus race-conscious language. The two approaches paint significantly different pictures for similar stories.[25]

Race and White Silence

It was difficult to get white community respondents to even discuss the issue of race and their views and ideas about black-white dating and marriage, which illustrates the relative lack of consideration this topic receives among predominantly white circles. For example, the white community respondents stated that they "never really thought about it" and "didn't know it was an issue." These responses could be read a few different ways. They may have been a semantic move to avoid discussing the issue, for fear of saying something wrong or being politically incorrect, since whites often view the new racial climate as forbidding the open expression of racial views.[26] Or, it may be true that these white individuals had rarely ever thought about the issue, since their families and social worlds were predominantly, if not exclusively, white. Whatever the reason for their claims of ignorance, these white respondents did not perceive interracial relationships as an issue or concern they wanted or needed to talk about; therefore, their discussion on this topic is limited.

In my interviews with white community members, interracial relationships were rendered outside the realm of what is speakable; in other words, interracial relationships were not part of the available discourse or script that they as a group drew upon.[27] Interracial relationships were not a concern for them—not necessarily because they did not or would not have objections, but rather because they did not even think it a possibility (or at least a possibility they wanted to discuss) that an interracial relationship could occur in their family or social circle. Interracial dating and marriage did not touch their lives, because interracial relationships in particular and blacks in general were outside these white groups' social worlds.

White Worlds

While the whites interviewed stated they hadn't thought about the issue of interracial couples much before, when asked about their views on these relationships in the group context, the boundary between black and white was clear. In one focus group, there was a dialogue that illustrated an underlying opposition to interracial relationships among the group. A white woman in her forties, Karen, discussed her job as a teacher in a school that had a "multicultural" student body. In describing the student body, she said, "Everyone is different, but prejudice is not dead by any means and [it is] mostly from the parents." At this point, Ellen, a woman in her sixties, interrupted to address the group: "Yeah, but would you marry one [a black person]."[28] The group did not immediately respond. Then, Sara, a woman in her thirties, answered, "I don't know how I feel, well would feel. I mean I have black friends," shrugging her shoulders (which I read as suggesting "no big deal"). "I don't know, I really . . . but I'm married, so it's something that I couldn't even answer," she said as she pointed to her husband, next to her, who did not comment throughout the group interview. What is most significant about this exchange is the way that Ellen's comment, which clearly implied racial prejudice as well as the view that blacks are almost completely outside her social experience, was not objected to by the group. When Ellen referred to a black person as one of "them," no one objected to her comment, and Sara legitimated her question with an answer. While this interaction occurred the other whites remained silent, with no one expressing outrage, disgust, or surprise.

But what does this interaction indicate about the group's views on interracial relationships? I argue that the group's responses to the woman's question can be understood as "the nature of the group," or, in other words, how individuals act in a manner appropriate to the group. Since racial groups are "primary groups," primary in the sense that they give the individual their "earliest and completest experience of social unity," there often exists a "group-nature," which is characterized as being more than an instinct one is born with but less than the "ideas and sentiments that make up institutions."[29] Often in a group context, "well-meaning" whites will remain silent when others are making a racist joke or engaging in a prejudiced action based on "interactional reasons."[30] Regardless of whether the other whites agreed with her statements, their decision not to address or confront her question allows "racialized" thinking—and in this case, the image of white-black relationships as deviant and undesirable—to go unchallenged.

"I Don't Have a Problem with It, but . . . ": Color-Blindness and the Denial of Race

The most common response among the whites interviewed when asked to comment on their own views of interracial relationships for themselves or their families was "I do not have a problem with interracial couples, but . . . ." The widespread use of color-blind language among whites is central to the ways they express their views on interracial relationships.[31] But what does it mean when whites say they are supportive of interracial relationships but they emphasize problems interracial couples may face in society and they do not personally know any black people? It is necessary to look carefully not only at what the white community members say about interracial relationships but also at how they say it and how it relates to what they do.

The white respondents' acclamations of neutrality or support were routinely followed by a "but," an explanation of reasons why interracial relationships do not work and should not happen, and descriptions of negative incidents they had heard about. Despite claiming not to have a problem with black-white unions, the white respondents discussed certain reasons why they thought interracial relationships might not work. In the community research, all of the respondents prefaced their statements with some version of the "I don't have a problem with it" disclaimer before outlining reasons they believed black-white relationships were indeed problematic. Jane, a married mother in her forties, stated that she wouldn't have a problem with it, describing it as *"their* choice, *their* life, if that's what makes *them* happy." This sentiment was echoed by others and reflects the ways that interracial relationships are perceived as something that happens to someone else, somewhere else.

Other community members further discussed their expressed acceptance by explaining why interracial marriage is so uncommon, illustrated in the following exchange prompted by my question on how they felt about interracial relationships between blacks and whites:

> JAMES: You just don't see it [interracial relationships]. Intermarriage isn't common 'cause people want to marry somebody like themselves.

> SUSAN [*agreeing with James*]: I personally don't think it has anything to do with race, it's not a race issue. [*She stops talking and I ask her what she thinks it is.*] It's more about, well, based on culture, you know, wanting to be with people with the same values and beliefs.

> LINDA: Listen, two white people have difficulty making a marriage work, so imagine the added strain of cultural differences, it's just too much, would be too difficult.

What began as the white respondents not having a problem with interracial relationships became a dialogue on the reasons why these relationships do not happen and, to some extent, why they should not happen and do not work. While one respondent explicitly stated that the reasons the relationships do not happen is not based on race, underlying the group's statements is the presumption of difference, which is based on nothing other than racial identity. Words like "culture," "values," and "beliefs" are used rather than "race" and "color," but this is little more than coding. Marrying within one's race is preferred and seen as a "natural," yet the reasons are described as not being based on racial preferences or prejudice.[32] The invisibility of whiteness and the existence of white privilege are key concepts to understanding why many members of the white community oppose interracial unions: whiteness is constituted as essentially different from blackness, with whiteness being the standard by which all others are judged inferior.

Another one of the main issues identified by the white respondents was that they felt they personally did not have a problem but "others" in society would still see it as a "problem." By emphasizing the existence of anonymous societal opposition, the respondents avoided discussing their own views and acknowledging their role in the opposition they said existed. They explicitly stated that they did not harbor negative views of African Americans, yet they also recounted reasons why African Americans were not suitable mates, or at least why white-black relationships did not work. These responses are part of a shift from blatant bigotry and overt demands for strict segregation and discrimination to a "laissez-faire racism," a progressive trend in white racial attitudes to advocate for integration and equality and against discrimination on a broad theoretical level while maintaining opposition to implementing practices that require day-to-day interaction or close proximity in their social circle to African Americans.[33] Therefore, it is not surprising that whites may state that they do not view blacks negatively but that they do not "prefer" to interact with blacks on a personal, especially intimate, level. Claiming not to have a problem with interracial relationships while offering arguments against it is understood as "symbolic racism," a way of disguising racist feelings or thoughts. It is the same as denying blacks are inferior but advocating against school busing.[34]

Black-White Couples in White Color-Blind Social Worlds

Based on the ways that whites discuss black-white relationships in nonracial terms, using language that simultaneously supports and opposes these relationships, it is not surprising that the black-white couples offer conflicting and opposing views on white communities' responses to interracial relationships. For example, the five black-white couples (discussed in chapter 1) who consistently denied the importance of race in their experiences also described the white neighborhoods they lived in as supportive of their relationship and family.

> OLIVIA: We just all of a sudden became part of the neighborhood. I think that we're pretty well liked and the two of us are pretty involved. I know there's some comments in this community, but I don't think . . . if it was negative it was never negative to our face. There must have been some negative commentary.

> FRANK: [A white friend who told him about the neighborhood] said one time [neighbors] asked why did they let us live there. Something like that and, okay, that was it.

> OLIVIA: I think we just became a part, people just got used to us being around and I'm sure if we were not good neighbors and neat neighbors and put our garbage out on garbage day and things like that then I'm sure people would have something to say . . . because we don't have wild parties and because the yard is neat, and the garbage goes out on the right day of the week.

In a later point in the interview, however, Olivia discussed her concerns about her two teenage sons driving home late because the all-white police force had pulled over each of the boys on different occasions, assuming they did not "belong" in their neighborhood. Nonetheless, Olivia characterizes the neighborhood as accepting and race as insignificant, focusing on nonracial factors such as being clean, good neighbors. Despite the all-white makeup of the neighborhood, the neighbors' questions about why they were allowed to live there, and the police incidents, they do not characterize their experiences as racial or motivated by opposition.

On the other end of the spectrum, four couples explicitly described how black-white relationships are problematic—at least for some whites—especially when it involves one's own family or neighbors. For example, three of the black-white couples detailed incidents when whites had a more difficult time accepting interracial couples in their own neighborhood or within a neighbor's family because it brings the issue too close to home.

> KAYLA: When I started dating [Jay], the more I started dating him, heads were turning. In my neighborhood [suburb in Maine] where I had grown up, people were talking, there was a local store up the street that was like "gossip central" . . . nobody would say anything to me directly, but people would say things to my parents. Nobody thought it was a good idea, yet nobody knew him or the type of person he was, just that he was black.

> JENNIFER: Here we don't have any problems, but probably because it is a mixed, and kind of rundown area, but I guess where I grew up [upper-middle-class white suburb in Connecticut] there would be an issue, I know my mom worries about what other people say, especially when I bring Lance home for holidays, and neighbors say things and I guess in places that you just don't see [interracial] couples or blacks there would be problems.

> AISHA: I was in the Upper East Side of New York and saw a white woman tell a black woman with a white man—you are dirty as the ground, dirty as the street . . . you two do not belong together, it isn't right. She was appalled that they could be in her neighborhood.

Within this discussion of white acceptance of black-white couples, the importance of the intersection of race and class emerged. Upper-middle-class neighborhoods tend to be predominantly white and often nonaccepting of interracial couples, such as Kayla's white suburban Maine neighborhood, Jennifer's white suburban Connecticut neighborhood, or the predominantly white section of the Upper East Side of Manhattan that Aisha discussed. Considering how the white community members reported a lack of exposure to interracial unions and a belief that it was something that happened elsewhere, it is not surprising that whites may have a more difficult time accepting black-white couples in their neighborhood because it brings the issue too close to home. Oftentimes, it seems that interracial couples such as Danielle and Keith, Jennifer and Lance, and Brittney and Mark have an easier time and face less opposition renting apartments in lower-income black neighborhoods. Couples who can buy a house also seem to encounter fewer problems than couples who rent, simply because if they can afford the house they can buy it; however, they may still have to deal with problems in the neighborhood. Even couples like Frank and Olivia and Sandra and David, who feel they have no problems in the middle- to upper-middle-class white neighborhoods they live in, recounted incidents where their white neighbors treated them like they did not belong.

Color Lines: Work, Play, and Prayer

Beyond their experiences in white neighborhoods, some couples stated that their relationship was never responded to negatively by whites they encountered. Yet these same couples recounted experiences, particularly at their workplace, where fellow white workers were surprised or confused by their black-white relationships. For example, the Robert, who is white, stated that his relationship with Nancy did not cause any problems at his job at the post office. Despite this account, he described almost having a physical altercation at the post office with a white man he works with who makes derogatory racial comments, sometimes specifically about black women. Sandra and David also stated they had never experienced any opposition to their relationship from whites in the workplace, though Sandra did discuss how white students in her classes routinely make racist comments. Since these racist remarks are not directed at the couples in particular, the couples did not interpret them as examples of opposition toward their relationships.[35] Another example is Lisa and Victor, who met at the middle school where they both worked as teachers. They stated that the other teachers, who were all white, did not have problems with their relationship, yet they did discuss coworkers' perceptions.

VICTOR: Being the only black teacher at school, I had been in those social circles, so yeah, I saw Blondie over here and I went, "Oh, God, young girl, she doesn't know nothing. I don't want to deal with it."

LISA: But I had dated black guys before, so I didn't have, he's used to people at his school having like a mystique . . . like [*names specific coworkers*]. [*Looking at Victor*] How do you explain it?

VICTOR: Curious. They're curious.

LISA: The curiosity factor, and *I* didn't have that. He was dating two other women and for them it was a new thing [dating a black man], and they were all ooh, aah over him.

Lisa and Victor stated that the white women they work with have a perception of black men and interracial dating as interesting because it is not the norm. Lisa differentiated herself from those white women who see it as a trend or cool thing to do. They also discussed that they both agreed to not start dating until her substitute position at that school had ended. When I asked why, they said it wasn't against policy, but they didn't feel it would be well received. In a later discussion, they made references to other things coworkers have said.

VICTOR: You know, my colleagues, my own [white] friends who I have known for years might say a comment [about our relationship], like "You're not really black you know?" . . . and I guess what they're saying, you know, you act white, no wonder you're marrying a white woman . . . you get your kicks, sure, but maybe there's an ounce of truth in it and you dismiss it or let him know . . . I'm sure I've had guys I worked with that certainly did not want it for their daughters.

LISA [*at a different point in the interview*]: Well, I know there are teachers at my school that . . . it's almost like when they told their parents or family members about me and Victor, well, some girlfriends just know their parents are prejudiced. Like they're really Italian and they have that viewpoint, so I don't . . . God only knows what their conversations are. You know she's probably—one friend will defend . . . "well, you know he's really cool" or . . . so I don't know . . . I don't know what they say.

When asked directly about their experiences at work and how they felt their coworkers responded to their relationship, Lisa and Victor stated that there were no problems and everyone was completely supportive, yet they recounted particular incidents where coworkers have made derogatory comments. In Lisa's case she expressed some doubt about what the women she works with really say about her and Victor.

Olivia also recounts an incident where a white coworker asked her questions about her family, not realizing that Olivia was married to a black man:

> OLIVIA: Once at work someone saw [her sons'] pictures on the desk and they asked me, "Where did you get them from, where did they come from?" so I say they're mine but they continue, "Yes, but what country did they come from?" so I say, "I gave birth to them, their father is black," and she just kind of looked at me like they're really your biological children.

Olivia interpreted her coworker's response as one of surprise and disbelief, which signifies that being married interracially and giving birth to biracial children was not what the woman expected of her. Olivia's experience may also point to another reason that some of the couples interviewed did not feel they had problems with others in society, particularly at work: they did not socialize with or engage in conversations or situations where the race of their partner or children would be revealed. While these four couples argue that they do not experience opposition, the stories they tell directly identify others who do not expect or fully accept black-white relationships. These couples have adopted a color-blind strategy for discussing and interpreting their experiences, and since the ways whites at their work (and in the larger society) express their views is color-blind, it makes it easier to maintain the idea that race does not matter.

Other couples discussed similar incidents, but they clearly described them as racial and defined them as opposition. For example, Brittney, a waitress, described how her coworkers reacted when they found out Mark was black:

> BRITTNEY: They were surprised. I think they look at me differently now. I just think they think, you know, they didn't expect it. They labeled me, as you know, because I don't act like, I don't know, and this young kid, you could tell because he used to pay a lot of attention to me, but then he was . . . disgusted, I guess just put off by it.

Keith discussed an incident with white coworkers that he believed ultimately cost him his job:

> KEITH: Before I started working at [her current job], I was working as a shift supervisor in the cafeteria of a factory, and one Saturday I was shorthanded, so Danielle came in to help, and we were definitely having a good ole time and whatever, and the next week my supervisor got written complaints, no names of course, saying how appalled they were at the way I groped my *white* employees and how inappropriate I was, and something to the effect that I harassed white women. Never before had these kind of things been said, but after the day my wife is there . . . and we may have been affectionate, I don't remember.

> DANIELLE: I don't even think so, it's not like we were kissing, I guess we acted familiar.

> KEITH: Yeah and it's after that the complaints come, and then it was one thing after another, and that's the first time I got fired.

Other couples described how they had never directly heard negative comments by others at work, but this did not mean they thought the others were supportive. For example, Stanley and Kim work in the same hospital, and they discussed how no one makes derogatory comments about their relationship to them directly, but they believe that they might indirectly. Kim attributed this to the negative comments she overhears other whites making about African Americans, whether or not they know who her husband is. Gwen also expressed these sentiments:

> GWEN: In my work environment, people know my husband is white, so it's never been, well our whole attitude is that if you have a problem with it, you should deal with it. It's not our problem, it's yours. I'm sure people have, matter of fact, *I know* people have problems.

Considering these experiences, it seems interracial couples can encounter overt or subtle difficulties in their workplaces; opposition, or the idea that being involved interracially is not the expected norm, is often implied but not directly expressed.

Although workplaces have become more diverse and it has become even more unacceptable to express problems with interracial relationships, friendship groups still remain predominantly of the same race. In chapter 1, the couples' narratives showed that interracial relationships often bring forth more opposition when they happen closer to one's own family or neighbor-hood, which brings up the question of how white friends respond. For ex-ample, while no one in the white community group acknowledged having been in an interracial relationship, all but one of the respondents mentioned they had black friends or expressed acceptance of friendships across racial lines.[36] Since many whites maintain that having friends across racial lines is acceptable, while intimate interracial relationships are not, the issue of friends, race, and interracial relationships is complex. The responses of the white part-ners' white friends to their black-white relationships, as well as how the white partners interpret these responses, reveals the ways black-white couples are viewed in white communities. One of the most illustrative examples involves Lisa and Victor, who described their white friends as completely supportive of their relationship, even though they had a close white friend who said he would not approve of an interracial relationship for himself or his family members.

> LISA: He was the best man at the wedding. He is young . . . younger than I am . . . he's white . . . okay, this is when we were talking about ethnicity and bringing home someone from a different ethnicity, so Jason comes out with, "Well, you know, when I get married, if my daughter brought home a black man, I've got to be honest with you, I'd probably be bothered by it."

> VICTOR: And yet . . . I couldn't see him being prejudiced, but he'd be prejudiced who's not doing something the way he wanted it done, so . . . I don't know.

Lisa and Victor stated that their friend Jason "does not have a problem" with their relationship and is not prejudiced. They understand his statement as a personal preference, not an example of opposition against interracial unions in general or their relationship in particular. Neither Lisa nor Victor question the racial meanings of why Jason would not want his daughter (who hasn't even been conceived yet) to marry a black man and what this says about his views on blacks. Jason is described by Victor as supportive of interracial re-lationships, but like the white community respondents, his support ends when it concerns his own family.

Lisa and Victor's friendship with Jason raises a central point: the dif-ference between interracial friendships and interracial intimacy. It was com-mon for couples to describe white friends they viewed as supportive, yet these "friends" made comments that were derogatory or in opposition to interracial relationships. Three of the white partners—Jill, Jennifer, and Victoria—had been friends with white women who had once dated black men but now were involved with white men and didn't want anyone, particularly their current white partners, to know they had been involved interracially. Kayla discussed how she had lost her white high school friends over her relationship:

> KAYLA: We tried going out with my [white] friends, girls I had grown up with, but I lost every friend I had at the time . . . I'm no longer friends with one person I was friends with then. They didn't like him because he listened to loud music they didn't like, and he was always playing ball and just didn't like that he was black. . . . They just stopped calling me, whenever I'd ask them to do something they would be busy . . . and [her high school boyfriend, whom she had recently broke up with] was mortified, he called me and said "I had lost it" and that I was just doing it to get him mad or embarrass him.

Not surprisingly, a number of couples discussed how they avoided predominantly white social circles, surrounding themselves instead with a diverse group of people who are supportive. Couples such as Kevin/Sharon and Chris/Victoria described how they had or sought out new groups of friends who are more racially diverse.

> KEVIN: We didn't have any problems from my friends, but the bunch I hang out with are all different, many different cultures, lifestyles.
>
> VICTORIA: It's not intentional, but I think it just happens. You gravitate toward people who think like you, or even look . . . I mean we don't recruit other [interracial] couples, it's more like if I meet someone cool at work and then see their spouse is another race it just gives us more in common and makes it more likely we may hang out.
>
> CHRIS: It has a lot to do with the things we do. We have this core group of friends who are not just diverse by race but that we share politics with, and I think that where we stand on issues lends itself to surrounding ourselves with people who are accepting [referring to involvement in civil rights organizations and working with an antihate crime coalition].

Gwen and Bill also recounted these sentiments, mentioning the diverse group that attended their wedding and how they associate with others who share the same political commitments, especially in regards to issues of race and gender. The choice to avoid predominantly white social circles or cultivate multiracial friendship networks reflects on the prevailing belief (and reality) that many whites do not accept interracial relationships, or at best treat them as an exception to the same-race norm.

Beyond friends, places of worship can also be a source of support and opposition, as described by black-white couples. Being that churches—like neighborhoods—are often racially homogenous, the issue of religion and the church can play a prominent role in the ways individuals conceptualize their views on black-white relationships. What first emerged in the couples' narratives was talk about "white churches," "black churches," and "diverse churches."[37] In particular, the black-white couples discussed the experiences and beliefs that they had involving certain churches or religions, viewing different religions and churches as significantly more and less supportive of interracial relationships, whether or not they practiced a religion.

Couples like Frank and Olivia and Nancy and Robert attend predominantly white Catholic churches, crediting Catholicism as something that brought them together. Frank and Olivia describe their common Catholic upbringing and beliefs as a common bond that was more important than race. They both stated that the Catholic religion and the members of their predominantly white church were supportive of their relationship, which they attributed to tolerance and acceptance of all people being taught within Catholicism. Nancy and Robert also attributed the strength of their relationship to their shared background in Catholicism, which "erased" any racial differences. They attend a predominantly white Catholic church with a small black membership and described the Catholic church as instrumental in their relationship.

> ROBERT: One day at her Mom's house I realized that I had more in common with her family than her brother's [black] wife because of religion.

> NANCY: Him being Catholic was much more important to me than what color his skin is. That's irrelevant.

Despite their perceived "unconditional acceptance," these couples did have some questionable experiences in their churches. For example, Nancy and Robert discussed how the white Catholic priest that married them counseled them on the difficulty of being a "couple from different races" and was "uncomfortable with the issue of children," asking them to really think about the issues involved in raising children in "this circumstance." By their own account, Nancy and Robert saw their religion as erasing all racial differences, but the Catholic priest did not. According to five of the fifteen couples, either they or people they knew had encountered opposition in predominantly white churches from either religious officials or church members. For example, when Kayla married her first husband, Jay, in a small Catholic church, the white Polish priest, who had known her family for years, did not want to marry them:

> KAYLA: He didn't think it was a good thing, and we had to sit down and convince him that we loved each other so much. He didn't want to be the one to marry us, but when we did get married, we had pews that were just placed in front of us because it's a mass that's held during the ceremony, and it was a long mass, and you're kneeling for a long time, and mine was padded but Jay's wasn't, it was ripped up, and we definitely thought it was on purpose.

It is not uncommon for interracial couples to recount these type of experiences in predominantly white churches. A recent example that caught media attention in 2000 occurred in Ohio, where Chastity Bumgardner, a white woman, and her black fiancé, Lawrence Henry, were told by Rev. Donald Ellis of the New Covenant Church of Christ that he would not marry them, claiming biblical justification for the refusal.[38]

Before I conducted the focus groups with the white church community respondents,[39] I attended three Sunday masses at St. Mathews. After one of the services I sat down with Father Carcieri, a white Catholic priest who stated unequivocally that religion, particularly the Catholic religion, accepts interracial relationships. He added that it is his job as the priest to make sure the message of acceptance and tolerance is understood and embraced by his parishioners. Father Carcieri takes what could be called an "individualistic approach" to racism and prejudice, articulating a belief in the authority of the priest and the belief that a Catholic priest could effectively legitimate the collective beliefs of his parish on issues of race and interracial relationships. Yet when asked about marrying a black-white couple, he did raise "pastoral concerns" that he would counsel the couple about before getting married. He mentioned "problems they may face" and "the issue of children," but he stated he did not feel these were reasons why they should not or could not get married. Father Carcieri's statement reveals a judgment that the "problem" of interracial couples is only addressed as a concern of the couples, something that he needs to make the couple aware of, not a societal problem. While he does not think that there would be any opposition from his parish or the community to interracial couples, he does think that interracial couples would need to be counseled on problems they will face in society in general. His statements and the responses of the church members show how individuals often do not acknowledge their opposition or negative views toward interracial relationships and that they are treated differently, but they address it either as a problem with the couple or with anonymous others in society. The ways that various white church officials feel it is necessary to counsel interracial couples about their relationship as different from same-race couples may not signal a lack of acceptance on the part of the priest, but it is an acknowledgment that interracial couples are "different" and that in society the couple will face problems. Furthering this notion of whites and blacks as separate, Father Carcieri attributes the lack of diversity in his parish to the upper-middle-class surrounding area, explaining that since this is not a lower- or working-class area, there are no African Americans living nearby. Like the community members, the priest places blacks and the possibility of interracial marriage safely outside their religious and social experience.

Based on a perceived lack of acceptance at predominantly white Catholic or Christian churches, a number of couples mentioned the Unitarian Universalist Association (or predominantly black Baptist or Episcopalian churches) as their church of choice. Sandra and David "don't have a religion," but they do attend a Unitarian Universalist congregation, where they also "baptized" their children.[40] Other white partners explained why they feel accepted within the Unitarian church:

> JILL: I like the church because it's spiritual but not into telling you what to do, or being judgmental . . . for [our daughter] I feel it's the best place to bring her, just more accepting of everyone.

> VICTORIA: We don't go much, but we like it [at the Unitarian Universalist church] because they're the only church that really promotes acceptance of all people, not just like read the scriptures, but actually like commit to issues, gay, lesbians, prison rights, antiracism. It's cool and for me, I was raised Catholic and still like a lot of things about it but can't accept what they say [no women priests, no abortion, no birth control] and Chris wasn't raised in the church, so he can relate to [Unitarian Universalist church] a little more.

Interracial couples reported that they are accepted at the Unitarian Universalist Association (UUA) because all types of couples and families are welcomed, which points to the lack of acceptance at predominantly white churches that prompted them to seek out the UUA churches in the first place.

Among whites, and in these white social realms, the pattern is clear: black-white couples are not common, and these relationships are not overly welcomed, yet whites (and some of the black-white couples) use color-blind language that masks the lack of acceptance. Among the white respondents, there was a tendency to discuss their views on black-white relationships in nonracial terms. The white respondents would clearly state they had no problem with black-white unions then contradict these statements by giving reasons why black-white unions are definitely problematic. Some black-white couples also adopted this discursive strategy. For example, eleven couples reported that, at least in some cases, others in society did not treat them differently because of race; however, they simultaneously reported incidents where they encountered problems with neighbors or coworkers who used racist language or behavior. If these white individuals did not directly say they objected to their relationship or did not directly make racist comments about their relationship, the couples did not identify their comments or behavior as oppositional.

Color-blind discourse and the refusal to acknowledge race is also common in popular culture,[41] such as the film *The Bodyguard* (1992), which is one of the most widely seen, mainstream films to feature a black-white couple. Randall Kennedy argues that in increasing numbers of films such as *The Bodyguard,* "interracial intimacy has been emerging as simply one part of a larger story in which racial difference is of little or no significance. . . . because presuming the normalcy of interracial intimacy—treating it as 'no big deal'—may be more subversive of traditional norms than stressing the racial heterodoxy of such relationships."[42] While *The Bodyguard* never addresses the issue of race, I argue that the depiction *does not* presume the normalcy of interracial intimacy; rather, in true color-blind fashion, it puts forth certain negative images of black-white relationships, all the time pretending not to be dealing with race.

In the movie, Frank Farmer (Kevin Costner), a white former Secret Service agent who is conservative and disciplined with rules by which he lives his life, is hired to protect Rachel Marron (Whitney Houston), a black music/movie superstar who is spontaneous, driven by her passions, undisciplined, and in need of protection. Though race is never mentioned, racial stereotypes are still perpetuated, such as the stereotype of whites as being in control and blacks as needing to be controlled. In one scene, we see Rachel surrender to Frank, and their relationship is portrayed as one of child and adult, with Frank tucking her into a bed filled with dolls that night. This imagery is important because it establishes who has the authority and power in the relationship.

Reminiscent of the days of slavery, interracial encounters are not threatening as long as the white man is in control. For example, she is the one who asks him to take her out, as well as the one who initiates the sexual relationship. Even though she is the aggressor, the control is quickly returned to Frank when Rachel says they should go out, but only if he wants to. This serves two purposes, it establishes her as the sexual aggressor while allowing him to be in control of their relationship. Also, Frank and Rachel's sexual encounter is not shown. The scene flashes from their first kiss to them waking up in bed together the next morning.[43] After spending the night together, he tells her that they can not be together. She gets upset and asks him "if he wants her to beg" or if she "has done something wrong." Although Rachel should be in the position of power because she is the employer, she is ultimately an object for sexual commodification, as she does not have control over Frank. Again, he is characterized as restrained while she is portrayed as desperate and needy. Further perpetuating the image of black women as promiscuous, in a later scene Rachel gets drunk at a party and seduces a white associate of Frank's to anger Frank after his rejection of her. This sequence of events reinforces the image of blacks as sexual and driven by their desires.

In particular, the role of bodyguard and client can be understood as metaphors for white and black, conveying the message that there are still boundaries that should never be crossed. As a bodyguard there are three rules that Frank lives by: "never let her out of your sight," "never let your guard down," and "never fall in love." Throughout history, these three principles have been a part of race relations between blacks and whites, manifest in the belief that blacks cannot be trusted, whites need to keep an eye on blacks, and that whites and blacks should remain separate. The movie ends with Frank and Rachel separating because they "both know that they don't belong together." Like the white respondents who discussed reasons why interracial relationships do not work, but who did so in nonracial terms, this movie puts forth the image, without ever mentioning race, that interracial relationships (or at least this interracial relationship) do not work.

Just because race is not discussed does not mean it does not exist. In fact, race, in its deliberate denial, is ever more present.[44] *The Bodyguard* does not have to mention that Frank is white and Rachel is black for us to see it. Like Victor and Lisa's friend Jason, whites do not have to say that they hold negative views of blacks or that they oppose interracial relationships, because their words and images still serve to convey the message that interracial couples are not desirable. As Henry Giroux argues about the interracial (and often sexually suggestive) Benetton advertisements, these depictions do not increase racial tolerance and awareness, but rather "decontextualiz[e], dehistoriciz[e], and recontextualiz[e]," which simply reproduces the dominant social relations instead of challenging them.[45] By avoiding discussing race, whites can express the idea that black-white couples are deviant without personally acknowledging that they "have a problem" with these relationships.

Black-White Couples as Deviant

In many white social worlds, black-white couples exist outside the boundaries, or at best on the margins, of what is perceived as acceptable. Regardless of whether whites acknowledge opposition or code opposition within a color-blind discourse, the words and actions of most white communities clearly frame black-white couples as outside the norm. In chapter 1, couples recounted the routine occurrences in stores, restaurants, and other public spaces of white individuals not recognizing them or treating them as a couple. Also, the white respondents' views that black-white relationships were not likely or acceptable in their social circles furthers the idea that black-white unions are deviant. In various societal realms, such as the workplace, the criminal justice system, and the general public, black-white couples have various experiences in white communities where others' responses mark their relationships as deviant—unexpected and unwelcome. Other studies have also documented the experiences of interracial couples who cite police harassment, getting pulled over a disproportionate number of times when together, and being told that "the [white] woman fits the description of a kidnap victim," or, in other words, that they just don't belong together.[46] Victoria and Chris recounted this disturbing incident involving two white police officers:

> VICTORIA: The scariest thing that ever happened was in [southern California] and we were driving to a shelter where I volunteered as part of an internship at college, bad area, gangs, drugs, so forth . . . we get pulled over and I'm driving, I have a convertible, and the officer is like, "Why are you here? What are you doing? Who is he?" [*pointing to Chris*] . . . I keep telling him, and I'm nervous and he still kept asking questions, so finally Chris goes something like, "Officer, why are you stopping us? What's the problem?" and ooh, that was it, they make him get out, the other officer makes him give his identification, and he has money from his scholarship check, so they grill him about that . . . meanwhile, I'm in the car and the officer is like, "I'm going to let you go, but you need to be careful, this is a bad area" and something to the effect you don't belong here

or with him. I forget his words, not exactly that but just like basically saying stay away from this black guy and then you won't have this trouble.

Victoria and Chris emphasized the role of race in this interaction, stating that the police targeted them because they were an interracial couple and driving into a predominantly black and Mexican area. They clearly interpreted the police's response as based on the idea that they did not belong together, especially not in that neighborhood, or, in Chris's imitation of what the officer was thinking, "'Why is this white girl with [*gasps*] a black in the hood?'" According to Victoria, the officer's attitude toward her significantly changed once Chris was out of the car, as if he was trying to help her avoid making a bad choice of being with a black man.

A similar scenario was depicted in *Jungle Fever.* One scene in particular highlights how whites and blacks are not viewed as eligible mates by the larger society and how black men are (mis)treated by the police. Angie, a white Italian woman, and Flip, a black man, are walking back from a date, joking around outside their apartment building at night, when a police car races up and two white cops jump out with their guns drawn. They report that they had received a call that a black man was attacking a white woman, retracting their guns only when Angie insists that she knows Flip. The prevalent belief is that when a black man is in close contact with a white woman, he is assaulting her or at least presenting a threat. The white police officers' reaction is symbolic of the ways that blacks, particularly black men, are targeted by the police and also, more important, of the historical tradition of white men protecting white womanhood from the black man, even if she does not want the "protection." While providing an accurate portrayal of what interracial couples can experience, the scene also serves as a reminder of the danger of being involved interracially and, in general, of being black in a white-dominated world. In this scene, Angie does not recognize the potential danger to Flip that is created when she keeps calling him her lover and Flip keeps saying, "No, no, we are just friends." Flip recognizes that to these white officers being her consensual lover is not much better than being her rapist. Though the police do not harm him, as they drive away they remark in disgust, "what a waste," signifying that this white woman had "value" before she became involved with a black man. This scene simultaneously exposes white racism and opposition to interracial relationships at its deepest level and serves as a deterrent against interracial relationships.

In the construction of black-white couples as outside the norm, there is an emphasis on the sexual aspects of interracial relationships and the idea that these couplings are deviant sexually. As mentioned, historically whites and blacks could be legally fined, imprisoned, or physically punished for having sex. Throughout American history there have been many images constructed around interracial sexuality. For example, there is the image of black women as being hypersexual or an exotic fetish who is satisfying the white man's desires, accompanied by the image of black men as sexual predators who seek out white women solely for sexual purposes. Although these stereotypes persist, the white church community did not acknowledge or discuss them, whether or not they knew of them (they did, however, figure prominently in the focus group interviews of white college students). In the couples' narratives, all but two of the couples interviewed described images of white women who socialize with black men as sexually promiscuous because white women only want black men for sex, black men only look for sex from white women, and relationships between black men and a white women revolve solely around sex. According to some of the black man–white woman pairings like Jennifer and Lance, whites see white women who engage in sexual relations with black men as low class, sexually promiscuous, and/or dirty.

> JENNIFER: I have heard all about that black men just want sex, and white woman want sex, especially, well that black men have, I don't know how should I say, are well-endowed . . . and white guys are disgusted probably thinking because I sleep with [a black man] I'm dirty, I don't know, that's how they make me feel.

Among the black woman/white man pairings, Gwen and Bill have experienced others viewing their relationship as deviant and sexual. For example, they discussed the assumptions others have about their relationship:

> BILL: There certainly is an idea of a sense of a kind of eroticism . . . you know, the sense of the other, mysterious, exotic. I'm not sure how that enters into my psychology, but not to the point where I harbor it as a desire, when I was attracted to Gwen, and that attraction existed on all kinds of levels, immediately intellectual.

> GWEN: It had to be, I assume my body wasn't, because I weighed less than 110 lbs. and was walking with a cane.

> BILL: For us it was definitely cerebral kind of . . . but I understand that kind of thing operates.

Gwen and Bill discussed the stereotype of black women with white men as inherently sexual, but they stated it was not a factor for them, even emphasizing how "nonsexual" her appearance was when they first met. Gwen and Bill also recount a number of incidents where white acquaintances of Bill have made "slurs about black women and sexuality" and have asked or implied how Gwen is sexually. One time in particular, a white man told Gwen he wanted a black woman like her, because Bill seemed to be having "a great time."

Gender Matters

Within this construction of deviance, there is obviously a different dynamic operating for black men with white women as opposed to white men with black women. From a historical perspective, there has been a difference in the ways that interracial unions were understood and responded to, whether it was a black man with a white woman or a black woman with a white man.[47] For example, as slavery was being legally institutionalized in Virginia in the mid to late 1600s, the public punishment of whites and blacks for "fornicating" was common, with white women and black men punished most severely; however, the much more common sexual exploitation of black women by white men was routine and rarely punished. The racial hierarchy, and more specifically the white male power structure, was not threatened by a black woman giving birth to a child from an interracial union, and it has even been argued that this was economically beneficial because it served to increase the slave labor force.[48] In contrast, a white woman who gave birth to a child from an interracial union would "pollute" the purity of the white race, thereby eroding racial boundaries and, most important, the power of white males.

In particular, the need to protect white women from black men became the justification for both the racial segregation of blacks and the severe formal and informal punishments inflicted on black men. "Within the white male's racist fear of the black male body a clear anxiety over the possibility of sexual exchange . . . [t]he fear is that some physical distance will be crossed, and the virgin sanctity of whiteness will be endangered by that proximity,"[49] evidenced in the lynchings of black boys and men for allegedly raping, touching, or even looking at a white woman like he wanted to rape her.[50] Defending the "honor and purity" of white women became a collective imperative, and the insistence of white men that they had to protect their women from the advances of black men resulted in frequent lynchings, castrations, and even destruction of whole black communities.[51] "White womanhood was the highly emotional symbol, but the system protected white economic, political, legal, educational, and other institutional advantages for whites, not just the sexual and racial purity of white women."[52]

Accordingly, the black man–white woman coupling is still the most disturbing in a society dominated by a white male power structure. While interracial relationships exist outside the norm in white social circles, the gender difference still exists. Reminiscent of slavery, a white woman involved with a black man is tainted and perceived as devalued, yet a white man involved with a black woman is not lessened; he is seen as at least having enhanced sexual prowess. The different intersections of race, gender, and sexuality are clear, where being a "good white woman" does not include dating or having sex with a black man.[53] Images of interracial relationships as largely sexual and deviant, as well as the different meanings attached to the coupling of black men with white women as compared to white men with black women, are still reproduced in contemporary mainstream movies.

Relationships between black men and white women are rarely depicted as long term or successful. Movies such as *Bad Company, Cruel Intentions, Freeway, Pulp Fiction,* and *Ricochet* include interracial sexual encounters or relationships, but they are submersed in a deviant world of crime, prostitution, and inner-city motels. Other films such as *One Night Stand* and *The Object of My Affection* also depict relationships between a black man and a white woman as deviant without ever mentioning race. In *One Night Stand,* even the title implies that the man and woman are not having a traditional date or relationship. Max, a married black man, and Karen, a married white woman, meet and have a one night stand. Then they meet up months later by coincidence and start up an extramarital affair. Their entire relationship evolves within an alternative lifestyle that mainstream society considers "deviant," such as homosexuality, AIDS, and drug use. The other example, *The Object of My Affection* (1998) revolves around a white woman, Nina (played by Jennifer Aniston), who is initially engaged to Vince, a demanding and controlling white man. After getting pregnant, she leaves Vince to raise her child with her gay roommate, George, with whom she eventually falls in love. Unfortunately for Nina, George still desires male companionship, so she finally accepts that they cannot be together. Ultimately, the film ends with Nina in a relationship with a black man but still in close contact with George and his lover. The movie revolves around the idea that Nina always chooses men who are not "suitable" for her, based on either personality, sexuality, or race. The final scene of the movie exemplifies this idea when Vince tells her, "You know, I was the only one who made sense." Since they shared no similar interests and were completely incompatible, it leaves the viewer to contemplate why they "made sense": was it simply because he was a white heterosexual man, while her other choices were deviant according to norms of sexuality and race relations?

Despite these films, the taboo of black man–white woman pairings has not faded, at least not entirely. Two prominent black actors, Cuba Gooding Jr. and Will Smith, have commented on Hollywood's tendency to avoid the issue of interracial intimacy and the hesitancy of white executives to place a black male lead opposite a white female lead for a romantic story line.[54] In Hollywood today, a black man kissing a white woman is still "the kiss of death," as far as studio executives are concerned.[55] Certain movies—like *The Pelican Brief* and *Kiss the Girls*—have even altered the storylines to eliminate any sexual tension or relationships between white and black lead actors, even though the original plots involved a romantic relationship.[56]

When Hollywood explores interracial love relationships, it tends to be from the perspective of the white man with an "exotic" woman of color.[57] There may be more films that take as their main theme the relationship between a white man and a woman of color, though even these films are few in number. In popular culture, the images depicted in movies such as *The Bodyguard, Bulworth, Mission Impossible II, Monster's Ball, Rich Man's Wife,* and *Swordfish* are worth noting for their depictions of relationships between black women and white men, yet again the depictions are deviant, sexual, or do not portray successful relationships.

Bulworth is a political satire about Senator Jay Bulworth (Warren Beatty), an aging white man who becomes disenfranchised with his political campaign and the political system in general. He begins pursuing a romantic/sexual relationship with a young black woman, Nina (Halle Berry), as part of a life transformation that includes substituting truthful remarks for his political speeches and adopting a hip-hop style through clothing and rap. Unlike the *Bodyguard,* the issue of race is addressed, such as Bulworth advocating a "voluntary free-spirited, open-ended program of procreative deconstructing" to eliminate the color line through interracial sex. Therefore, while the topics of race and race relations are addressed, they are still coded within a color-blind discourse that suggests interracial sex can solve the racial inequality. This movie can be read as an attack on the American power structure and the rigid hierarchy of the racial and class status quo of the political system, but it also exposes certain dominant ideologies about interracial relations. For example, only within a groundbreaking transformation and renouncement of his former position, as well as of his previous (white) supporters, does a prominent white man align himself with a black inner-city woman who also happens to be much younger and extremely attractive. Yet this relationship still affirms the white male power structure and brings to mind the history of white men "eroticizing the bodies of African-American women, especially light-skinned women like Halle Berry,"[58] rather than suggesting that interracial relationships are acceptable.

The same can be argued about *Monster's Ball*, where once again Halle Berry's character,[59] Leticia Musgrove, becomes involved with Hank Grotowski (Billy Bob Thornton), another white man undergoing a life-changing transformation. The story involves the execution of a black death row inmate who is Leticia's estranged husband and father of her son. Hank is the supervising correctional officer. After the execution, Hank's son, who was also a correctional officer, commits suicide and Hank quits his job. Hank meets Leticia after her son is hit by a car. He sees them on the side of the road and takes them to the hospital, where her son dies. The relationship begins with a very graphic sex scene that Leticia initiates. Like *One Night Stand*, the relationship is framed within a circle of deviance, including death, execution, poverty, family dysfunction, and deception (in particular the fact that Leticia does not know that Hank was a part of the execution of her son's father). Despite the emphasis on a black-white relationship, racism plays a significant role in this movie because Hank and his father are very racist. As Leticia and Hank's relationship develops, though, the issue of race is virtually never discussed (other than a fight after his father refers to Leticia as "nigger juice"). The movie portrays the relationship in color-blind terms and reproduces stereotypes, especially with a scene at the end where Hank tells her he will take care of her and she agrees that she needs to be taken care of. In both *Monster's Ball* and *Bulworth*, white men abandon their previous white social worlds and deviate from the norm, which involves entering a relationship with a (light-skinned, attractive) black woman while reproducing the images of these relationships as deviant and sexual.

The interracial relationship is always seen as a deviation from the norm. This view of interracial relationships as deviant has existed throughout America's history; therefore, it is not surprising that most films depict interracial sexual relations as outside the realm of acceptable behavior. The portrayal of interracial relationships as unsuccessful and/or deviant is a means of privileging same-race unions and maintaining white dominance. In the films, as well as in society, crossing the constructed racial boundaries and leaving the confines of a white social world has its price, at work (as with Keith and Jay Bulworth), with the police (as with Victoria and Chris and the couple in *Jungle Fever*), and in a million small ways throughout society, from questions and stares to outright opposition.

Conclusion

There are common ideas about interracial relationships that dominated the couples' narratives, communities' statements, and popular cultural images. Most whites employed a discourse that interracial unions are unnatural, non-traditional, and otherwise uncomfortable. The words whites use to discuss interracial relationships—such as, "I don't have a problem with it, *but* . . . "— can be understood as "discursive buffers" that allow individuals to say something negative about interracial relationships without being accused of opposing these unions based on race.[60] These "speech acts" express the socially shared knowledge of groups about the rules and conventions of acceptable behavior, or, in other words, "scripts,"[61] which are culturally defined and managed according to cultural norms and expectations.[62] Speech works as a "move in a game" that signifies more than the simple meaning of the words;[63] for example, when whites (and blacks) state they personally would not marry interracially but do not care if others do, they are still reproducing their racial group and the boundaries that separate white and black. Although they said they did not have a problem with interracial marriage, they also made comments that implied opposition. In addition, their own social worlds are predominantly, if not exclusively, white. These discursive strategies allow whites to maintain that they do not see race and that they do not object to interracial relationships, while simultaneously discouraging these relationships through their discussion of the problems of these relationships.

While race or racial difference was rarely discussed, other reasons and explanations to object to interracial relationships were given, and these responses were remarkably similar. For example, couples discussed how others were concerned about (1) how society would respond, (2) the couples' children, and (3) the general "difficulty" of being with someone of a different race. These same issues also figured prominently in the communities' reasons for questioning interracial relationships. In each of these responses, emphasis was placed on how *they* did not have a problem with interracial unions and how *they* did not think there was "anything wrong" with blacks, often using certain language like, "I don't care if someone is red, blue, black or green." A number of the couples also embraced these color-blind ideas, arguing that their white families and communities were supportive despite stories that seemed to imply something different. Some couples straddled the border between acceptance and opposition, at times espousing a color-blind discourse and at other times clearly stating that race did play a role in the responses of others. Still other couples clearly stated they experienced opposition from white friends, families, neighbors, and strangers. Based on the couples' stories, I argue that at the very least interracial relationships are not expected or preferred. The white community members' responses support my argument through their lack of thought on the issue, their avoidance of the issue, and the problems they perceived existed with interracial relationships. Similarly, the infrequent yet growing interest in portraying interracial intimacy does not render interracial relationships less deviant. Mainstream film (even in the depictions of black-white couples) does not depict acceptance; rather, it reveals a social structure that privileges intraracial unions. The images in these films provide certain ways of thinking about or understanding interracial relationships that serve to reproduce racial boundaries, even when attempting to challenge the existing racial hierarchy. By pulling together these different white responses—while not generalizable—a collective white opposition can be identified and characterized: avoidance of the issue of interracial relationships, possibly in hopes that it does not happen to them; a common discourse or use of language that deemphasizes race while emphasizing the "problems" with interracial couples; a tendency to explicitly state that interracial relationships are acceptable while implicitly showing through words ("not my preference," "nothing in common," "what about the children") and behavior (all-white families, friends, and neighborhoods) that interracial couples are not encouraged, expected, or accepted.

CHAPTER 3

Crossing Racial Boundaries
and Black Communities

Benedict Anderson discussed communities in terms of the members who "will never know most of their fellow-members, meet them, or even hear of them, yet in the minds of each lives the image of their communion."[1] In terms of race, blacks are more likely than whites to think and talk in terms of racial communities, since many whites refuse to even name their own identity in racial terms, much less acknowledge that they think of other whites as their community—even though their words imply that they do.

In black communities, there is a painful and complicated history attached to black-white unions, and the roots of the opposition are markedly different from white communities. Whereas white communities often become silent around racial issues, interracial sexuality and marriage are topics that can provoke heated discussion and debate among black communities. Reflecting the ambivalent state of interracial relations, the discourses on black-white sexuality and marriage are multifaceted and complicated. The opposition of black communities to interracial relationships seems to derive from a historical and collective "memory" of violation by whites and in many ways can be discussed in collective terms. Interracial marriage is understood and discussed as a politicized social issue within black communities, linked to the contemporary debate over multiracial identity and the push by multiracial organizations—often formed by white mothers of biracial children—to add a multiracial category to the 2000 Census. Numerous black communities and organizations such as the NAACP oppose a multiracial category because it is viewed as a way for some to distance themselves from black communities and as a weakening of the black community—economically, socially, and politically—that ties in with the opposition to interracial marriage. To explore these varied perspectives, I bring together the views of black communities, the experiences of black partners interracially involved, and black popular film images to illustrate how black-white relationships are viewed and characterized. The emphasis on experiences and interpretations within the research comes out of a wide array of theoretical approaches— critical race theory, cultural studies, and symbolic interaction—acknowledging that individuals interact according to the meanings attached to their social relationships, and this interaction or "lived experience" is connected to the cultural images and representations that are produced in the various realms of society.[2]

Interracial Relationships and Black Communities in Historical Context

Contemporary views on black-white unions must be understood within a historical context. Black history has been characterized by centuries of slavery, oppression, and segregation with the rich and complex cultural heritage of black Americans not being recognized by whites as culturally valuable, at least not until relatively recently.[3] Even though "black" is a social, political, and surely an emotional construction, it is also a powerful and effective part of what we call American society. Historically, blacks as a group have dealt with their devaluation by whites and the effect it has had on their collective identity in various ways, which has undoubtedly shaped their attitudes and responses to intermarriage.

The historical impact of interracial sexual relations on black communities is well-documented. The frequent abuse and lynching of black men for allegedly raping or desiring sexual relations with white women,[4] as well as the widespread rape and sexual abuse of black women by white men,[5] all play an integral part in the sociohistorical construction of race and the rules of race relations. As W.E.B. Du Bois writes: "The red stain of bastardy, which two centuries of systematic legal defilement of Negro women had stamped upon his race, meant not only the loss of ancient African chastity, but also the hereditary weight of a mass of corruption from white adulterers threatening almost the obliteration of the Negro home."[6] This systematic rape of black women during slavery can be understood not only as a historical tragedy but also as a "spirit injury" that still has deleterious effects on the black community today.[7] For example, many black writers discuss their personal family histories and the legacy of miscegenation: legal scholar Patricia Williams recounts how her grandmother, who was a slave, bore children by her white master (who used her for sexual practice and eventually gave her to his future wife).[8]

While black women were physically and sexually abused by white men, the image of black women and black femininity was also being devalued by white Eurocentric standards of beauty and femininity.[9] Due to this devaluation of black femininity, as well as the lack of power that women—particularly black women—have in a patriarchal system relative to men, black women have been portrayed as promiscuous and immoral and unattractive compared to the white ideal.[10] Within these ideas of racial purity, the white woman was constructed as the virgin and the black woman as the whore.[11] At the same time, black men were elaborately constructed in our folklore, pornography, and laws as violent, dangerous, and possessing a natural tendency to rape.[12] These depictions of black men as sexual predators of white women evolved into the myth of the black rapist. Images of black men as morally and intellectually inferior sexual predators was in stark contrast to the projected images of white men as intelligent, civilized saviors.[13] In a white male power structure, this enabled white men to justify the sexual exploitation of black women while simultaneously protecting "their" white women from black men. "Lynching emerged as the specific form of sexual violence visited on Black men, with the myth of the Black rapist as its ideological justification."[14] Countless stories of beatings, lynchings, and killings for alleged interracial offenses inflicted on black men, women, communities, even children still haunt today. In particular, the story of Emmett Till—a fourteen-year-old boy who, while visiting the South in 1955, was brutally beaten and murdered by a group of white men for allegedly whistling at a white woman—is still routinely referenced in contemporary popular culture.[15] Ironically, while white men were "protecting" the sacredness of white womanhood from black men, the sexual exploitation of black women by white men was common and widespread. Since the time of slavery, the presence of a large population of visibly mixed individuals has served as proof of the sexual coercion and abuse.[16] These painful events in the history of race relations between whites and blacks remain relevant, especially in black communities, for understanding contemporary interracial relationships, because they still serve as a frame of reference.

Race Talk in Black Communities

While white communities have produced certain images within society about black-white unions, the images and meanings attached to black-white unions in black communities are often much different, though undoubtedly—at least to some extent—a response to the attitudes and beliefs of whites. Despite (and some argue as a result of) white racism and oppression, a sense of a black community has developed, and black individuals have constructed an identity for themselves to replace the negative images and stereotypes prevalent among whites.

Unlike the white respondents, black respondents spoke extensively about their views on race, even beginning the focus group with a general discussion of racial inequalities and the persistence of racism. Kelly, a single woman in her twenties, stated that relations between blacks and whites are still segregated and "not so great," with "not much intermingling." Lydia, a married mother in her forties, agreed that race relations are "not good, and it's getting worse, not better." Alice commented, "On the surface it may appear we are living together, but racial prejudice still exists." Leslie, who is single and in her thirties, also discussed how race relations are getting "more institutionalized," comparing her mother's experiences growing up in the South, "where at least you knew they [whites] didn't like you," to what she sees as the contemporary situation where "we say it is getting better," even though subtle racism still persists. Jean, a married mother in her fifties, concluded that "racism is alive and well; it is thriving." She also stated that among whites there is "no open-hearted acceptance of blacks," and even though she gets along with whites, she feels there is still "a division." All of the black community respondents employed a race-conscious discourse, agreeing that relations between blacks and whites are not good and attributing this to the prejudiced views, racist thinking, and discriminatory actions of whites. Each respondent discussed numerous incidents of "racism" in which they encountered difficulty buying a house in certain neighborhoods, were denied opportunities at work, had to work harder because they were black, or experienced overall negative treatment by whites in society. This view of white society had a significant impact on their views of black-white relationships.

While the black community respondents were clear on the significant role that race played in their lives and opportunities, among the interracially involved black partners the perceptions of racism differed depending on the discourse they employed. For example, black partners who adopted a color-blind approach tended to state that race played a very small role in the way they were treated; for example, Victor described being the only black teacher at his school as a positive aspect that was not racially based. Black partners who deemphasized their racial identity and opposition to their black-white relationships were less likely to report encountering incidents of white racism, which may have affected their views on interracial dating. On the other hand, black partners who emphasized their racial identity and the role of race in their experience were more likely to report having experienced or witnessed significant racism.

The black partners in the study differed in their views on racism, though each had become involved with a white individual, which undoubtedly affected their views in some way. Among the black community respondents, no one was involved interracially and their views on interracial relationships were complex, yet often expressing opposition. When looking at the responses of black communities and the perceptions of black societal responses, the discursive strategies are slightly different. In his recent work on interracial intimacy, Randall Kennedy argues that there are three camps on interracial marriage among black communities: those who see interracial marriage as a positive good; those who see it as a private choice of the individual; and those who repudiate mixed marriages as a distancing from the black community.[17] Based upon my research, I argue that there are not necessarily three separate camps, but rather most black individuals adopt any of these three different strategies depending on the person, situation, and their knowledge/closeness of the relationship. The black responses were complex, ambivalent, and sometimes contradictory. Whereas the white community respondents claimed they accepted interracial marriage but then described the problems they had with it and acknowledged having exclusively white social and family networks, the black community respondents were more likely to report they did have a problem with interracial relationships but then listed various interracial couples among their friends and families who they accepted.

Black on White:
Contemporary Interracial Images in Black Communities

Unlike the white community respondents who were hesitant to speak on the issue of interracial relationships, the black community respondents were vocal and eager to speak.[18] Jean captured much of what the others stated: "I've got no love for interracial marriage, no interest in it. I don't want to be judgmental, because I certainly don't care who goes to bed with *whom,* but I draw the line at interracial relationships." Her use of language is relevant because she starts out strongly declaring her opposition to interracial marriage but then adds a disclaimer by stating she is "not judgmental" and "doesn't care," which is similar to the contradictory language whites use. Jean further explained her views by mentioning her daughter, who went to an elite private school that was predominantly white. She discussed how her daughter was accepted, but she resented the fact that she had all white friends. When it came time for her daughter to go to college, she insisted her daughter go to a black college because she felt strongly about her being in a black social circle. Jean stated that she wanted her daughter to find "a black husband," because there is no reason for her child "to go over to that other group that don't want you anyways." She added that she doesn't want her daughter "in that situation where she could get hurt." The group agreed with Jean that it was acceptable, even necessary, to discourage interracial relationships for loved ones.

Kim, another black community respondent, stated she "still can't walk past an interracial couple without looking at them," and she doesn't know how she would feel if someone close to her "chose a white person; it would be hard." All but two of the black respondents confirmed these were reasons they did not consider interracial dating a personal option. Kelly, for example, said she didn't care what others did, but she wouldn't date interracially, particularly because she wondered if "when they're angry do they call you a 'nigger.'" For these black respondents, interracial relationships were an issue that had generated much thought (it was evident that this was not the first time they talked about it) and something they felt was a growing concern in black families and communities. As Patricia Hill Collins argues in *Black Sexual Politics: African Americans, Gender and the New Racism*, "norms of racial solidarity . . . posit that African American men and women should support each other in every way," identifying marrying within one's race as "an important African American community norm."[19] According to the black community members interviewed, choosing to date or marry interracially is frowned upon because it is seen as an effect of white domination and the internalization by black people of a complex and debilitating prejudice and self-hatred against themselves that makes them perceive whites as superior, and that by associating with whites they can elevate their position.

Despite the overwhelming agreement that interracial relationships were not a preference for one's self, family, or friends, Alice's response illustrates the complexity of the views expressed, and the reported opposition:

> ALICE: I don't let myself get bothered by it [interracial couples], but I just say there's just more in common with your own race. . . . I don't have a problem with interracial couples, I mean I have, even have a friend who is married to a white man, very nice. They have a child, a girl, she's eight [shaking her head] she's very confused, but that's another story . . . but I don't tell them that I'm uneasy [with interracial relationships], because I really do like them.

Alice, like the other black respondents, employs a discursive strategy similar to the white "I don't have a problem with it, but . . . " by offering some disclaimers that they "do not care," "have no interest," or "aren't bothered" by interracial couples, followed by a number of reasons why interracial dating is problematic. The difference is that Alice does have a number of interracial couples in her family and among her friends. Unlike the white respondents, the black community members did not see interracial dating as outside their social circle; rather, it was discussed as something that did occur but often had negative implications, even deleterious consequences. These responses touch on the central issues that emerged from the focus group— interracial relationships are particularly unacceptable for oneself and one's family because of lingering racism, which prevents whites and blacks from being able to come together. In general, there was a sense that interracial relationships are problematic, as well as questioning of how whites treat the black partner and the problems the children face.

Within the discussion of interracial relationships, an interesting exchange took place when two of the black women expressed support for interracial relationships. Jackie, the youngest woman (age eighteen), and Ella, the oldest woman (in her eighties), both disagreed with the opposition of the others. Jackie expressed her belief that "where there is more knowledge" there is "more tolerance." She discussed her experiences in high school where "everyone is friendly" and "young people are more open-minded." She also mentioned that some of her family members are married interracially and her family taught her "to be open and love everyone." She stated, "the problem is parents and grandparents who enforce ideas on children" and that she "may be too idealistic," but she believes "if interracial couples branch out there could be more acceptance." Ella commented for the first time, stating that she "thinks that [Jackie] has a better view" and "is more up-to-date." She stated, "Each of us has part of someone else's blood from slavery." Looking at the other church members, she said, "You don't know whose blood you have." She discussed her memories of a time when blacks and whites weren't allowed to marry, so, according to her, interracial dating and marriage should now be viewed as a positive thing, "as long as there is love there." Jackie and Ella adopted a color-blind approach, arguing that interracial couples were a sign of improving race relations and could even lead to greater racial tolerance. They emphasized the importance of love and its ability to overcome racial problems, similar to the color-blind discourse employed by some of the couples.

Immediately, a number of the others began to speak, but Will got his response to Jackie's remarks out first. He stated that he was not trying "to disillusion" her, but when he was younger he also went to a white high school, dated white girls, and thought "everything was fine." According to Will, even though "everyone is friendly" in high school, "when you get older you see people as adults, and it is different. You learn that those same whites look at you different." He discussed how he went to a historically black college and now has experienced the difficulty of being the "only black male in the corporate office." Will also commented that "once you get out in the world you see interracial dating in a whole new light." Alice added to the discussion by mentioning her child, who has always been the "minority" in a predominantly white school. She remembered how all the children played together when they were younger, but when her child got older she was no longer invited to the white children's parties. Alice described how this reminded her daughter that "she is black and that she is different from whites." Leslie also recounted her experiences growing up in a school system where she was "always one of the only black kids." She stated that she used to "feel kind of optimistic, but as you experience life you get more jaded," and as she looks back now, "things weren't necessarily as I thought." She explained that now, in her "thirties and single," she looks around and sees interracial couples, which is "hard because I'm looking for someone and all I see is black men with white women." Based on their experiences, the other community respondents stated that Jackie's optimism is a result of her limited experiences in high school. Once she gets out of school and enters college or the workplace, she will realize what they have—that whites no longer treat you as a friend or equal, and certainly not as a potential mate. Furthermore, all of the community members, except Jackie and Ella, rejected the color-blind discourse that posits black-white relationships as equivalent to better race relations.

Interracial Choices: Ulterior Motives, Deviance, and Sex

A significant piece of the opposition from the black community members centers on the problems associated with why black individuals choose to date interracially, what the motives for becoming interracially involved are, and the implications for black communities. Among the black community respondents, Leslie discussed how it "bothers" her to see interracial couples because she wonders "what brings them together," adding that she is "curious and stares." Will also agreed, "I don't care what you do on the surface, but underneath I ask why?" A recurring theme among the black community groups (and some black partners) is that blacks are often suspicious of interracial dating, questioning the motives and the sincerity of the white individual. The black community respondents brought up the issue of how whites in general mistreat blacks and in particular of how a white individual may use racial slurs, disrespect the black partner, and not understand what it means to be "black in America." Until blacks have achieved full equality in this country and whites and blacks as groups can form coalitions, many black communities, such as those interviewed, question whether blacks and whites can form true and equal individual relationships.[20] Such distrust of interracial relationships has its roots in history, where black institutions such as the church opposed intermarriage; for example, Cornel West argues that there is a longstanding belief in the black community that the legalization of intermarriage is not representative of whites' belief that blacks are equal but rather a way "to make black bodies more accessible to white bodies."[21]

Black filmmaker Spike Lee's *Jungle Fever* (1992), which involves a relationship between a white woman and a black man, encompasses images that are prevalent among black (and white) communities—such as interracial intimacy is a sexual animalistic attraction, likened to a disease that can be caught and cured. While Spike Lee's films usually challenge the racial hierarchy and racist images produced by white society, when portraying the issue of interracial relationships his depictions of the ways black and white communities respond to these relationships also reproduce the idea of interracial unions as undesirable and problematic.[22] The difference lies in the justification for the opposition: Lee documents an oppositional black perspective based on "black political ideas ranging from Afrocentricity and black separatism to a subtle refrain of black neo-conservatism."[23] Lee even dedicates the film to Yusuf Hawkins, a black teenager killed in the Bensonhurst section of Brooklyn in 1989 by a group of white teens who believed he was coming into this predominantly Italian section to see a white Italian girl. He does provide a sharp critique of the racism that exists in white communities and the strong opposition against interracial relationships that still exists among whites.

In *Jungle Fever,* Flip, a successful married black architect and Angie, his new white temp secretary, develop a relationship over late-night takeout dinners at work, which leads to a sexual encounter on top of his desk. Lee does deviate from dominant Hollywood strategies by including an erotic and highly visual interracial sex scene in *Jungle Fever,* yet it only serves to emphasize the sexual aspect of interracial unions, in contrast to the "routine, missionary position lovemaking scenes between Flipper and his black wife that open and close the film."[24] This sexual encounter results in Flip's wife throwing him out of the house, while Angie is severely beaten by her father for her indiscretion with a black man. The relationship begins as an extra-marital affair and seems to have nowhere to go from the start, since Flip loves his wife, not Angie. The temporary nature of their relationship is conveyed through the scenes showing that the apartment the two are staying in is never unpacked or decorated. In *Jungle Fever,* the interracial affair begins because Flip and Angie are "curious" about one another, as evidenced in their initial conversations about her ability to cook spaghetti and lasagna, Harlem, and skin color. Sexual stereotypes are also explored; in one scene she asks if it is true that black men do not like to give oral sex, and he replies that it is a myth, same as the myth that white men have small penises. Through a gradual process of overcoming prejudice, comparing experiences, gaining confiden-tial insights, and becoming familiar, the two are drawn together.[25] Flip con-tinues to spend time with Angie, even after his wife finds out, taking her to his family's house and various spots such as a black soul food restaurant in his neighborhood. Angie breaks up with her longtime boyfriend because of her relations with Flip and even raises the question of children with Flip. Yet when Flip ends the relationship with Angie, he tells Angie that she got with him in spite of her family only because she was "curious" and that he was "curious about white." Flip and Angie's relationship does not last, and the two ultimately separate, with Flip returning to his wife and Angie returning to her family house. Though Spike Lee shows how complex the responses to interracial unions may be, his portrayal of Angie and Flip's relationship (like other films) still serves to reproduce the image of interracial unions as sexual and not based on love and respect.

Even the progressive HBO series *Sex and the City* reproduced these stereotypes of the sexual prowess of black men. During the fall 2003 sea-son, one of the main women characters, Miranda, becomes involved with a black man in her building who is a doctor for the New York Knicks. The affair is short-lived because Miranda is still in love with her white ex-boyfriend and father of her child, to whom she returns. After the breakup, the black doctor angrily tells her that she used him for sex, mentioning how she had told him no one had ever gone "so deep." In a later scene, the white boyfriend confronts the black doctor after Miranda thinks he is sabotaging her because he is so devastated by their breakup: when the white boyfriend gets to the doctor's apartment, he is with two black women about to engage in a threesome.[26]

These images of black-white unions based on sex, financial motives, or curiosity are found not only in film and television but also within black communities. Gwen and Bill discussed the stereotype of black woman–white man relationships as inherently sexual, but stated that it was not a factor for them. They even emphasized how "nonsexual" her appearance was when they first met, which illustrates how this image (even though they know it does not fit their relationship) is one they must confront. Other black man–white woman couples interviewed responded in light of black communities' views.

> MARK: Like at this black comedy show we went to, like [the comedian on stage] says "who's doing the white girl?" [*referring to Brittney*] He's like "Ah, you see, sisters, they'll always tell you it's hard to find a good man, that a white woman always takes your man, and obviously she's doing something right," and he's making a sexual motion, so then a black girl in the background is like . . . "she's going down on him or something like that" . . . [and the comedian] just kept going on about white women . . . basic comments about sex and that type of thing. Where everybody always thinks it's something sexual, but it's not; they always think it's financial, but it's not.

When Andre discussed the beliefs about interracial unions that he knows of, Sara expressed surprise. She was not aware of any of these images.

> ANDRE: They say a black man is going to date a white woman because of some socially, some social status move, or maybe it's ingrained from slavery that the black man wants what he's never been able to have or a white woman. There's all those disgusting stereotypes of black sexual prowess . . . maybe that's why whites date . . . want to date blacks you know, black men have bigger penises, they're better in bed. I think it's all bullshit . . . they say that white women are easier in bed . . . easier to get in bed . . . even stereotypes against black women. They're too controlling, that they're too, you know, they're stuck up.

While Andre strongly disagrees with the stereotypes about motives, in Victor's discussion of why he has almost exclusively dated white women, he referenced these images of white women as being "easy" compared to "difficult" black women:

> VICTOR: It's not like I would go out and say, well I'll only go out with white women, but I will also confess that with us males, if you don't have to work so hard, why should you? If you sit back, if you went to a party and there were black and white women there, it was easier to make conversation and easier to get the white women

interested in you than it was with the black women. Because [white women] are already curious to begin with, and it is this curiosity factor that you could play upon. The black women already knew you in a sense; she knew a thousand men like you. It was much easier to know there was this crowd of [white] women who wanted to talk to you. They were coming to talk to you. They were curious. Then you had this crowd of [black] women over here who, well, anyway, why work so hard?

While this is not a psychoanalytic study of the couples' motives for becoming involved, Victor's narrative supports the black community respondents' views that some blacks, particularly males, date and marry white women based on certain beliefs and motives that white women are easier.

Based on historical realities and contemporary situations, the issue of motives and reasons for dating interracially is viewed differently whether it is a black woman or a black man. While black men and women have fought to be free from racial subordination and oppression, the connection to interracial sex is markedly different for black women and black men. For black women, racial equality included an escape from the interracial sexual exploitation of white men; for black men, racial equality was an escape from the lynching and abuse that surrounded real or alleged interracial sexual relations with white women. As Patricia Hill Collins argues, "African American women in interracial love relationships face the stigma of being accused of being race traitors and whores, whereas African American men engaged in similar relationships can find their status as men raised."[27] These gendered opportunities and choices surrounding interracial dating were addressed by the black community respondents, emphasizing the motives of black men and white women. Jean discussed her belief that skin color plays a big part in the decision for black men to date interracially, which prompted the following dialogue:

> JEAN: Every Valentines' day, there's a debate between the [black] students, where the black guys say they want a white wife because they like light skin, good hair, and want light children with good hair.
>
> [*There was a silence, and I asked the whole group, "Why do you think this is?"*]
>
> JEAN: It's just self-internalization of racism, that's what it is, those [blacks] who want to date a white person must perceive *themselves* as unattractive.

TERI: I always hear [black] women talking about how white women are taking all the men, but personally I don't care, take the men.

LYDIA: It's funny, I can remember hearing from my mother that since white men have been taking their women so that's why now black men do it.

ALLEN: Not all black men [he smiles], only black men who are re-moved from [their] race; black men who date white are weak. They want a weak and subservient woman.

ALICE: I agree. I agree it comes out of discrimination they face grow-ing up. Why not just be proud of their race?

Most responses in the discussion of the problems of interracial dating were directed toward the black man–white woman couplings. This is due not only to the larger numbers of black men who date interracially as opposed to black women, but also to the underlying reasons behind the disproportionate number of black men compared to black women who date interracially and the dis-tinct meanings associated with these relationships.

Selling Out?

In black communities, interracial relationships are often seen as a sign that one is removed from the black community. More important, they indi-cate a negative image of oneself as a black individual and of black commu-nities in general. Black communities can act as a deterrent to interracial unions, since these relationships are constructed as incompatible with black pride, cultural affinity, and fighting racial injustice. In other words, to en-gage in an intimate relationship with a white person means that one is sell-ing out to white society and in the process has sold out the black community. When it comes to interracial unions, blacks who cross the color line are of-ten accused of sacrificing their blackness for a white ideal. In general, it comes from a belief in the existence of an "authentic" black experience or identity "unmediated by exposure to 'white' cultural influences . . . usually in oppo-sition to hegemonic theories and practices that are perceived as denying the existence of African-American culture."[28] This belief is supported by the works of early black writers such as E. Franklin Frazier, Langston Hughes, Amiri Baraka, and Frantz Fanon, who argued that black men who sought white women suffered from a devaluation of self and a desire to be white.[29]

Contemporary black scholars such as Lawrence Otis Graham also argue against interracial marriage, stating "the cumulative effect is that the very blacks who are potential mentors and supporters of a financially and psychologically depressed black community are increasingly deserting the black community en masse, both physically and emotionally."[30]

Black community respondents addressed the belief that black individuals who intermarry or who engage in intimate relations with whites are "sellouts." Interracial couples were not problematized as individual relationships but rather discussed collectively as representative of a lack of economic and moral commitment to the black community. Among the black community respondents, an integral part of the sellout image revolves around the issue of class, with the sense that successful black men choose white wives. For example, Kim brought up the issue of money and status, stating that "white society approves" of an interracial relationship if it's "a black man with money," but "if the black man is poor, then whites say forget it." She mentioned that she doesn't like certain sports figures because they date white. She wonders, "Why don't [they] just find a sister?" Kelly expressed conflicted views on the issue: "I definitely understand the economic but do think love is important . . . I hate to see blacks putting their money into the white community" and "just wish more black men wouldn't go over to the white community so much." Will offered his perspective, stating that interracial dating is "not genuine," especially because it is usually powerful black men who date or intermarry. He added that "white women don't like poor black men," citing sports figures involved interracially.[31] Again, among the community respondents the idea of selling out primarily was discussed in relation to black men. Black men who date or marry interracially were questioned as to their motives for becoming involved interracially and their commitment to the black community. The issue of money and status was raised as a reason why couples come together. The group argued that mainly successful black men choose to date white women and that whites only accept blacks if they are highly educated and/or wealthy such as sports figures.

Images in black popular culture also reproduce this image of black men selling out, in movies such as *Jungle Fever* and *Waiting to Exhale.* In *Waiting to Exhale,* a popular film in the 1990s based on the best-selling Terry McMillan novel, Bernadine, a married mother of two, finds out that her husband is leaving her for another woman. She asks her husband if it is the "white bitch" from his office, and her husband asks if it would be better if she were black. Bernadine responds, "No, it would be better if you were." His blackness is questioned because of his relationship with a white woman. Similarly, in *Jungle Fever,* when Flip cheats on his wife with a white woman, his wife accuses him of always struggling with his dark skin and blackness, which she feels is why he chose her, with light skin, and now a white woman.

This sellout image is also used for comedic effect in black comedies such as *Undercover Brother* (2003), *Bamboozled* (2001), *The Brothers* (2001), *Living Large* (1991), *Don't Be a Menace* (1996), and *Mo' Money* (1992), which all show a black man with a white woman as a way to illustrate his lack of commitment or loss of allegiance to the black community. *Living Large*, a popular 1990s film, depicts a young black man from an inner-city neighborhood who becomes a newscaster by being at a scene of a breaking news story. In his pursuit of success, he loses touch with the black community. To illustrate he has "sold out," he has an affair with a white woman, speaks formally with proper English, and begins to "act white." When he looks in the mirror, even his appearance whitens. In Spike Lee's *Bamboozled,* the main black character creates a new minstrel show for television that features all the negative stereotypes of blacks and mistreats his black colleagues. After telling his black female assistant that he should have never slept with "the help," meaning her, she replied that if he hadn't been busy sleeping with Mary and Susan (drawing on names that are seen as white), he would have been better in bed and presumably would not have sold out. *Undercover Brother,* a mainstream comedy that was successful at the box office in 2003, tackled a number of racialized stereotypes, including the images surrounding black men, black women, and white women. Satirizing the blaxploitation films of the 1970s, the black hero is out to fight the "man," who is responsible for oppressing blacks. Yet when he goes undercover in the white corporate world, the "man" uses a white woman, referred to as "black man's kryptonite," to bring him down. He cannot resist her and slowly changes the way he talks, the music he listens to, and the foods he eats. When he returns to the black undercover brotherhood organization he is working with and the other black men hear that he has been with a white woman, they respond like adolescent boys, asking how it was, then quickly reverting back to their professional composure and criticizing him for "selling out." The black woman member of the organization is the main source of opposition, and she ultimately rescues him from the white woman's house and influence. Calvin Hernton, in *Sex and Racism,* draws upon these same ideas when he argues "that to almost all black men, no matter how successfully they hide and deny it . . . there arises within almost all blacks a sociosexually induced predisposition for white women. The fact that few blacks will readily admit this is due more to their knowledge that black women and whites in general bitterly disapprove of it, than to their honesty."[32] Regardless of whether these images and ideas are true, they are reproduced and influence the perceptions and understandings of black-white relationships.

Interracial relationships are seen as an unacceptable alternative that allows black individuals to turn their back on their family and community and escape into "white society." Therefore, blacks who do cross the racial divide to date are accused of "selling out" the black race and of not being "black" enough. Overall, their commitment to the black community is questioned as a result of their relationships with someone white. Like the premise of *Undercover Brother*, interracial relationships are viewed as a betrayal of the black community, and what makes the betrayal more painful is that the black individual is betraying the race with the "enemy," who is a member of the group that has oppressed them for centuries.

In many ways, black communities (to speak holistically of a complex and varied group) challenge the identity of any black individual in an interracial relationship, viewing that person as *less* black or even antiblack. Like the films depict, black individuals who intermarry are subject to a line of racial reasoning that questions if he or she is *really* black, black enough to be supported or just black on the outside.[33] Among the black community respondents interviewed, statements that only blacks "who are removed from their race" or those who are "weak" engage in interracial relationships were common. Black college student groups also emphasized the importance of "keeping it real," which includes having a black partner and staying in the "black community." The issues of black identity and commitment to the plight of black Americans are tied to intimate relationships, with the decision to date interracially equated with a weak black identity and less commitment to black communities.[34] These beliefs are communicated in many ways. Recently, an interracially married African American friend of mine took me to meet a group of his high school friends, who he hadn't seen in years. During the conversation, these old friends, who were all black, were asking him about his decision to leave an area of the country they viewed as much more desirable to live in. My friend replied that he preferred an urban setting with a larger black community. Immediately, one of the women asked him, "Is your wife black?" As an outsider to this group, I read her question about the identity of his wife as a question to his commitment. While he was verbally stating his commitment to remaining grounded in black communities, the woman, through her question, relayed the idea that his commitment, or at least her belief in it, was based to some extent on the race of his wife.

This "litmus test of loyalty to the race" is widespread and intergenerational, with black individuals who are interracially involved often confronted with these ideas and beliefs.[35] Although the black partners had different ways of addressing the issue, they all discussed their struggles with identity and others' views of their identity because of the dominant belief among other blacks that they are sellouts. While some black partners dismissed these views, other black partners were obviously deeply conflicted by this belief, describing how they had to work that much harder to be taken seriously with their access to leadership roles and ability to represent the black community.

All of the black partners were aware of the image of "selling out," but they discussed the topic in different ways. Five of the black partners disregarded the stereotype that interracial dating or marriage is selling out by emphasizing how limiting and ignorant the belief is.

> AISHA: I've been called a sellout by black men, but . . . it doesn't make me feel bad because whites don't owe me anything, so I can't imagine what [I'm] selling out to.

> ANDRE: I don't think that [I'm a sellout]. I kind of think I'm better than those people, you know? Like, I'm on a higher intellectual plane than them . . . if you're just going to alienate me [as a sellout] because who I date or what music I listen to, or because of my views, then I got no time for you, really. If you know your history, then you know you've been biased and prejudiced against, so why are you going to be prejudiced against someone else. Again, that's defining me by my skin color and my hair texture to what I'm supposed to do, like I'm not preprogrammed because of, and no one is preprogrammed because of, their race to live a certain way, to think certain things, to date certain people.

> VICTOR: I don't even subscribe to that. Like I said, I have always resisted being thought of as a color, so I'm not going to let anybody do that. I am a human being. I'd like to say sometimes to people when they say, "You're not black," and I look at them and I go, "Wait a minute, I'm any color I want to be, who I want to be, where I want to be, how I want to be," and they catch on. Sometimes my own friends might say a comment, white or black might say a comment like that and that's my retort to that question.

> MARK: Yeah, people think that way about selling out, but if that's the case, I was always a sellout, because I was born a sellout. I was

never black, quote unquote. [*I asked him to elaborate.*] First of all, yeah, I'm black-skinned, that's why I don't understand about this, you know I'm not into all this racial stuff because I'm black. I'm just me. I can only be me, [I can't] try to cater to everybody else's whims or their needs or what they need to see.

These black individuals challenged the sellout image by articulating a color-blind discourse and emphasizing their membership in the *human* race. Randall Kennedy also puts forth a similar argument: "I myself am skeptical of, if not hostile toward, claims of racial kinship, the valorization of racial roots, and politics organized around concepts of racial identity. I am a liberal individualist who yearns for a society in which race has become obsolete as a significant social marker."[36] Kennedy, along with the black partners in this study, maintain that they do not have any obligation to act a certain way or to have a partner of a certain race because they are individuals, not a race.

Among the couples, two of the partners argued against the sellout image. They maintained they had a strong black identity while asserting that their choice in partners was irrelevant to their racial identity.

FRANK: I'm a black male, it's important. I know who I am . . . I've earned that and I won't be anything else. Just treat me with respect, I can't change the color of my hair, the texture of my hair, nothing. I selected her because I loved her. How can you question it [his blackness] it's visible . . . but it's not going to dictate where I live, who I love, what I think.

SHARON: I am a strong black woman on my own; it's about the man, not the color.

Both Sharon and Frank stated they have a strong black identity that is not compromised by their relationship with a white person. They did not feel their actions were dictated by race, nor could they be used as indicators of how "black" they were. Sharon's response reveals ambivalence because she didn't feel that her relationship with Kevin impacted her sense of identity as a black woman or that it should matter who she was with. Her response emphasizes race when discussing her own racial identity, yet it deemphasizes the importance of race when it comes to her white partner. Four of the black partners addressed the sellout image and argued that they were not sellouts, but not because race doesn't matter.[37] Rather, they reaffirmed their racial identity in terms of their commitment to racial issues:

KEITH: I've definitely heard of sellout, but no one has said it to me, but I think it's because I work like everyone else, we live in the neighborhood [a predominantly black neighborhood], and just don't really act like I'm better because she's white.

Keith discussed how his racial identity was not compromised by his relationship because they lived in and were a part of the black community where he had grown up. Others mentioned activities or organizations they were involved in to counter the sellout image.

CHRIS: Sellout, that's what blacks like to say when they don't like the way you are living, whether it be with a white person, or your job, or your neighborhood. I feel secure in my identity, so when people say things like—that's why you got a white wife, or you think you're white—I just try to educate them. One of the biggest obstacles to blacks succeeding is this mentality, you know, that you got to be one way to be black. I'm black, and don't challenge my authenticity because I am educated and I'm with her. Judge me on where I stand and what I do. I am involved in the NAACP. Are you? I give to the United Negro College Fund. Do you? But I also am not going to let my life be dictated, like, "Oh, you can't vote that way. You're black," or, "You can't like them because you're black" . . . that's ludicrous. To me, selling out is when you do something that contributes to the negative images of blacks.

GWEN: If people have questioned my credibility, they've questioned it behind my back. I don't think people would dare question it to my face. The stuff that I have done [both her academic credentials as professor on race and her community work for racial justice], I mean, it's such a dumb question on credibility. However, that doesn't mean that when controversial issues happen [like a recent shooting of an off-duty black policeman by a white officer], I'm sure some people would say—well she has this perspective because her husband's white—I don't object to people making that statement, but I know I'm more likely to step up to the plate than a lot of them are.

Gwen discussed how she even had to struggle with feeling like a sellout and that some interracial relationships justly fit the term, especially involving black men who only date white women.

Gwen: I used to think that, too, I thought for a long time that I was selling out. It was also that you didn't see people of your own race as being attractive and desirable and worth being involved with. I don't think that anymore. I don't think all of us sellout, I think that those of us who are married to whites who are actively involved in the black community feel we must do it, and more likely throw ourselves into it. We might be trying to prove ourselves a bit too much, but there are black males who fit the stereotype [thinking of a few in particular that she knows] that will never date a black woman. I think they are insecure and do anything they can to distance themselves from black, does whatever he can to lighten up his gene pool.

Both Chris and Gwen stated that they were not sellouts, yet it is evident that they struggled with this image and that it had impacted them greatly. Both drew upon their participation and commitment to the black community to contradict this image of a sellout. Among black communities, including the ones interviewed, black individuals who intermarry are no longer trusted and often lose "credibility" among black communities. Therefore, Gwen acknowledged that she may work harder in the black community because of not wanting to be discredited among blacks. This scenario is not uncommon, and there are many stories of black individuals who, because of their interracial marriage (among other allegations of selling out, such as their political beliefs), are discredited by blacks, such as Supreme Court Justice Clarence Thomas. Imamu Amiri Baraka, formerly known as Leroi Jones, left his white wife, Hettie Jones, in 1965 at least partly because of the racial solidarity arguments against interracial marriage and his involvement in the black nationalist movement.[38] Similarly, a successful black psychologist I spoke to described how he had been in a number of interracial relationships and had recently gotten divorced from his white wife and mother of his two biracial sons, partly because of his changing views on his black identity. Now engaged to a black woman, he described how he had been ostracized from the black professional organizations while married interracially. He felt he was not taken seriously, and his marriage was often raised when others disagreed with him. His growing friendships with a number of other black individuals, as well as other nonracial problems in the marriage, also contributed to the divorce. He described how he had felt like a sellout, or at least now looks at interracial marriage as a desertion of the black community and as indicative of a lack of commitment to other blacks.[39] This points to the complexity of interracial relationships—most important, how societal views impact individual views and interracial relationships. Most black views on interracial marriage rarely seem to be completely supportive or opposed but rather shift over time, circumstance, and situation. Even among blacks who are interracially married, such as Gwen, there remains an element of fighting the image yet seeing other blacks, especially black men, as selling out, affirming that this is a reality, not just an image.

The Myth of the Angry Black Woman

Black women are often scripted as the only "legitimate" mate for black men. This role is reinforced in magazines geared toward the black community, such as *Ebony*, which clearly endorses the importance of black men being with black women.[40] Given the emphasis by community members and even media and popular culture on black men–white women relationships, I look specifically at the views of black women, real and perceived. Black women frame their view of intermarriage within a historical context of slavery, sexual abuse, and exploitation. For black women in particular, there exists an explicit and immediate sense of connectedness with the past.[41] Though this disturbing history of sexual relations between black women and white men may contribute to the collective opposition of black women to intermarriage and the low rates of intermarriage among black women, the issue is much more complex, encompassing more recent economic, social, and sexual aspects.

According to the black women in the community research, interracial relationships are an option that they *do not* accept because of contemporary racism as well as the history of sexual relations between blacks and whites. Yet it is also an option they *cannot* choose because of the white standards of beauty that deem them unsuitable mates to whites (and black men who also choose white women),[42] as illustrated in Jean's comments about young black men at the university where she works seeking white or light women. While all the black women in the community research (except Ella and Jackie) stated that when black men engage in interracial relations they are rejecting the black race (which underlies their opposition to interracial dating and marriage), they also discussed how the majority of white men do not find black women attractive or acceptable as mates. Black community members like Leslie, who are single and in their thirties, referenced their own marital status and options in relation to their views and concerns over interracial marriage. The views of the black community women resonate with the writings of black scholars and writers, such as Gloria Wade-Gayles, who has described how seeing a black man with a white woman makes black women feel: "We see them, and we feel abandoned. . . . The truth is we experience a pain unique to us as a group when black men marry white women and even when they don't. It is a pain our mothers knew and their mothers before them. A pain passed on from generation to generation because the circumstances that create the pain have remained unchanged."[43] Bebe Moore Campbell, a successful African American writer also discussed how she and some friends felt when they saw a prominent black actor come into a restaurant with a white woman as a date: "For many African-American women, the thought of black men, particularly those who are successful, dating or marrying white women is like being passed over at the prom by the boy we consider our steady date, causing us pain, rage and an overwhelming sense of betrayal and personal rejection. . . . For sisters, the message that we don't measure up is the nightmare side of integration."

The existence of opposition among black women emerged in the couples' narratives, especially the black men–white women couplings. Four of the white women partners described in detail their perceptions of black women's opposition from their experiences:

> JENNIFER: We have had a lot of problems especially with black girls, some he knows but most just strangers who stare, or say something nasty to him and me.

> JILL: I think black women have a problem with it, obviously, more than I think black men . . . or maybe just show more of a problem. . . . I think that you know they are mad, I'm taking him away, especially like if it's someone good-looking, then they have a problem with it.

> KAYLA: [When she and Hank visited California] black women I heard all the time, saying to him real loud, "What are you doing with that or what's wrong with your own color, what's wrong with your own kind."

> BRITTNEY: I've had [black] women be blatantly pissed off and I'm like you don't even know me . . . and they want to know why can't he go with his own race . . . they don't like from the beginning. They don't even know me. . . . It's just the fact that they are looking at the color of my skin and that . . . I just found them to be real ignorant. I just find they're just not knowledgeable. They're just mad be-

cause they can't have a man, basically, and it's usually the ones that don't, that's just bitter women, they're just angry people, and they're blaming black men for their life, so they have to put their anger somewhere so they put it toward a white woman.

These white women describe the negative treatment from black women as personal and offer little understanding of the larger situation, which angers black women. Furthermore, Brittney argues that these black women are judging her by color, which she feels should not matter. Their views fit in with the color-blind discourse that argues that love is color-blind and it should not matter what race one is. This line of reasoning does not recognize that the issue does have racial implications, with a disproportionate number of black men choosing white partners, compared to the smaller number of black women. Patricia Hill Collins has argued this point, critiquing Maria Root's work on interracial couples as "far more concerned with protecting White women from blame for social relations that leave African American women without partners . . . views such as these not only leave political and economic factors that frame the new racism unexamined, they conveniently let white women off the hook."[44]

Olivia and Frank, who described white individuals and communities as supportive, identified black women as the only ones who ever gave them problems.

> OLIVIA: Of course you go to your friends' houses and they have other friends that you're not necessarily that close with and there were a few [black] women at that barbeque . . . and made a few comments. You know, "Why are you with her, and if you're with her, you must not have anyone good that was black, and you don't know what you are missing" . . . [another time] we go to the theater and there's three black women sitting there and him and me. The one woman closest starts, "Mmmm you sure do smell good," and he said, "Well, thank you very much, but I'm with somebody" . . . then they started, "That's the problem. Why do you have to be with her? Whenever you get the money in your pocket you've got to spend it on a white woman."

Similarly, Victor, who is black, described whites as relatively supportive but black women as opposing:

> VICTOR: I don't think it has happened in along time, but it's mostly black people . . . they will definitely shut you off . . . because you're

with a white woman, because they think you betrayed them. . . . So
that's where, if I'm going to have a problem even now, that's where
there might be a problem . . . walking together somewhere and
there'll be a black girl . . . she'll shake her head like who do you think
you are, and I'll just act like I didn't see her . . .

Victor's comments reveal that he disregarded the views of black women and
his response seems to support the black community views of black men who
intermarry as distanced from black communities. Other couples viewed this
perceived opposition of black women differently.

GWEN: I would think not all black women have opposition to it, but
there are some black women who do, and that's because the number of available black males is very small. Available black males who
are employed and not in prison is very small . . . so black males who
go to predominantly white colleges and marry white women, you
have a lot of educated black males being taken completely out of
the pool and you have these [black] women who . . . and white men
weren't dating the black women . . . so they had little chance for relationships, so there was some resentment toward white women because of that. There is some wondering why that when a black man
makes it that he all of a sudden thinks that white women are more
desirable.

VICTORIA: I think about it differently now than when I was say, seven
years ago. . . . I understand that it's not personal. I mean black women
have legitimate concerns . . . and in general black women, and for
that matter men, might tell you how they feel against the relationship, but at least it's honest, upfront, and not like, "Oh, you're not
good enough" [to the white person], more like why do you have to
take a good black man from the community, because we're hurting
and it's all white people's fault already. I understand it, not that I
think opposing interracial marriage is the answer, but I see where
the black community is coming from.

As a black woman, even though she is interracially married, Gwen understands the responses of black women and how the opposition is based on
realistic concerns about the small number of available black men (and the
small number of white men who date interracially). As a white woman,
Victoria discussed how her views have changed from those of the other white
women, including Kayla, Jennifer, and Brittney, to where now she understands
why black women might have a problem with interracial unions. Victoria's

husband, Chris, also discussed how his marriage to a white woman made his sisters and other women in his family feel like somehow he was buying into the belief that "white is right," like many of the black men they encountered who only wanted to date white. Interracial marriage, along with incarceration, drug abuse, and homicide, is often viewed as the cause of the shortage of marriageable black men, which makes intermarriage further resented because it is seen as responsible, at least partly, for the large number of single women in the black community.[45]

In black popular culture, the opposition of black women to interracial relationships has been depicted in a number of films. One of the best examples is *Waiting to Exhale* (1995), which addresses the issue of interracial relationships from the perspective of black women. Bernadine, one of the four black lead characters, finds out that her husband is leaving her for his white secretary. Later another white woman is a barrier to Bernadine's happiness when she meets a man with whom she immediately bonds and is attracted to, then it is revealed that he is also married to a white woman. Both *Jungle Fever* and *Waiting to Exhale* contain a scene where a group of black women discuss black men and relationships, focusing on the "problem" of white women. For example, in the scene from *Jungle Fever,* Flip's wife, Drew, and her friends discuss the "low-class white-trash white women" who throw themselves at black men. The issue of black men's obsession with white women and light skin is explored, with the black women referring to the white standards of beauty and femininity that have been used to devalue black women. The women conclude that if it wasn't for the "29,000 white bitches . . . who give up the pussy" and are "stealing" all the black men, they would have men to date and marry. Intermarriage is understood as a rejection of blackness and an internalization of the dominant belief held by whites that blacks are inferior. In *Waiting to Exhale*, the same issues are raised and the conclusion is that white women (along with incarceration, drug abuse, homosexuality, and homicide) are the reason they cannot find a "good black man." Through these different images, opposition to interracial unions among black women, collectively speaking, is conveyed. Based on the views of the black communities interviewed, these scenes offer a realistic portrayal of the ways interracial relationships affect black women.[46]

Color Lines: Friends, Neighbors, and Communities

Just as white friends and neighbors were often perceived as supportive despite their personal views against interracial relationships, so were black friends and neighbors. In particular, couples discussed the responses of black friends by differentiating between their views of the couple's relationship as opposed to their personal views on interracial dating for themselves or their family. The couples' narratives of their black friends also support my argument that views on interracial relationships vary greatly depending on the person, place, and situation. It is common for friends to express support for the couple's relationship yet not necessarily endorse interracial relationships in general or for themselves. Examples include friends who have made comments that they or their family would not and should not date interracially.

> MICHAEL: We mostly do things by ourselves, like dinner, movie, and whatnot. . . . she does go out with *her* [black] friends to clubs or functions, but that's not something I would really participate in. . . . they don't care that she's with me, but they wouldn't.

> LEE: My friends are cool with it, it's not a problem for them.
> JILL: Well what about Trevor [Lee's black friend]?
> LEE: He doesn't care, he likes Jill, but just for himself personally he wouldn't, it wouldn't be him, he feels it shouldn't be that way, you know, all that white people have put [blacks] through.

Michael describes Aisha's friends as not caring that she's with him but objecting to interracial relationships in general. Lee describes his friends as supportive of the relationship even though they would not date interracially. Jill clearly viewed Trevor—who wouldn't date interracially—as opposed to their relationship. This reveals the different interpretations of others' responses between the couple, which is easy to explain given the multilayered responses of blacks like Lee's friend Trevor, who supports someone's relationship in practice but in theory objects to interracial dating.

Another example of these changing views involves a story Gwen and Bill told about a black colleague of Gwen's. He invited Gwen to bring her husband to dinner with him and his wife, mentioning to Gwen how excited he was to meet Bill and hang out. His wife was white, so Gwen didn't even think there was a possibility that her husband being white would be a problem:

> GWEN: We got invited to dinner, and I never, I mean I never discussed because I didn't see any reason to say, "Oh, by the way, my husband is white," . . . so we rang the bell, and when he opened the door and saw Bill, his face fell off.

BILL: . . . and we never got invited back.

GWEN: I guess it was okay for him [to marry a white woman], but it wasn't okay for me. He really expected to see a black male walk in with me. Never in a million years did he expect to see a white male. I remember to this day the expression on his face. Wow, it was so obvious, he couldn't hide it.

This example highlights the complex way that individuals respond to interracial relationships and emphasizes the way individuals may endorse interracial relationships on one level (in this case for oneself) but not on other levels or for other people. It also points to the importance of gender and how certain couplings are more offensive to certain groups (men opposing women of their race with men of another race, and vice versa).

Some couples, however, described their predominantly black circle of friends as overwhelmingly supportive:

KEITH: We live in a black neighborhood and that's where we hang out. I still have the same [black] friends I grew up with. It's not a choice, but I couldn't see us living in a white suburb. That's not what Danielle wants, either.
DANIELLE: We met because I knew his friend's girlfriend who are black, and we work in the city. We definitely feel more comfortable in a black community.

BRITTNEY: I don't have any friends from moving so much and just growing apart, so we don't have many friends, but if we do they're Mark's friends.
MARK: I grew up in Brooklyn, so I still have some [friends] there, and then there's a few guys I work with . . .
BRITTNEY: And they're black.
MARK: Yeah, they're all black.

Both couples stated that their social circles are predominantly black due to their neighborhood, their jobs, or their childhood, only minimally addressing this as a preference. Certain couples also expressed that because they lived in predominantly black or racially diverse areas, they had no problems in their neighborhoods.

> STANLEY: I constantly told Kim about not wanting [our son] in certain areas . . . even when there was the opportunity, I wouldn't have him bussed to school in a rich neighborhood so he could be some token.

Stanley and Kim chose a predominantly black neighborhood to live and raise their child. When they bought their house in the 1970s, their "friends and most of society thought it was a bad decision," because the neighborhood was deteriorating and cheap due to "white flight." Both have professional medical careers at a hospital and they have a middle-class income, yet they choose to live in a lower-income black neighborhood rather than a predominantly white middle-class area because they feel more accepted.

Danielle and Keith and Brittney and Mark chose to live in a predominantly black neighborhood because of both their financial ability and their personal preference. Their narratives reveal, however, that this may have been their only choice.

> DANIELLE: We want to live here, I don't care if people say it's the inner-city or—oh, it's a bad area—that's just because it's black . . . yeah if we could afford a big beautiful house we would, but right now we rent and I'm not gonna pay hundreds of dollars more somewhere else.

> KEITH: Even if we had more money I don't know if we would move. I grew up right near here and this is where we feel comfortable. I just see us trying to rent in [an upscale predominantly white area], forget the money, no one would rent to us.

Danielle and Keith indicated that they feel more comfortable in a predominantly black neighborhood, but Keith also implied that it would be difficult to move into a white neighborhood. Brittney and Mark also recounted this experience.

> MARK: We live here but a lot of that has to do with that we couldn't rent anywhere else. It's not like we didn't try . . . it's obvious when we show up that this [white] guy isn't going to rent to us, me being black, I'm with her and she's white . . .

> BRITTNEY: Where we live is fine. You know, it would be . . . well to be able to live in a nicer neighborhood, not that's all white but that's all you have here . . . we even had a real estate agent say that she thought certain places wouldn't rent to us, she was nice and was just trying to let us know how things are even though it's not said upfront.

Mark and Brittney's experience illustrates how interracial couples can encounter problems when trying to rent an apartment, and it also points to the segregated nature of many areas where neighborhoods are either predominantly minority or predominantly white, with not many diverse areas, especially outside of major metropolitan areas like Los Angeles and New York.[47]

Another issue that emerged through the couples' discussion of neighborhoods is the importance of the intersection of race and class. Oftentimes it seems that interracial couples such as Stanley and Kim, Danielle and Keith, Jennifer and Lance, and Brittney and Mark have an easier time living in black neighborhoods or lower-class areas. While a few couples, such as Frank and Olivia and David and Sandra reported that their predominantly white communities were supportive, they also told stories of incidents that contradicted that support. The couples who lived in all-black neighborhoods described them as accepting and did not report any incidents in their neighborhoods that signaled differently. While opposition or negative views toward interracial marriage may exist, Keith's explanation of living in the black community where he grew up and of not changing because he married Danielle makes it seem plausible that they are accepted.

Black churches, like black neighborhoods, were also viewed as relatively more accepting than white counterparts. The issue of religion and the church played a prominent role in the couples' relationships. Whether or not they practiced a religion, many couples had strong views on religion and the church's role in supporting or discouraging interracial relationships. Furthermore, in black communities black churches have traditionally occupied a central role: the black church has been the "spiritual face . . . in some sense a 'universal church,' claiming and representing all Blacks out of a long tradition."[48] The idea of black churchgoers as symbolic of black communities has historical relevance, with black churches like Trinity Baptist Church, where the black community research was conducted, still providing a sense of community and common meeting ground in black neighborhoods.[49]

Many black-white couples attended, or perceived as most accepting, predominantly black churches (whether black Baptist or Episcopalian).

> SHARON: I grew up in the Baptist church . . . and I think that would be most accepting, though don't get me wrong, [interracial couples] would still get looks, but not like some white church.

> AISHA: We don't go to church right now. Michael works on Sundays . . . we want to go to this [black] church in Harlem where the minister who married us is.

MICHAEL: I took a class on "the Black Church," and it really opened my eyes, sort of changed the way I think about race relations . . . there's a lot more problems than I realized. It really interested me in getting involved [in a black church].

Despite the idea that black churches are more supportive than white churches, some couples discussed how the black priest or minister counseled them on their relationships and the problems that they might encounter. This was the case with Aisha and Michael, who were married in a predominantly black Episcopalian church:

AISHA: The minister counseled us on being interracial . . . having children, like what would we do if the child comes home and had been called an "Oreo," what would we do? Things like that.

The minister seemingly wanted to make sure Aisha and Michael were aware of the racism they (and their future children) might face.

What is interesting about the issue of church is that despite the perceived higher levels of acceptance at black churches, the black church community respondents I interviewed expressed significant opposition to black-white relationships and gave many reasons why they saw these relationships as problematic. The Reverend Mildred Johnson of Trinity Baptist Church stated that interracial couples would not face any opposition at her church, since her congregation is "a very accepting church," where "more weight is given to character than color."[50] Reverend Johnson explained that blacks are painfully aware of the "reality of racism" and prejudice of the larger white society; therefore, she believes black churches are less likely to judge others based on race or racial difference. Nonetheless, when marrying interracial couples, she addresses issues such as "the challenge of being interracial, the additional challenges they face." Although for her the "bottom line is if they love each other," the reverend also tells couples "to count the costs before entering into this union" and to think about issues such as children, where to live, and what group of people to be with.

It is relevant to note my own experiences while conducting the research. During the extended time I spent observing at the church, all parishioners were warm and welcoming to me, despite my outsider status as a white woman (who they later learned was married interracially) and a non-Baptist. Based on this acceptance, and the inspirational services emphasizing Jesus' acceptance of all people, especially those ostracized for whatever reason from the larger society, I anticipated that the responses of the black community members would probably be generally supportive. Nonetheless, attitudes within the black community are complex. Although I was accepted and the official discourse was to accept everyone, the black community respondents did not favor black-white unions.

Opposition in Black and White

The basis of opposition in black communities differed significantly from white communities. In general, interracial relationships were viewed as detrimental to the black group and a threat to the "survival" of the black community. Due to the relatively small size of the black population in the United States compared to the white population, the existence of the "black community" and "black culture" are threatened by intermarriage, particularly considering that when race boundaries are crossed, it is the black community that gets "polluted" with the interracial families and biracial individuals.[51] Based on contemporary racism, the painful history of race relations, and the importance of maintaining the black community, interracial marriage was understood and discussed as a politicized social issue in black communities, not as an individual relationship judged on its own characteristics.

Gender also played a role in the opposition among black communities, yet in different ways than with the white communities. The painful history of miscegenation in black communities is based on black women being raped by white men during and after slavery and on black men being brutalized or killed by whites over the accusation of interracial sexuality.[52] In contemporary society, the context of interracial relationships is different. They are consensual love relationships. Regardless, black families and black communities oppose marrying a white person because it is seen as rejecting the black race and buying into the dominant belief held by whites that blacks are inferior. Based on the couples' narratives, a number of black partners, particularly the women, recount the importance of the painful history of race relations in their families' views of the relationship. Since black men were lynched and killed because of the implications of an interracial encounter, many black families cite concern about the safety of black men involved in interracial relationships as the reason for their opposition (as Spike Lee depicted in *Jungle Fever*). This concern is based, at least partially, on the violence inflicted on black men by white men if there was even a hint of sexual contact, or the desire for it, between a black man and white woman. Also, since black women were sexually exploited for centuries by white slave owners and employers, the idea of a black woman engaging in a relationship with a white man also opens up these historical wounds.[53] The fact that the black community members addressed with strong emotion the issue of interracial relationships reveals how this issue has impacted these black individuals and communities. The community's opposition undoubtedly has roots in this history, as well as the contemporary realities of racism. To them, black women risk being mistreated by their white partners, while black men coupled with white women are lost to the white community.[54]

The "loss" of black men to intermarriage is seen as more detrimental to the African American community because of the lack of available black men and their potential to earn more money and status. It is assumed that a black man with a white woman is wasting his success on the white woman and in the white community. The black community respondents raised legitimate concerns about the future of black communities. For black women there is the question of whether there will be a black man to raise a family with because of the shortage of black men.

According to most couples, however, black communities and black families, despite any opposition or derogatory images, are still more accepting of interracial unions than whites.[55]

> LEE: Me, I think blacks accept more. They'll accept it quicker than whites will . . . white opposition is just total racism . . . but black people may just not like whites because of what's been done.

> GWEN: I mean [black and white opposition] is very different. The black opposition for the most part has to deal with, at least for black women, what's going to happen to us if there are no black men to date, we won't have relationships, we won't have kids. . . . The other opposition when blacks oppose black women with white men, it really is rooted in the history of rapes that occurred on the plantations . . . it really comes [to] the abuse and misuse of black women. It has a strong history and I would say that my mother's reaction to us had a lot to do with the fact that she was afraid that I'd be hurt by this relationship . . . but [white] opposition to it has a lot to do [with] racism . . . thinking that it's impure, it's unnatural, that kind of thing.

The couples stated that blacks are most vocal about their opposition but that "whites have a problem . . . but are afraid to express it because of fear of blacks in general."

Conclusion

On a number of levels, black-white relationships threaten black communities: these relationships are viewed as detrimental to the black family structure and the survival of the black community, as well as representative of a self-internalization of racism among the blacks that engage in these relationships. The image of "sellout" encompasses much of the oppositional views of blacks, where choosing to date or marry white is equated with a rejection of the black community and an attempt to position oneself with whites in the racial hierarchy. This image not only represents the opposition but also acts as a deterrent against engaging in interracial unions. Black communities (and black popular culture) often view a black person in an interracial relationship as "less black," and the community questions the motives and sincerity of the relationship. Black individuals in black-white relationships often struggle with issues of identity and develop different discursive strategies for negotiating being black and interracially involved.

The opposition and ambivalence surrounding the issue of interracial couples is evident. Unlike the white individuals, families, and communities interviewed, the black individuals, families, and communities had extensive knowledge and views on black-white relationships; interracial unions are something that they have experienced and seen firsthand. While the black community members (and black popular film images) explicitly outlined problems with black-white relationships, these same individuals often knew and had friends or family members who were involved interracially. The research reveals how individual whites and interracial couples may be welcomed into families or communities, even though on many levels black communities have significant problems with interracial relationships.

More times than I can recount I have encountered black individuals—students, colleagues, acquaintances at community events, even the black community members I interviewed—who opposed interracial relationships yet embraced me and my children. This is largely because opposition to interracial relationships in black communities has less to do with their views on whites and more to do with what interracial relationships symbolize—a weakening of black identity and community. This ambivalence is evident in Reverend Johnson's closing statements after having listened to her parishioners' responses that expressed opposition to black-white couples: "Blacks are more accepting than other races. . . . we come to accept this as the person we love, when we see interracial couples we don't treat them differently we embrace them . . . I think of Martin Luther King . . . and we are accepting people for who they are . . . judge by character . . . sometimes we have to try

to understand interracial relationships but most times we can accept them."
Reverend Johnson maintained that people are judged by their character, not
the color of their skin, at least in the black community. While adopting a color-
blind approach in some aspects, her statements also reflect the ambivalence
of the black responses of opposition to interracial relationship. Whereas white
opposition to black-white unions is primarily based on a racist belief that
blacks are inferior and less desirable (socially, culturally, and economically)
as marriage partners, black opposition is primarily based on the knowledge
that these racist beliefs exist and that whites are seen as unacceptable partners because of the way whites treat blacks—and not necessarily something
inferior or undesirable about white individuals—as well as the perception that
black individuals who are involved interracially have deserted the black community. However, interracial couples may be accepted once they are known
and viewed as different.

CHAPTER 4

Families and the Color Line

MULTIRACIAL PROBLEMS FOR
BLACK AND WHITE FAMILIES

Black-white couples come together across the boundaries of race and perceived racial difference seemingly against the opposition of their communities. This is not to say, however, that the couples are free from racialized thinking, whether it be in their use of color-blind discourse or their own racial preferences, such as to date only interracially or to live in all-white neighborhoods. Nonetheless, these couples create multiracial families, not only creating multiracial families of their own but also changing the racial dynamic of the families from which they come. What significance does this have for the institution of family, and how does this play out for the white and black families to whom it occurs?

It might be expected that the family is the source of the greatest hostility toward interracial relationships. It is in families that the meanings and attachments to racial categories are constructed and learned; one's family is often "the most critical site for the generation and reproduction of racial formations."[1] This includes who is and is not an acceptable marriage partner. In white and black families, certain discourses are used when discussing black-white relationships that reproduce the image of these unions as different, deviant, even dangerous. Interracial relationships and marriage often bring forth certain racialized attitudes and beliefs about family and identity that otherwise may have remained hidden. The ways that white and black families understand and respond to black-white interracial couples and the racialized discourses they use are inextricably tied to ideas of family, community, and identity. White and black families' (and communities') interpretations and responses to interracial couples are part of these available discourses on race and race relations in our society. Many times, black-white couples provide the occasion for families to express and play out their ideas and prejudices about race and sex, which is integral to understanding the social construction of "interracial couples" within America today.

All in the Family: White Families

Among whites, the issue of interracial marriage is often a controversial topic, and even more so when they are asked to discuss their own views or their family's views.[2] The white community respondents in this study were hesitant to discuss their personal views on family members becoming involved interracially. One discursive strategy used by the respondents was to discuss other families they knew rather than their own views. For example, during the white focus group interviews, the first responses came from two individuals who had some experience or knowledge of interracial couples or families. Sara discussed a friend who adopted two "very dark" black children and how white people would stare at her and the children in public. Anne mentioned her niece who married a black man and said "the family is definitely against it," which causes them problems.

In group interviews with white college students, a number of the students also used stories about other interracial families they knew to explain why their family would prefer they marry someone of the same race. One college student said her family would have a problem with her marrying interracially, explaining that their opinion is based on their experiences with an interracial family in their neighborhood. She had babysat for this family and, according to her, they had "social issues because the dad was *real dark* and the mom was white, and the kids just had major issues." Her choice of words reveals the importance of color and the use of a discursive strategy such as referring to the children as a problem and not the relationship itself.

Like the white community respondents, interracial couples like Frank and Olivia also avoided discussing their own families directly, instead discussing the responses of other families. Frank talked about the family of another white woman he had dated before Olivia.

> FRANK: I was dating this Italian girl and [the family] invited me down for dinner. I was a detective [at that time], and I'll never forget it. It wasn't that it was derogatory, but her father sat there, he excused the women, and I'm sitting with the brothers. I'm sitting next to [the father] and he goes, "Frank, it's not that I don't like you, but I just

can't let my daughter marry a nigger." Then he said, "now you have dinner, enjoy, but don't ever mention this to [my daughter]." So I ate dinner. But it was just the Italian hard line . . . I broke it off. I gave my word and I didn't tell her why, because I would not break that trust. I don't think it was out of fear . . . he wasn't nasty about it, though. He let me sit at his table.

OLIVIA: The more removed generations just don't understand the concept and it doesn't even have to be racial, just out of your own. I don't really think it's so much that it's an antiblack thing as stepping outside your family.

FRANK: Yeah, that's the way I felt.

In their discussion of this incident, both Olivia and Frank deemphasized the importance of race in the father's words and actions, choosing instead to view it as a question of family. Even when confronted with blatant racism and racist language, Frank's interpretation is color-blind. This story also points to the importance of gender and, more specifically, how patriarchy works where men (often fathers) make the decision about who their women can date.

White "Concern" and Preference

For the white college students interviewed, the role of family is key and certainly influences their decisions not to date interracially. The majority of white students expressed verbally or by raising their hand that their parents, white parents in general, would have a difficult time with an interracial partner for a number of reasons. Yet their parents' opposition was described in nonracial terms, much like their own views. For example, one white male student said, "All parents find something wrong [with the person their child chooses] if they're not exactly as they imagined. My parents would be *surprised* because [an interracial relationship] is not what they are expecting, so it would be difficult in that sense." Many students simply stated something to the effect of "my parents aren't prejudiced; they just wouldn't want me to marry a black guy."

Other students described their families' views against interracial dating as based on the meanings of family and marriage in general. For example, one male student stated that his parents would have a problem with an interracial relationship, because "they brought me up to date within [my] race. They're not like racist, but [they say] just keep with your own culture, be proud of who you are and carry that on to your kids." Some students cited the difference between dating and marriage. As one female college student said, "It becomes more of an issue when you get to be juniors or seniors, because you start thinking long-term, about what your parents will say, and dating a black person just isn't an option." Another student described dating interracially in similar terms: "Dating's not an issue, they always encouraged [me] to interact with all people. For the future and who you're gonna spend the rest of your life with, there's a difference between being with someone of the same race and someone of a different race, [interracial marriage] is not like it's wrong but . . . just that it would be too difficult."

In one of the discussions of family with the white college students, an interesting incident occurred. One of the male students, who was vocal throughout the focus group, sat listening to the other students and looking around the room. Finally he interrupted the discussion: "Are you kidding me? . . . parents would shit, they'd have a freaking heart attack. [*He dramatically grabs the front of his shirt and imitates a growling father's voice*] "Uhh, son, how could you do this to us, the family?" Everyone laughed at his performance, but this student's use of humor to depict his father (or a white father in general) having "a heart attack" is an interesting discursive strategy. Although he presented it in a comical way, his statement does not seem unrealistic to the group. Often, jocular speech is used to convey a serious message in order to avoid being labeled racist or prejudiced.[3]

When asked why their families would respond in these ways to an interracial relationship, the group largely cited the "opposition of the larger society" as the reason why they and/or their family personally would prefer that their family not become involved interracially.[4] Among the white college students, parents were described as "concerned about how difficult it would be." The following two comments illustrate the students' responses:

> My parents are *not* prejudiced [*her emphasis*] . . . they are completely open-minded, but [their concern] comes out of how others would act.

> My parents would just worry and wouldn't want me to make my life harder than it had to be.

These students saw their parents' concern about societal opposition as legitimate and did not question or imply that their families opposed interracial unions simply for themselves. This concern and desire to spare their chil-

dren the difficulties of interracial marriage illustrates white privilege and reveals how white families, without mentioning race, acknowledge that they
do not want their family member to experience the racial discrimination and
lessened opportunities that blacks face.

Among the white community respondents (who were primarily older
than the college students and had children of their own), societal opposition
was also blamed for their own decisions to avoid or discourage interracial
relationships in their families. For example, Linda stated that the "problems"
interracial couples face are the reason she would "say no" on the issue of
interracial relationships. In particular, she mentioned the problem of the children, stating that "it's just not fair to the children." James discussed how his
children married individuals of the same race and ethnicity, not because he
would have cared or told them not to, but because "that's where they feel
comfortable." He added that he has heard that children from interracial unions
have "problems," expressing the confusion over their identity with such questions as "are they white, half and half, will they be accepted?" These responses
reflect an opposition to interracial relationships, yet the blame is placed on
society and not the individual's personal views. A number of white partners
also used this discursive strategy when discussing their familial responses,
which will be examined later.

In general, the responses of the white student and white church communities were very similar. The white students discussed how their parents
would be concerned or disappointed if they became involved interracially,
yet they often deemphasized or minimized the racial aspect. The students
seemed to find it important to convey that their parents were not racist and
did not hold prejudiced views, despite their parents' opposition to interracial
dating and marriage. In addition, their parents' desire for their children to
marry within their own race is not interpreted as opposition, just an expression of concern or a pride in their own culture. Many students shifted between stating that race and/or color is insignificant to them and to their parents
to acknowledging that race would be an issue, at least to their parents. Also,
the white students all stated that they did not think it was likely that they
would date outside their race. Similarly, most of the community respondents
stated that they did not oppose interracial relationships; they just didn't want
it for *their* family. The white students and community respondents indicated
that their families were not opposed to interracial relationships, but they did
not feel one would happen in their family or social circle. By rejecting the
idea of interracial marriage for oneself or one's family, racial boundaries are
secured by reproducing the image of blacks as not the same as whites.

When White Families Become Interracial

While the white community respondents subtly expressed the idea that black-white unions were not acceptable or at least not a likely possibility in their families, there is a difference between interpreting how individuals *would* respond and how they actually *have* responded. Therefore, it is interesting to compare the black-white couples' narratives on the white family responses with the white communities' responses. In general, the couples had similar experiences and incidents of opposition in their families, yet the ways these couples interpreted the familial responses seemed to differ based on whether the couples adopted a color-blind discourse that deemphasized the role of race or a race-conscious approach that emphasized the role of race.

Six of the fifteen black-white couples interviewed stated that their families were completely supportive of their relationships. For example, Sandra and David said their families had no issues with their relationship. Despite this statement of support, Sandra later described how her grandparents felt:

> SANDRA: My grandmother had certain views . . . mostly from TV that made her uncomfortable . . . so they didn't come to the wedding, and it wasn't until the baby was born [after ten years of marriage] that she sent us a check. . . . now we exchange Christmas cards but haven't visited, I don't know if I say it is that she *opposes*, but she is just from that older generation that doesn't understand . . . but that's not how my mother was raised.

Rather than acknowledge that her grandmother "opposes" the relationship, which seems clear from the grandmother's response, Sandra chooses to discuss her grandmother's views as reflective of her generation. Similarly, Jill hesitated when asked how her family responded but did ultimately answer that they were supportive. In later discussions she said that there are some members in her family who do not approve and that with others she may not know their "honest feelings, but they don't *say* anything negative."

> JILL: I mean, my grandmother doesn't really approve . . . and I just think that's what their beliefs are and I love them and they're around, but they're not really in my life all the time, so it's kind of like life goes on. She's nice to Lee, and I don't necessarily think like she sees him and goes, "I want to break this relationship up." I don't think it is that big of a problem. My grandmother and grandfather are getting older, and I don't know if they know what's going on anyway.

Jill explains her grandparents' response in the same way Sandra did, by minimizing their opposition and excusing their views, at least in part because of their age.

Overall, these couples' responses were similar to the community responses. They described the white families as supportive and discussed any negative reactions to their relationship in nonracial terms. The way Lisa described her family's response exemplifies this strategy. She stated her family has been supportive but describes her father in the following way:

> LISA: My parents divorced when I was thirteen, but growing up there were never any racial slurs; yet, as I found out later, my father is more the prejudice one and since he has remarried, they actually reinforce each other, him and his new wife. There was one time, those once-a-year visits where he happened to see the picture [of Victor, whom she was dating at the time] and his whole head and neck, everything turned red. He was furious. Well, they, he and his wife, use the "n" word, but I didn't want to hear it, and later, when I told him I was engaged, he asked what kind of name is that? [Victor's last name] and I knew what he meant, but I didn't tell him [that he was black], so I ended up putting a photo of us in his invitation to the wedding, and if I could have been a fly on the wall then. . . . but he didn't respond, even though I did write that this was going to be one of the happiest days of my life and I'd love him to come if he could overcome his views . . . but I never knew what the real reason was. I mean, he had always been an alcoholic asshole, so I never knew what he thought . . . but, you know, with my situation it really isn't a race issue, because he isn't a father to me anyway, so it's not like I'm expecting anything different. You know, if I married an Irish boy with red hair, he still wouldn't be calling me or in my life.

Lisa interpreted her father's reactions as due to his character rather than his views on race. She clearly stated that he is "prejudiced" and uses racial slurs, but she did not believe his decision to miss her wedding was racial.

The ways that whites articulate their views on black-white relationships often creates an ambivalence that some partners feel about their family's response. Kayla discussed how her family reacted to her current relationship with Hank as well as to her first interracial relationship with Jay, her ex-husband and father of her two children.

> KAYLA: When [Jay, her ex-husband] was going to pick me up for a date at my parents', where I was living, I felt weird even having to

tell them he was black because really what's the big deal, but at the same time I did because if I didn't they would have been a little surprised . . . my mom, especially, and *again not prejudiced* at all but just being like you need to make sure this is what you want to do, and I want you to be aware of other people . . . Then they started worrying because they thought I only was around blacks now . . . and then I had to tell them I was pregnant [and not married yet] and my father just bawled, and my mother, *again who's not prejudiced*, just didn't speak, actually for two weeks . . . but finally they accepted that I was having the baby, but my mom cried the whole time we got married, and not tears of joy, though they were there for me when I needed them . . . then after all [the second baby, marital problems, and divorce] she was kind of happy, because I said I wouldn't be with a black man again, now *she's not prejudiced* at all, but just seeing what I went through and she hadn't seen it with white guys.

Later, Kayla and Hank discussed how her family feels about their relationship:

KAYLA: He's definitely like part of the family, and my parents accept him with open arms, so it's nice to see the support that way, just because he's been wonderful to me, people don't see color anymore, and I think maybe it wasn't because Jay was black but because our relationship ended so badly.

HANK: Her family is cool, I feel welcome in the house, I mean I can't really say they have ever been disrespectful.

In general, these individuals minimized the opposition of the family and deemphasized the importance of race, focusing on other reasons to explain the familial attitudes and behaviors. Kayla's language (similar to a number of the college students') revealed how she tried to balance out the seemingly oppositional words and actions of her mother, by emphasizing three times that her mother is "not prejudiced." She had a close relationship with her mother and seemed to want to protect her mother's image from others as well as herself and quite possibly Hank. Also, when she discussed her family's feelings about her current boyfriend, her views of how her family reacted to her ex-husband shifted. She blamed their negative reaction on the bad relationship, even though they objected to him long before the relationship went bad. Using a color-blind discourse, Kayla and other white partners interpreted their families' responses in a way they felt was nonracial and less oppositional.

Like Kayla, many whites (white partners and white community respondents) reported that their parents and families were not prejudiced and had not raised them to judge others by the color of their skin. For example, Jane, a white community respondent, said she raised her family to be color-blind: "it's not the color of their skin, it's what in their hearts." Yet when asked about the possibility of her family members marrying across racial lines, Jane clarified that "marriage is a different situation." Despite her color-blind beliefs, she acknowledges that she would not be comfortable with interracial marriage, "not because there's anything wrong with blacks," but because of the issues that marriage brings, such as children. Jane's views are similar to Jennifer's experiences with her family. Jennifer's parents found it difficult to accept her relationship with Lance, despite the way they had raised her.

> JENNIFER: Well, my father told me . . . they'd always raised us not to judge people on the color of their skin, and my dad always said he didn't care if someone was purple, yellow, black, whatever, as long as they were nice . . . but he has a hard time dealing with my relationship [with Lance] . . . my mother raises concerns, like she will say, "I'm not being racist, I'm not saying there is anything wrong with interracial dating, but I want you to take into consideration the stress and impact it's going to have on you. It's not going to be a normal relationship." She was just trying to clue me in to the problems it might cause in the future as far as children, buying a home, and things like that . . . but I think they like Lance.

Jennifer was unclear how to interpret her parents' response. They raised her to accept everyone, so she struggled to understand their reservations about the relationship because it seemed like a contradiction. Jennifer's mother's response was similar to the white community responses, in that societal opposition was cited as the basis for her own personal concerns. By doing this, the mother did not have to acknowledge that she might have held prejudiced or racist views. Interesting to note is the way color was described as insignificant ("purple, yellow, black, whatever"). The very reason people make these types of statements is because skin color and race do matter, most often to those who espouse a color-blind discourse.[5] For Jennifer, however, it was difficult to reconcile what her parents told her growing up with how they now felt about her relationship. Jennifer also described her brother's response:

JENNIFER: My brother at one point was like, "What is it about white men that you wouldn't like?" . . . it was like he was offended, he took offense, but I think he got over it, because he really likes Lance.

Jennifer's brother did not directly state he had a problem with his sister dating black men; instead, he discussed the issue in terms of her rejection of white men. By doing this, her brother avoided expressing opposition to his sister's interracial relationships, yet his problems with her choices were clear. From a white male perspective, her brother may have seen Jennifer's choices in men as a rejection of him, and even a sign of the deterioration of white male privilege, which is heard about in discussions against affirmative action.[6] This notion ties in with the gendered nature of familial responses, as evidenced in one white college student's discussion of her family. The student admitted her parents would have a problem if she wanted to marry a black man, even though her brother is married to a black woman. When I asked her what the difference was, she stated that her father would never accept her "coming home and saying, 'I'm marrying this black guy' . . . because, I'm his [her father's] little girl." The gender difference was given (and accepted by the other students) as a reasonable explanation for her parents' seemingly contradictory views. The importance of gender and its intersection with race is clear, highlighting how the historical images attached to black men (with white women) still play a role today.

Negotiating Family Responses

Brittney and Mark's story is an interesting example of familial response and whites' use of color-blind discourse to mask opposition. They both described Brittney's family as supportive of their relationship, but they tell a particularly complex and difficult story.

MARK: I was raised, you know, to judge people for who they are not for what they are, you know what I mean? It didn't matter if you were black, white, green, whatever the case might be. As long as you treated me with respect, you'd get the same thing back . . . I actually have interracial couples in my family.

BRITTNEY: As long as he treats me well. That's all they . . . they don't care if he's purple, green, or blue, you know what I mean? As long as, I mean . . . a white guy can be just as bad as a black guy can be just as bad . . . so as long as he was good to me and I was happy they don't care . . . my father and mother were very, you know, open to . . . they weren't judgmental . . . they love him to death, you know, nana and papa, and yeah, they all say it doesn't matter. . . . When they saw [our son] in the hospital for the first time, everyone was like, I can't believe how beautiful he is . . . and I guess they had been unsure, because he was biracial, how he would look.

MARK: Well, my outlook on her family . . . they're just down-to-earth people . . . nobody treats me differently than they would treat their own. . . . It's just at that time there was a lot of things going on and nobody wanted to face up to it, so they had to put the blame on some-body, and I was the most likely candidate . . . in a way, I do think it was racial . . . but I don't know, if it wasn't race or anything it was because who am I.

Mark was referring to a very serious incident that occurred less than a year before the interview. Brittney had given birth to their son prematurely and the baby had tested positive for cocaine. Mark and Brittney were together but were living two hours away from each other because Mark had not yet been able to relocate with Brittney. Upon finding out that Brittney had been using drugs, her mother turned Mark into the police, claiming he was a drug dealer and making unspecified "racial" remarks. Similarly, Brittney's grand-parents (her deceased father's parents) also expressed serious concern that, despite Brittney's denial, Mark was also involved in drugs, because he was black.

MARK: [Brittney's mom] tried to use the drug situation against me to the point where she had the whole family about ready to . . . let's go get a rope and a tree and let's get that joker . . . but they've all come around to the point where I'd do anything for those people . . . and I'm pretty sure they would do the same for me.

According to Mark and Brittney, her family eventually became completely supportive of their relationship. The family "came around" only after the baby was taken from Brittney and Mark, Mark was subjected to three months of random drug testing, which were negative, and *he* regained custody of the baby. Mark's reference to a lynching is in stark contrast to his comments that they now treated him like family. Without the perspective of Brittney's family, it is impossible to know their motivation. However, considering how the situation was racialized and how Mark's character was challenged, despite the absence of any evidence of drug use, it is difficult to accept their claim that race did not play a role.

Six of the couples described their families as supportive but contradicted their statements with examples of opposition. The rest of the couples discussed how their (or their partner's) white families opposed their relationships to varying degrees. Oftentimes, the family ultimately accepted the relationship or the individual but still had issues with interracial dating and marriage in general. In the white partners' families, some white individuals recalled racist remarks or actions growing up as initial signs that their family might not have been completely supportive.

> KEVIN: My father was blatantly racist, Archie Bunker style, and, well, my mom was more just passive. . . . but both died many years ago so it wasn't even an issue, but basically my whole family [aunts, uncles, and cousins] disowned me for in general hanging out with people of color. I was always ostracized growing up, but it made me accepting, because I saw all the lies [about why nonwhites were inferior], so I was constantly battling my family about racist remarks.

> SARA: I shouldn't laugh, but . . . I'm more comfortable with it now . . . my father and especially the way he's . . . what he speaks and what he says about other people of all kinds of other people has always been derogatory. I grew up thinking "Puerto Rican" was a bad word just from the way he said it. My mom doesn't have too many opinions on it, but she, yeah, I've grown up hearing that [racial slurs].

Sara further described how her family reacted to her relationship with Andre in particular.

> SARA: I knew presenting myself and my relationship with Andre was going to be . . . I knew it was going to be a challenge with my family but . . . it's more subtle than overt . . . I didn't experience the overt, you know, "You can't date him." I didn't get any of that. It's more subtle. It's more like, "Well, you don't understand." I'm close to my mom, I wouldn't really say she's supportive, but she's not antagonistic . . . my mom's big thing is that she's trying to understand and I get frustrated. I'm like, what are you talking about? What are you trying to understand, you know . . . my mother's thing is that if I'm happy then she'll be happy for me, but she, I think, can't understand how I might be happy in this way, and I think that's what it is, and my mother's big issue is if I got married and had kids. My

parent's disapproval or whatever, the first question is, well, what if you marry him?

Andre described Sara's family as not accepting and offered this perspective:

> ANDRE: I don't know how I feel about it. I think it's very insulting. I mean, that's an insult to me. I don't . . . but I don't pay much attention to it. I'm not really going to be out there trying to bridge gaps. That's not, not going up to the family, her parents or father and be overly in your face. Try to get to know me and accept me. I don't . . . that's not really my style, it's not my responsibility. Like I don't . . . I'm not going to sell myself to you.

Sara and Andre acknowledged the white parents' opposition in different ways. Sara stated that her parents have problems with her relationship but attributed the trouble to a lack of understanding and a concern for what the relationship might bring. Andre said the parents' response was based on a belief in the inferiority of blacks and that he is not good enough for their daughter because he is black. Black partners, and black individuals in general, such as the college students interviewed, often have a different perspective on white familial opposition. A number of black students recounted incidents, in explicitly racial terms, in which black individuals were not accepted by white families or were not even given the opportunity to meet the white parents.

Chris and Victoria discussed the response of her white family, highlighting the complexity of familial views and the fine line between acceptance and opposition. They described her family's responses as one of opposition, at least on some level, even though their opposition was often expressed in more subtle ways, such as questioning the relationship, expressing concern, or making derogatory comments. These responses often came as a surprise.

> VICTORIA: Well . . . how do I describe my family? I don't know. It's hard. My parents have always said they have no problem with Chris being black, but I guess they say offensive things, without even knowing it, like not about us, but, whatever, blacks on talk shows or just little sarcastic remarks . . . [*I ask her if she can think of any specific examples.*] Hmm, I'm trying to think, like, "Oh, what did they serve? Chicken and watermelon?" [referring to a summer vacation they spent with Chris's family], but then in fairness, they get angry when others in my family like my aunts and uncles or cousins are disrespectful or say things . . . which was a big problem for

us, because many in my family didn't acknowledge our wedding or come to it, and we aren't invited to certain family functions. Though it's not my parents, but they get it and then again, well, they don't.

CHRIS: [*laughing*] Her family is crazy. I have to say her parents have been really supportive of us. I mean, helping us out in a lot of ways, but I think they, of course, harbor certain, you know, ideas, or prejudices, and so it's hard. But the rest of her family, basically we don't see because she's always been like if they don't accept me then forget about it, and I think that's where her parents get a problem, because it breaks up the family and they sometimes place the blame in the wrong place [on Chris and Victoria].

Even family members who are viewed as basically supportive by the couples, like Victoria's parents, may make derogatory comments or not fully support the couple when faced with opposition or exclusion from other family members.

For some couples, the white family's opposition was so clear that they severed all ties. For example, Stanley and Kim have had little contact with her family because her father could never accept or even acknowledge his grandson. Couples like Victoria and Chris and Jill and Lee have limited contact with their family because of their families' views. Though none of the couples I interviewed described the white family as reacting violently, it does occur. In *Jungle Fever,* when Angie, a white Italian woman, becomes involved with a black man, she is repeatedly punched, kicked, and beaten with a belt by her father. He calls her a "disgrace" and says he did not raise her "to fuck a nigger." Angie's brothers pull the father off her, and as she is being kicked out of the house, he says he'd "rather die than be the father of a nigger lover." Underlying Angie's father's violent reaction is the same message of opposition that the white partners' families and white communities send: interracial relationships disrupt family unity and threaten the social status of white families, not to mention the racial purity of whites in general.

This opposition is expressed by families in a number of ways. Eleven of the fifteen couples acknowledged that certain family members do not allow the black partner in their house. By doing this, the white family rejects the possibility that this individual could become part of the family and, by not allowing them in the house, they are maintaining their image as a "pure" white family, which protects the family from losing any status or privilege with other whites.[7] The white college students and the white community respondents referenced the idea that they or their families preferred they not marry a person of different color because they would not want their child to experience problems, which can be read as an acknowledgment of white privilege—unearned advantages that whites experience—which could be lost if the individual or family was "unwhitened" by the relationship. Couples also discussed how family members did not attend their weddings, or, if they did attend the wedding, how they symbolically expressed their opposition. For example, Kayla's mother wept throughout the ceremony. Many families also "disown" the white member who dates interracially, a declaration that the person is no longer a member of the family (and of the white community in general). At least six of the couples discussed how they no longer had contact or had limited contact with various family members who could not accept the relationship. All these responses can be understood as attempts by the white family to protect their family from "blackness" and prevent the union of black and white, two irreconcilable opposites. Ultimately, many whites choose to marginalize the white member of their family rather than accept a black individual into their primary group. While some of the white families expressed outright opposition, I argue that most white families' responses reflect what I call a "supportive opposition." Individuals who are supportively opposing claim to be supportive of interracial relationships in general while expressing negative views, questions, and concerns in nonracial terms about interracial relationships in their own families.

It's a Family Affair: Black Families

Black families, like white families, can operate as a deterrent to interracial relationships. A family member becoming involved with a white individual is seen as problematic on a number of levels, yet the black families often raised different issues than the white families, such as the importance of "marrying black" and the negative meanings attached to becoming involved interracially. These issues figured prominently among the black partners, the black community respondents, and even black popular culture.

Among the black college students and community respondents, a main issue was the emphasis on marrying within their race, explicitly identifying race as the issue, unlike the white communities. Most students discussed how their parents would have a problem. One black female student stated, "My family would outright disown me" (which received a number of affirmations from the group). Another college student commented on the beliefs her family instilled in her: "My family raised me to be very proud of who I am, a black woman, and they instilled in me the belief that I would never want to be with anyone but a strong black man." Other students described incidents or comments they had heard that let them know they were expected to marry black. Similarly, Leslie, a black community respondent, stated she was raised by her parents to date anyone, but they were "adamant about me marrying black." She added that they told her not to "even think about marrying interracially." Allen also stated that his parents told him that "high school dating is fine but not marriage, ohhh nooo!" Couples like Gwen and Bill, Chris and Victoria, and others also recounted how the black partner's family had more difficulty accepting the relationship when they realized that the couple was getting married as opposed to just dating.

A significant piece of black familial opposition involves the perceived racism of whites in the larger society. Black families were described as having a hard time accepting a family member getting involved with a white person because of lingering racism and a distrust in whites in general. For example, one black college student stated that her family would have a problem if she brought home a white man, "because they would always be wondering what his family was saying, you know, do they talk about me behind my back?" Other students' responses echoed these views, such as one student who remarked, "My mom would have a problem with it. She just doesn't trust white people."

Also, black community members such as Alice and Jean argued that their opposition to a family member getting involved with a white person was based on the belief that the white individual (or their white family/neighborhood) would mistreat their family member. All but two of the black community members expressed the concern that since white society is racist there is no reason to become involved with a white person. Films such as *Zebrahead, Jungle Fever,* and *Waiting to Exhale* depict black family opposition based on the same reasons the community members stated. For example, in *Zebrahead,* Nikki, a black teen, starts a relationship with her cousin's best friend Zachary, who is white. Even though they know and like Zachary as Dee's friend, Nikki's family are opposed to his relationship with Nikki because of the racism that exists among whites. This reflects the different meanings attached to friendships across racial lines as opposed to interracial dating, as well as the significance of gender in these interracial meanings. Another example is *Jungle Fever,* where the parents of Flip, a black man who has become involved with Angie, a white Italian woman (mentioned earlier in the section on white familial responses), express their opposition when Flip and Angie come over for dinner. Flip's father lectures the couple on the historical oppression of blacks, while white women were placed on a pedestal and white men raped black women. He accuses his son of "fishing in the white man's cesspool," utilizing a common stereotype that the only white women who get involved with black men are those not desired by white men. The father questions Flip's motives, implying that Flip has internalized white racism and the belief that white women are more desirable.

Similarly, among the couples, black partners discussed their family's concern with the motives of the white partner or the depth of the relationship. There was a belief among some of the families that the white partner would at some point, especially during an argument, use racial slurs.

> AISHA: My mom told me she thought Michael would call me a "black bitch" or some other racist slur.

> SHARON: My grandmother was completely against it. She said it's just like slavery. He must be using you . . . My parents didn't really care, not like a big issue, but I guess a little shocked.

Sharon also discussed how her brother and sisters would never be involved interracially and had mixed feelings about her marrying a white man.

> SHARON: My brother has white friends, so he really didn't say anything, but my sisters, well, my older sister was shocked . . . and my younger sister accepts the relationship but not interracial in general. . . . She just doesn't think white and black should be together, she always says [*imitating her sister*], "It is hard for me to relate to someone of a race that has killed, belittled and continues to come into the black community to break it up. I couldn't do it."

Among black families, the issue of rejection is also mentioned, with opposition based not only on the racism of whites but also on the decision of the black individual. Black male partners such as Mark, Lee, and Chris discussed how their sisters or female relatives often felt offended by their choice of white women as partners, seeing it as a rejection of them. Chris's statement typifies this response:

> CHRIS: My family likes Victoria as a person and they respect her . . . but I can't say that they don't wish she was black, or really that I married a black woman on a number of levels. My younger sisters especially feel hurt by my choice, because they feel all too much they can't get a date because all the [black] guys are dating

white, so I think it's hard that I did . . . and then it's about thinking whites are just different. "Oh, white people cookout, they don't barbeque, they're uptight, they can't get their groove on," and all that . . . so I think they feel sort of confused at why I married a white woman, like "Don't I like my own people?"

The opposition—expressed as disappointment, confusion, and hurt—that Chris described does not seem to stem from a belief that whites are inferior but rather that intermarriage is seen as a sign that black individuals feel their own race is inferior. According to his narrative, another part of this opposition comes from a belief that blacks and whites are "culturally different," making the idea of having a white person in the family undesirable and uncomfortable.

This preference of black families to marry black because it is more "comfortable" was also articulated by the black community respondents. For example, Alice stated that she preferred members of her family not to marry interracially. She added that "there's just more in common with your own race." Similarly, Kayla, one of the white partners, discussed her views on why her ex-husband's family opposed their relationship.

KAYLA: Jay's family was totally against us getting married. They didn't fly in for the wedding. . . . They just thought blacks should be with blacks and whites white . . . and when we did visit and our oldest daughter was one and a half, they made comments about me the whole time, just I couldn't cook, I spoiled my daughter, basically I'm white.

The black families related to this study objected to having a white person in their family and intimate social circles because they viewed whites as the "enemy" and their presence as a sign that the black partner is not committed to his or her community or family. Not surprisingly, black individuals opposed interracial marriage much more than interracial dating, primarily because marriage represents a legitimation of the union and formally brings the white partner into the family.

Despite such opposition, the black college students argued that black families are still more accepting than white families. A number of students talked about interracially married family members. One woman described a family reunion where one of her relatives brought his white wife and "everyone was tripping over her being there" but eventually "got over it." On the other hand, a number of black individuals described their families as supportive of the relationship, but the support was often unclear. For example, Victor described his mother as supportive of his marriage to Lisa, but he discussed some issues she had raised.

> VICTOR: I think there is some worry in the case of my mother. She wonders if we are okay, what problems we have to deal with.
>
> LISA: She likes me better than the first wife [who was also white].
>
> VICTOR: This is true. She did . . . you see . . . some of these questions I think were asked about the first wife, but it's like I said.
>
> LISA: He didn't . . . well, he didn't have . . . you've got to say that . . . well, Victor didn't have contact with [his mother] for ten years because of his wife.
>
> VICTOR: Yes, but you know, it really wasn't, it wasn't because of race. It was she didn't think this woman was right for me. She just didn't want to hear it.

Victor acknowledged that his mother had objections to his first wife, who was also white, yet minimized the role of race. Instead, he argued that she just didn't think the woman was right for him, but he was not able to explain the "real" reasons, which remain unclear.

Lee, another black male partner, also stated his family has been supportive, but Jill disagreed. Lee acknowledged that his family, especially his mother, often makes jokes about the relationship.

> LEE: She does say things . . . she'll say things jokingly, but I'll know she's joking. One day she said I shouldn't have sent them to that "white" camp. I knew she was joking. . . . but [Jill] took it in a different way.
>
> JILL: I took it in a different way from what she said from the beginning . . . you'd tell me different things that she would say, how she didn't approve of it, she didn't like it.
>
> LEE: Ideally, any race wants you to be with a person of your own color. You know, that's just the way everybody thinks it should be . . . my brother had a problem with me talking to white women . . . he just doesn't like white people, and he just doesn't think that's the way it should be.

JILL: It's not comfortable to go have a family picnic at [Lee's family house] because they're all sitting around making fun, saying, "cracker this and cracker that," and it is awkward, even though they don't mean me personally.

Lee's assertion that his family is accepting of the relationship is in contrast to Jill's perceptions and his own statement that everyone (including his mother) prefers same-race unions, reflecting an ambivalence about interracial unions. Even among the black respondents, discussing family's views on race and their own interracial relationships seems to pose difficulties.

Some black partners stated that their families' expressed opposition to their relationships came as a surprise. Gwen described how her family responded when she brought Bill to her family's house for Christmas and told them they were getting married.

GWEN: I told my mother that he and I were getting married, and my mother continued to talk as though I'd never said anything. That surprised me because my mother would always tell us that you don't judge someone by what they look like. You judge by their character. It was something about marriage. It's a totally different ballgame. So, not only did my mother have difficulty, I think she made it so that my family had difficulty with it, so the only people who would acknowledge his presence was my father and younger brother [who was eleven or twelve at the time], no one but me and my father would give him a Christmas present . . . and Bill would sit downstairs with my parents and watch TV with my brothers, and they'd act like he wasn't there. They'd carry on a conversation and wouldn't include him. And there were all these little statements being made, not to us so much, as to each other and then my little brother would tell me everything, so we found out what was being said from my little brother because he hated it.

Gwen and Bill rarely visited her family in the early years of their relationship because of her family's problems accepting the relationship.

BILL: [Her family's reaction] obviously bothered me to the extent that it bothered her.

GWEN: I stopped going home after that.

BILL: Yeah, and I thought we weren't spending much time with them anyways.

GWEN: But that was deliberate. I mean, if they couldn't treat him fairly then neither one of us needed to be there.

BILL: Then when we did get married, we didn't invite any of the family, and I don't know if that helped or hindered the relationship.

GWEN: That was not because I didn't want them there. First of all, my father had just died right before we got married, and I was just feeling that because my father was the one who really wanted me to get married and was supportive of our relationship and I just didn't think I could have the family there without my father there.

Gwen, who always employed a race-conscious discourse, had difficulty discussing her family, particularly her mother's response. Like the white partners who were raised to be color-blind but then told by their parents they did not approve of their interracial relationships, Gwen was confused by the contradiction in how her mother raised her to judge people by their character but then objected to Bill because he is white. Gwen chose to exclude her family from her wedding primarily because of their lack of support.

While white families discourage their family members from engaging in interracial relationships to maintain white privilege, black families discourage these unions to maintain the strength and solidarity of black communities. Black families view interracial relationships as a loss in many ways—the loss of individuals to white society, the weakening of families and communities, and the devaluing of blackness.

What about the Children?

Interethnic and interracial families make different choices concerning the identity of their children, but for black-white interracial families the choice is much more socially restricted: "black-white marriages are still relatively rare and are not likely to reach very high levels anytime in the near future."[8] As Omi and Winant argue, "the determination of racial categories is thus an intensely political process. . . . the census's racial classification reflects prevailing conceptions of race, establishes boundaries by which one's racial 'identity' can be understood, determines the allocation of resources, and frames diverse political issues and conflicts."[9]

In my community research, both whites and blacks discussed the issue of children as a central concern and reason to question and/or oppose interracial unions. While the white and the black community respondents identified the potential offspring of interracial couples as an issue, they could not or would not elaborate on why these children are a concern. Some white respondents stated "it's just not fair to the children" and discussed their belief that offspring from interracial unions have "problems," such as confusion over their identity and lack of acceptance among whites and blacks. White families of the couples interviewed vocalized the same concerns, regardless of whether or not the couples had children. White partners Danielle, Sara, Kayla, and Jennifer all mentioned how their families expressed concern about the children. Kayla's parents even suggested abortion.

> KAYLA: They told me they didn't think it was a good idea because all the things I would have to go through raising an interracial baby in Maine . . . that other people would be too cruel and that I had to think of the child and that it is not fair to bring a child into this world, interracial, knowing what was going to happen. They told me if I had the baby I was selfish.

> DANIELLE: I don't have a really close family, so it's really just my parents, and they have been okay, and I think a lot of it is that Keith treats me a lot better than any other guy I was with, but they did talk about worrying about the kids. That was before we had [their daughter], and it was wanting to be sure I understood how "difficult" it would be to raise black kids being white, and maybe some of it was they were worried what our children would be like, look like, or even how *they* would be with black grandkids.

Among the black respondents, the same sentiments were echoed. For example, Jean stated, "The problem is the kids you bring into it" and the difficulties they face, such as, "Am I black? Am I white?" Alice summarized the views of the group: "The children definitely bear the brunt because it is difficult being black and white when some people don't want you as either." Black partners like Aisha and Keith discussed how their families mentioned the children as an issue.

> AISHA: My mom said, "What do you think kids will be like . . . it is wrong to bring kids into a situation like this. Kids will be confused. I Don't Want Polka Dot Grandkids!

KEITH: My family didn't really have a problem with us together, but their main concern was with how are you going to raise the children . . . mainly, they asking are you gonna raise them black? Because I don't think they could picture having some white grandbabies or just that they couldn't relate to.

Race was not explicitly stated, but Keith and Danielle's experiences with their two families illustrates the racialized nature of the concerns involved. Danielle's parents were troubled about having black grandkids; Keith's parents feared the children being raised white.

The apprehension of Keith and Danielle's families ties into the historical beliefs and practices surrounding biracial children. Historically, children of black-white unions were accepted into the black community and participated as members within it.[10] The white community, however, created the one-drop rule and "forced all shades of mulattoes into the black community where they were accepted, loved, married and cherished as soul brothers and sisters."[11] Though both whites and blacks discuss the issue of children as a reason to object to interracial relationships, the underlying arguments are different. Whereas whites seem to object to the creation of "black" children through interracial unions who may be inferior or "pollute" the white race, black opposition seems to stem from a concern with maintaining the black community.

When the community groups (as well as some couples) discussed concern for biracial children, they often described them as having "problems," referring to them as confused, maladjusted, or "mixed up."[12] The white community members expressed concern that children produced through racial mixing are believed to be flawed.[13] Individuals who based their opposition to interracial marriages on children seemed to draw on this traditional image of "tragic mulattoes" predisposed to emotional and psychological problems. The word "mulatto," which is still used by many today, is actually a Spanish word for mule, the sterile byproduct of a horse and a donkey. This designation implies the belief that blacks and whites represent two different species who should not reproduce, and it undoubtedly still plays a role in the belief that children of white and black couples are essentially different. This opposition to biracial children is based on the concept of group identity and is justified with various excuses, such as biology, the absoluteness of racial differences and the existence of distinct and separate cultural communities.[14] Whites have always maintained that children from interracial unions are to be considered black rather than white, which comes from social and legal traditions that construct the white race as a biologically pure group. Even one drop of black blood is thought to taint the individual.

Many in the black community, however, also argue that children from interracial unions should identify as black, since they will be treated as "black" by both whites and blacks. Claiming a biracial identity is seen by black communities as a way to be "less black" and an internalization of white racism. Yet attitudes that exist in black communities toward children from interracial unions further reveals the opposition toward interracial relationships. As Patricia Hill Collins argues, "Currently, however, the birth of biracial and mixed-race children to so many White mothers raises new questions for African-American women. Even in the face of rejection by Black men that leaves so many without partners, ironically, Black women remain called upon to accept and love the mixed-race children born to their brothers, friends, and relatives. By being the Black mothers that these children do not have, these women are expected to help raise biracial children who at the same time often represent tangible reminders of their rejection."[15] Furthermore, the recent trend of children from black-white unions to identify (or be identified by their parents) as biracial, and not black, contributes to the opposition among black communities to these relationships.

It seems that a significant piece of the opposition to interracial relationships is that these relationships "produce" biracial children who blur racial divisions. Since racial boundaries and, in essence, racial communities are maintained only through mutually exclusive racial categories that reflect and reinforce the all-pervasive power of race and its classifying character, biracial individuals are a threat to these racial boundaries and groupings, as well as to social, cultural, and political institutions, because their very existence undermines the assertion that race is a mutually exclusive grouping. Naming the "children" as a reason to question interracial relationships reveals the complicated and layered meanings attached to interracial relationships and the ways that opposition is coded within particular arguments, such as those concerning children. Arguing other points takes the emphasis off the relationship and focuses it on the potential harm being done to children. It can also be understood as color-blind discourse. Rather than admit race is the problem, it is easier to oppose interracial couples based on concern for the children they may or may not have.

Individuals also referred to the problems biracial children would face in "society," although they were unwilling to admit that they *themselves* were part of a world that treated children badly. Instead, they used an "alienated discourse," revealing an inability or unwillingness to construe race relations as something that they participated in or could change. There was no discussion or acknowledgment that any "problems" the children might have would clearly be a result of how individuals and communities responded to interracial families and biracial children.[16] Furthermore, the concern for the children conjures up the image that these children will have to "pay" for the parent's actions, reminiscent of "the biblical injunction that 'the sins of the fathers will be visited on the sons.'"[17]

But, Really, What about the Children?

Considerations of the children do figure prominently for some couples, not because they believe their children are fundamentally flawed but because they worry about societal treatment and acceptance. The issue of raising children is an important part of the neighborhoods and schools that the couples choose for their children. Frank and Olivia chose to move to an all-white neighborhood.

> FRANK: The game plan was this: you communicate by participation, first day they attend school. So the idea I said, I participate, the children are the connection. Once the children connect, all you do is participate. I was the only father in PTA. It's human nature to be afraid of something that you've never experienced, and if you only read, or what the media puts in the paper, if I do what you do what's the difference. We control the environment . . . if you put [a biracial kid] in an all-black neighborhood, I think he'd be ostracized more.

Speaking of his teen sons and their social experiences, he said:

> Well that's been another thing. All these questions, I totally, that's the one part of my grand plan that I failed to consider, being that they never dated black females.

> OLIVIA: That's probably because we live in a white neighborhood. There aren't any black females in the schools . . . it just happens there aren't any black females in the community. That wasn't a purposeful selection on our part . . . it's not a problem for them and it's not a problem for the [white] girls. I think both boys have met or heard some resistance from the parents of some of the girls they took out. The same kind of hesitance like . . . you know, it's not an Italian boy. It hasn't affected the kids 'cause I'll tell you what, this house is full all the time.

Later in the interview, when talking about being a mother, Olivia offered this perspective:

> OLIVIA: I'm always concerned for my sons, because I don't want. . . .
> I'm afraid for them when they're driving out at night. Oh, God, some-
> body is going to pull them over because they're black in a white
> community and it's happened, so that certainly has heightened my
> awareness, because for my fear for what happens to my kids. I'm
> not sure if parents have fear for their kids, kind of like a white kid
> going into a black neighborhood is going to have the same fear on a
> different level.

Olivia and Frank's statements were complex. They claimed their children were completely accepted, yet their sons are the only students of African American heritage at their school, they have limited or no contact with African American peers, and they have encountered problems with the white parents of girls they have dated in high school. Olivia expressed concern because her sons had been harassed by the police in their neighborhood due to their dark skin. Frank and Olivia maintained, however, that they "control the environment" with the belief that if they do what the white neighbors do (go to work, take kids to school, put out the trash), then there will be no problem. Race and racial prejudice is deemphasized. Rather than worry if their children will be accepted, they see their children as a way to foster friendships in the area.

Sandra and David's two sons are very young (three months and three years old), so they have not thought about how their predominantly white neighborhood will affect them.

> SANDRA: We do talk about teaching the boys about being biracial . . .
> they don't look black, more like a beautiful tan, with big soft
> curls . . . so we couldn't raise them black . . . but we definitely make
> an effort to have them with other biracial kids.

For Sandra, "not being in an all-white environment" was the same as "raising her children black," which she did not consider an option. Instead, she attempted to diversify her children's world by introducing them to other biracial children. Similar to many in the multiracial movement, Sandra looked at diversity in terms of constructing a world of multiracial people and interracial couples, and distanced herself from black communities. Her husband did not comment on this issue, but he seemed to agree (all of his friends were white at the Ivy League university where they met).

Gwen and Bill chose to live in a diverse neighborhood but sent their child to a predominantly white private school.

> BILL: At school most of his friends are white, so what we attempt to do is to expose [him] as much to black experience and culture as possible . . . we took him to see an African dance troop from Harlem . . . and his trip to South Africa for the summer with Gwen.

> GWEN: His percussion instructor is Latin but looks like him, which is important, and we spend time with a black family that the children attend the same school as [our son] and also the fact that this woman and I together formed Families of Color for families who have children of color at [the private school that their son attends], so we get the kids together so the kids can get to know each other. So there are things we do to try and make him feel a part of the community [of color] while at the same time not downgrading his white side.

> BILL: We made a decision to send our son to [this private school] because of what we wanted, education and opportunity for him. Rather than let the status quo exist, [Gwen] has organized parents of color, run fund-raisers, had cultural events . . . putting pressure on the administration to increase scholarships to bring in more children of color . . . become actively involved within the institution to bring about some change to the institution that will benefit by bringing a more racially diverse group.

> GWEN: If we weren't in these schools we wouldn't be at the table and therefore would still see those people who are succeeding on major levels in this country coming out of schools like this, and I won't deny my son that.

Gwen and Bill's remarks reflect the politicized way they view their choices and the emphasis that is placed on the importance of the role of race. Their choice in where they live and the school they send their son to is explicitly racial: they sent their son to a predominantly white school, not because race does not matter but because they wanted their son to have the opportunities whites have so that he could succeed and make changes.

Family Matters

Families occupy an interesting role within the reproduction of opposition to black-white relationships. According to the couples' experiences, many of the white families had difficulty accepting the black partners, though their "concern" was often described as nonracial. A family member's objection to an interracial relationship was not interpreted as racist or even racial; instead, the racial aspect was minimized or justified by explaining it as a preference, a concern, or a natural occurrence. The white community respondents were less direct, yet their opposition was evident from their avoidance and discomfort in discussing the issue, their statements about the problems with interracial couples, and their limited contact with blacks.[18] Black families were also described by the couples as holding strong views against interracial marriage, and the black community respondents supported this view with their own concerns and problems with the relationships.

The familial responses discussed throughout the research clearly demonstrate how images of oneself and one's family is linked to the concept of race and otherness, especially within the construction of families, both white and black. White families often objected to the idea of a member dating interracially, not because they met the black individual and were confronted with overwhelming "racial" differences, but because they were merely responding based on their ideas and beliefs about interracial relationships and blacks in general. For example, Kayla's parents objected to her relationship with Jay, her first husband, before they even met him; many couples' families had a problem with the relationship even though the black partner was highly educated, successful, and a good mate. Black families also expressed opposition toward black-white relationships based on negative experiences with whites or a belief that the relationship was problematic. The couples discussed their families' responses in different ways, either emphasizing or deemphasizing the importance of race, yet *all* couples seemed to have more difficulty discussing family members (as opposed to others in society) as racist or opposed to the relationships because of race. Many white partners (and some black partners) had difficulty reconciling the views of their families as "good" and "loving" with their families' responses and reactions to the relationship. Regardless of personal attributes, a black individual was often not viewed as "qualified" to become part of a white family because of *perceived* irremediable, alienating differences.[19] Race is understood as a "tribal stigma" that "can be transmitted through lineages and equally contaminate all members of a family," which plays into the added concern expressed about the biracial children these unions can produce.[20]

The issue of children is often thrown into the discussion on interracial relationships, and it is viewed as a legitimate concern that is not racist. Both blacks and whites use offspring as a basis for opposition, often blaming the couple for having children rather than blaming society for making it difficult to be both black and white. This opposition reveals one of the central sociopolitical oppositional responses to intermarriage: the threatened outcome of the mixing of the races, a blurring and confusing of racial groups in society. The 2000 Census was the first to allow individuals to choose multiple races, and these choices will undoubtedly have important bearings on the future of intermarriage in both white and black communities.

Being in an interracial relationship often brings forth problems within families, since white and black families overwhelmingly want to remain monoracial. For example, Stacey, a white twenty-year-old student, and Danny, a twenty-two-year-old African American student, came to talk to me separately after breaking up their two-year-relationship because of Stacey's father. In sum, Stacey's father did not accept the couple's relationship and would not let Danny into the family home. The father maintained that he didn't have a problem with Stacey having black friends, but he didn't believe that whites and blacks should be involved intimately. At first, this didn't pose much of a problem because Stacey and Danny lived on campus, but as the relationship progressed, Danny became frustrated at what he saw as disrespectful treatment from Stacey and her father. Stacey explained that she was torn because she felt she was being asked to choose between her father and the man she loved. She explained that one time Danny dropped her off at her father's house. Before she got out of the car, Danny went to give her a hug and a kiss, but she refused because she thought it would enrage her father and would be disrespectful toward him. Danny, however, was the one who became angry, because *he* felt disrespected. At the same time, Danny was getting pressure from other African Americans who felt that as a strong black man Danny should not subject himself to this treatment and, in particular, that he should be with a black woman. While from the outside the role of race is clear, from talking to Stacey and Danny there was much confusion. First, Stacey had difficulty stating that her father was racist, even though he would not accept or acknowledge her relationship with a black man. She often mentioned how he let her black girlfriends in the house but just didn't believe that whites and blacks should mix. Also, she felt like she had to choose between her father and her boyfriend. Though she adamantly disagreed with her father's views, he was still her father, and it was difficult to separate her love from him and the offensive views that he held. Whereas Danny clearly saw her father's racism, he was less clear on how the views of his family and friends were also racially based. While he demanded that Stacey take a strong stand against her father, he was not willing to argue against those who told him he should be with a black woman.

This scenario highlights how difficult it is to negotiate issues of race and family. Discussing race and, more important, views on interracial relationships in nonracial terms often makes it even more difficult for individuals to challenge and confront their family's views. By using phrases such as "It's not my personal preference" or "I just worry about the problems you will face in society," families and individuals are able to oppose interracial relationships without appearing prejudiced or racist. A family member's opposition, however, is also tied to the issue of identity—the identity of the family and the individuals involved. Families express concern over the identities of the biracial children who will be produced, and in many ways there is a tendency for white families to worry that the children will be "too black," and the black families worry about the children being "more white." The white individuals who enter into a relationship with a black person are seen as "less white" and as tainting the white family, while the black individuals who get involved are seen as "not black enough" and as leaving their blackness behind. All of these fears and beliefs demonstrate the centrality of race to the constructions of families and identities and, more important, the socially constructed nature of race, if one's relationship can change one's "race" in this society still divided by racial boundaries. Ultimately, black-white couples and biracial children are forced to exist somewhere in between, with or without their families.

CHAPTER 5

Racialized Spaces

COLLEGE LIFE IN BLACK AND WHITE

*T*here are many stories about race on college campuses—debates over affirmative action, race in the classroom, as well as diversity issues among the faculty and student body.[1] In media reports, particularly, the university campus is most often heralded as a place that promotes interracial relationships, primarily because it has an ethos of tolerance, the assumption that education decreases negative racial attitudes, and the belief that the younger generations are more open about race. For example, a 2002 *New York Times* article reported that "in a world brimming with bad news, here's one of the happiest trends: Instead of preying on people of different races, young Americans are falling in love with them. . . . Whites and blacks can be found strolling together as couples even at the University of Mississippi, once the symbol of racial confrontation."[2] Amidst these color-blind stories, there are also reports—some media and more academic—on the persistent (self-)segregation of college students.[3] In particular, while universities may have racially diverse student populations, they do not have an integrated, diverse social environment.[4]

The question remains, does the college social environment foster interracial relationships between blacks and whites or simply contribute to the maintenance of racial boundaries? College campuses then are a prime social space to explore the meanings attached to black-white couples since campuses may create the opportunity for meaningful social interactions across racial boundaries—although they do not ensure it.

Race on College Campuses

The racial climate of a college campus and the frequency of black-white dating differs based on the college, the student body, and other factors, such as geographical location and affiliations. Most colleges place an emphasis on diversity and promoting (at least in theory) cross-racial interaction, though the college campus can be described as both a place that promotes and discourages interracial unions. While it is not uncommon to see black-white couples across college campuses nationwide, much of student life is still highly segregated.[5]

Certainly the official discourse that a university employs—or, in other words, the ways that the university and its officials address and deal with issues involving race—can be important in how race relations in general and interracial dating in particular are viewed by the students. Universities often take different approaches, as evidenced on the three campuses where I conducted student interviews. In light of this fact, I interviewed an administrator who monitors issues of diversity and student life to get a sense of the impact of the university's perspective.[6] At Collegiate University (an Ivy League school in the Northeast), Cooper, a professor and director of a race/ethnic research center, described the university as going through "a transition phase," where "rhetorically the university is very committed to addressing issues of race on campus yet students would question this commitment." She explained that the students often feel their concerns and issues are overlooked, citing the "recent demand" from students for a new academic program devoted to ethnic studies, although "the university said the resources weren't there." At St. Stephen's University (a private Catholic university in the Northeast), Willis, the director of the Multicultural Program, described the racial climate as "fair," with the "greatest negative" being that issues involving race are "not addressed." According to Willis, many within the university adopt a color-blind approach by "wish[ing] it would just go away, so they ignore it hoping that will erase any problems." Willis acknowledges the university has realized "the need for greater expansion and more inclusion of students of color," which has led to the redesign of her position and a new emphasis on promoting multiculturalism. At Central State University (a large public university in New England), Merritt, a professor and dean of Multicultural Affairs, stated that the university is "very committed" to issues of race relations and diversity, citing the recent revision of the General Education requirement to include courses on race and ethnicity and the creation of his position.

These administrators' views reveal how even if race is being addressed, it may not be sufficient or it may be a more recent phenomenon, as evidenced in the new positions that have been created. The (lack of) ability of the university to address racial issues undoubtedly affects the racial climate in the classroom and among the students. According to Cooper, universities can serve as "a place to cut across racial lines because of the numbers, the exposure to other groups." Though, she adds, "people prefer to be with people they feel comfortable with," and when groups are racially mixed it tends to be "black and Latino, not black and white." Similarly, Willis described race relations on the St. Stephen's campus as "fair," stating that if students of color said how they felt, they would say "the university is not accepting of all races." She discussed how the campus has had some ugly incidents like racial epithets sprayed on students' doors in the dorms, adding that she believes there are problems between students in "face-to-face interaction that are not reported." In contrast, Merritt described race relations at Central State University as "actually quite good," adding that "probably two-thirds of students feel relations are good." (This view, however, will be disputed by both white and black students later in the chapter.)

With a growing emphasis on addressing issues of diversity, and a growing multiracial population, many universities have even addressed the issue of interracial dating, hosting forums and sponsoring multiracial events. College newspapers often address the topic of interracial dating, such as the University of North Carolina online college edition, which ran a debate piece bringing together the views of two students: a black women who writes for the student publication *Black Ink* and a white man who writes for the main student paper, *blue & white*.[7] It would seem that university handling of racial issues affects or at least reflects racial interaction on campus. For example, Bob Jones University, a conservative southern Christian college, came under media spotlight in the late 1990s for its policy that banned interracial dating among its students. It overturned this policy in 1999 but still requires students to get explicit written approval from their parents before they are allowed to engage in an interracial relationship. While this may be considered an extreme example, it illustrates how a university's official response can have an effect on the frequency and acceptability of interracial relationships among its students.

College as the Land of Interracial Opportunity?

Research within the social sciences has long discussed the connection between college education and interracial marriage, finding that those who intermarry and/or support interracial marriage in general are more likely to be college educated. Among the black-white couples interviewed, however, there are contradictory views on what role the college campus plays in encouraging or discouraging interracial unions. Some couples, such as Lisa and Victor (though they did not meet at college), stated that the college campus was a place that brought blacks and whites together.

> LISA: When I was living at home I did not meet any black people, just because of where I was living. So then I go to college. I think that may have something to do with it . . . say I didn't go to college, I might end up staying in the same circle of people, the same friends. So the fact that someone goes to college, it broadens their horizons and education, it all has something to do with it. It's just meeting different people.

> VICTOR: It just seems that the interests I had in college, and that's where it starts mostly, there just weren't a lot of black women there. Period. I mean I was in the band at [college]. I was on the radio station at [college], even in the dorms that I was in I found no black women around, so I found myself in the company of white women mostly all the time. Even the biology majors. There were no black people at all in biology. In the sciences, they just weren't taking those courses, you know, physics courses and stuff.

College was Lisa's first exposure to other races, though she didn't establish any relationships with any black individuals at that time. Victor also focused on the opportunities college provided for him to meet white women, yet he did not address the significance and meaning of the lack of African Americans in his classes, dorm, and social activities.

Sandra and David, who did meet at a university (a prestigious Ivy League school), described their college experience as accepting of interracial couples. Despite this perceived acceptance, the couple discussed how "blacks and whites didn't really mix . . . it was a divided campus."

> SANDRA: Well, in the lunch area, blacks mostly kept to themselves, but . . . well, David had mostly white friends, just because, well, he was in theater, and the band, oh, and water polo.

Neither one addressed how or why their relationship was accepted and "ordinary," despite their reports that it was not common or ordinary for blacks and whites to hang out. Both couples (Sandra and David, Lisa and Victor) consistently used a color-power evasive discourse and deemphasized race in their narratives.

In contrast, other couples expressed very strong beliefs that the college campus did not foster interpersonal relationships between blacks and whites, even if they had met at college. Kayla described her college experience as segregated, without much opportunity for interracial dating.

> KAYLA: Where I went to college in Florida, I found that interracial dating just wasn't common. It was prejudiced, but a lot of African American students seemed prejudiced too . . . it was more like "how ya doing" friendly, but nothing more than that, and I was really attracted to black men at that time.

Similarly, Jennifer discussed the college campus that she attended as an uncomfortable place for interracial couples.

> JENNIFER: I don't hang out at school that much, mostly because Lance and I don't feel comfortable . . . I mean, I have mostly black friends and probably because white students don't relate to me or Lance . . . and on campus, it's like this organization throws a dance, so it's all white students, or the black student union throws a dance and it's all black. Yeah, the only time you get a mix is for athletics, like basketball games, but then even the get-together afterwards are mostly one or the other [white or black]. We go to black parties because it's better for the music, the atmosphere, I guess.

Victoria and Chris, who met as undergraduates at a large state university in California, described their collegial experiences as an interracial couple in great depth, touching upon many of the issues that will be addressed by the college student group interviews.

> VICTORIA: We went to [a college in southern California], and you definitely saw blacks and whites together, but not really couples.

> CHRIS: We were one of the few serious . . . committed, uhh, [interracial] relationship, most times there might be dating but more just "hooking-up" for the night or just casual. We definitely went through a lot, probably more her than me . . . thinking about it now, I see how things were at the time, though in school I don't think I realized what a problem our relationship was . . .

> VICTORIA [*interrupting Chris*]: . . . put it this way, white guys were like "why throw it away on a black guy, he's just using you," and black girls would harass me, call me names, and always act like Chris

was with me because I had money or did things for him, which I didn't, and I think I let it get to me, but he definitely did worse, when all his [black] friends and their girls would tell him, "how could you make her your girl," or just try to break trust . . .

CHRIS [*interrupting Victoria*]: We did have a lot of problems, and I think when we were younger, it's like you do let what friends say kind of change the way you feel . . . I think for me another part of it was this perception among the guys I played with [college basketball team] that she would sleep around because that was how a lot of the white girls who liked black guys acted.

VICTORIA: One of the hardest things in college is you can't really get away from it, because you have a group you hang out with, and for us even more so because Chris played basketball, so he hung out with them and most of them were against him being with me, and then even worse because a lot of [black] girls hated me because I was with him . . . I wouldn't join a sorority because they were part of a totally different world, all white, and it would just have been weird. We met at school, but I think the fact that we are still together has nothing to do with what we went through . . .

CHRIS [*interrupting Victoria*]: . . . probably in spite of it.

Chris and Victoria's story paints a picture of a college campus racially divided, and of white and black students vocal about their opposition to interracial relationships. Furthermore, this is not a story from the past, in some remote area of the South. These individuals were undergraduates in the mid-1990s in California, where interracial couples are seen as common.

The black-white couples interviewed have divergent views, envisioning the college campus as a place that either provides the opportunity for individuals of different races to meet or discourages serious relationships between blacks and whites. However, these views, which are seemingly in opposition, may not be mutually exclusive. In what follows, contemporary college students' views on interracial relationships, and the discourses they draw from to explain these views, will shed light on the couples' experiences and issues such as the absence of African American students, the segregation between whites and blacks, and the meanings attached to interracial dating.

White Students Speak: For Whites Only?

The general consensus among white students at all three universities was that friendships across racial lines were common and completely acceptable. As one student put it, "No one would even suggest that it was okay not to be friends with someone just because they were of a different race. That's just old-fashioned racism." Yet the definition of "friend" seems rather vague and does not necessarily refer to an individual one is close to, but rather any individual that one is friendly with, which seems to be an important distinction. There may not be hostility or tension between racial groups, but the students also do not seem to feel there is a significant amount of close interaction. As one of the male students stated, "Most people [in college] have friends of another race. Maybe not your core group that you go out with every night, but definitely friendly." Nonetheless, the idea of interracial friendships was viewed as ordinary, even mandatory if one didn't want to be perceived as racist or prejudiced.

Despite their tolerant views on interracial "friendships," white students readily acknowledged that interracial dating between blacks and whites was not common or widespread. They offered varied reasons, such as the predominantly white campuses and the self-imposed segregation of black students. Yet the majority of students maintained that their campuses were "definitely like a liberal, open-minded environment." For example, students framed the lack of interracial dating initially as a problem of there not being enough black students, not as a reflection of their actions. They also attributed the low number of interracial couples to the role and responsibility of students of color. As one male student said, "There's a mentality here where students from other countries hang out together, and same for blacks and Latinos." In particular, students referenced organizations formed around racial and ethnic heritages, "which is meant positively yet may decrease interaction." Not surprisingly, there was no acknowledgment or discussion of white self-segregation or organizations that were predominantly white. One male student added, "It's not that black students are into dating whites, either. They think the same. They prefer to stick to their own." The general consensus was that "blacks just like to stick with other blacks." While acknowledging that little interracial dating occurs, white students placed responsibility primarily on black students and a lack of diversity on campus.

The students also agreed that interracial couples would face problems on campus and in the larger society. Whereas not being friends with someone of a different race was viewed as "old-fashioned racism," not wanting to date interracially was acceptable. At Collegiate University the following exchange occurred:

> FEMALE 1: It's not a problem for me, but probably in general there's definitely some issues involving race on this campus . . . unfair treatment or discrimination, reverse discrimination.

> MALE 1: I'm not sure what is acceptance, but any time there [is] something outside the norm, people will look, or even maybe be curious.

Among the white students there was consensus that "it would be awkward for couples, and probably some people who might say things." In general, interracial dating was "not overly welcomed." From all three universities, the white students' responses were virtually the same. They concluded that interracial dating among blacks and whites was still a problem, at least to some extent. In general, the white students expressed the general belief that interracial dating might cause problems, discomfort, or elicit stares and comments. The lack of interracial couples and the larger societal opposition were seen as contributing to the opposition on campus.

Furthermore, the lack of interracial dating was described as being based on personal interest and associations, not on ideas of racial difference or inferiority. Like the white community respondents discussed earlier, the white students used the "I don't have a problem with it, but . . . " discursive strategy. The majority of white students stated that they did not care about *others* dating interracially, but they stated reasons why *they* would not or should not. Like the white church community members, some white students mentioned how they had never even thought about interracial dating before. One student put it like this: "Nothing wrong with interracial couples . . . to be honest, I never considered dating outside my race. The situation has never presented itself. I don't find a lot of black men asking me out or anything."

Most students, in nonracial terms, described interracial dating as not a "preference," stating that they were not attracted to African Americans. As one Collegiate University female said, "I think it's great, but I probably couldn't see myself dating interracially, not because they're black; it's just not my preference." Similarly, a St. Stephen's woman responded, "interracial dating is not a problem. Most people just aren't physically attracted to other races. I know I just don't find black guys attractive." One of the male students concluded the discussion in the following way:

> There is a big difference between *having a problem* with interracial dating and just not doing it yourself. I don't notice a couple, like, "Oh, he's black, she's white!" It doesn't even register. I personally would not date a black woman. Does that mean I'm prejudiced? No! I wouldn't date a man, but that doesn't mean I hate gays.

Other students explained their preference not to date interracially because it was unnatural, untraditional, and they simply wouldn't have anything in common with a black person. For example, one St. Stephen's male student said he did not "have anything in common, don't like the same music, nothing in common." Other students described interracial dating as "untraditional, a problem of cultures clashing." Some said they would not date interracially because "there's a comfortableness with people who are the same as you. I'm more comfortable with whites." One student from Central State University referenced her upbringing as giving her a preference not to date interracially: "Where I grew up, interracial relationships are just not common . . . I couldn't see myself doing it for that reason. It's not how I grew up." Another Collegiate University student's response encompassed much of what all the students were saying about interracial relationships: "If that's what you do, cool! It's a matter of what you like, blond hair, tall, short, certain personality . . . people like what they know. If I grew up in a black neighborhood, I'm sure I would like black guys."

These white students stated that they did not have any problems with interracial dating but simply would not do it themselves. Their decisions were based on what they identified as individual reasons, such as personal preference, not being attracted to blacks, a lack of common interests, or the way they grew up. Despite the students' statements that race was not an issue and that they did not harbor negative views of blacks, their statements that they did not find any black individuals attractive and did not have anything in common with them is racially based. Furthermore, these racialized views were coded in nonracial terms, such as preference and upbringing. Eduardo Bonilla-Silva and Rogelio Saenz's study of white college students on their views on race relations also found that though most students claimed they were "color-blind on love matters, their own answers and lifestyle suggest that their approval of interracial associations is (1) conditional and (2) has little implications for their own individual likelihood of establishing primary associations with blacks."[8]

The white students' discussion of why interracial dating was not a personal option for them clearly included various prejudices and racialized ways of thinking. For example, at St. Stephen's, a male student discussed why he wouldn't date interracially, drawing on derogatory images of black women: "I'm sorry, but I just don't find black girls attractive. I mean, put Tyra Banks in front of me and I wouldn't touch her. She's got this forehead like an ape, big lips" [*the other students laugh*].

Students used a racialized discourse when explaining their decisions not to date interracially, reproducing the idea of whites and blacks as essentially different. One female student remarked, "Blacks are just different, like they have a different way of talking, walking," quickly adding, "not in a bad way, but I mean I just couldn't see myself in *that* type of culture." In particular, the image of black men as sexually deviant is referenced by the college women, describing black men as "athletes with attitudes" and "dogs who only want to hook up."

Throughout the group interviews, the white students maintain that interracial relationships are not a problem and that race is insignificant. Yet within these affirmations of support for interracial dating, the students' personal decisions not to date interracially and the racialized images of blacks they expressed seem to contradict this "support." While it was considered socially unacceptable to say one is opposed to others' interracial relationships, it was perfectly acceptable to state that one personally would never date a black person and that he or she finds black people unattractive. In general, the white students had either not thought about the issue of interracial dating much or, if they had, they expressed the general belief that interracial dating is personally undesirable and causes problems and/or discomfort.

The lack of interracial couples and the larger societal opposition were seen as contributing to the opposition that possibly existed on the college campus. In particular, peer groups played an important role in perceptions of the acceptability of interracial dating. While a number of the white students stated that their friends would be supportive if they decided to date interracially, they also said it was unlikely they would make such a decision. For example, one white woman at Collegiate University said, "I don't think friends [are] an issue because [one chooses] friends who are similar in activities and ideas. . . . I've never dated outside [my] race, but if I met a really great guy who was cute, smart, interesting, and whatever else but *happened* to be black, my friends would be cool about it, but the places we go I just don't see that happening." Some students expanded on this idea, stating that their friends would not have a problem with an interracial relationship itself, but rather "it may be awkward if you all went out, like just kind of change the way things are, you know at a party or something." Again, the white students' language denied race was an issue but emphasized other factors such as commonality and comfortableness; yet race, or more specifically perceived racial difference, was the only basis for the lack of commonality and comfort cited.

The white students also implied that their friends might not oppose the relationship, but they might still make sarcastic remarks and jokes or harbor negative views. For example, one white male student said that since none of his friends had black girlfriends, they would probably "say things to be funny . . . the main issue would be sexual, like, 'So what's it like?'" A female student also described how she did not "think friends would be, like, 'Why are you with him?' but they may make little comments, just kind of joking."

Other white students acknowledged that their friends might not say or do anything negative, but that did not mean it would not be a problem. For example, one woman added that she did not think friends would say anything, "because it's embarrassing to say you're opposed to it even if you were." However, she did acknowledge that "it would be an issue, like wondering what they really think." Another woman added that she could "definitely see it being a problem for some people," in terms of what their friends would say or how it would affect their friendships. At Collegiate University, only one woman mentioned having a friend who had a relationship with "a black guy" and how her other friends "took an attitude and just kind of didn't feel comfortable with the situation for whatever reason."

Among the white men, the consensus was that black women are generally not perceived as attractive. At St. Stephen's, the male students argued that "you're not going to date someone who you know the guys aren't gonna think [is] pretty or won't like her," expecting that friends would ask "why are you with a black girl?" A small number of students even stated that their friends would openly express, even degrade, someone who dated interracially. From these discussions, it is evident that the students' perception of how their peer group would respond played a role in their decision not to date interracially.

In general, the white students stated that dating interracially might be a problem among friends. Even students who did not think their friends would respond negatively explained that their response would be based on the belief that expressing opposition is wrong, not that opposition does not exist. Since their social circles were predominantly or exclusively white, many students stated that their friends might have a problem with an interracial relationship. It was considered unlikely that they would date interracially, especially because it would cause "uncomfortable" social circumstances.

These viewpoints were not seen as based on race or racial prejudices, but rather on "natural occurrences." By adopting this color-blind discourse, the white students were able to deny the role of race while expressing their personal aversion to interracial dating.

An integral part of socialization involves "generating norms—that is making things seem or appear natural and timeless so that people accept situations as well as particular ideologies without ever questioning their socially and politically constructed nature."[9] When white students discussed their reasons for not dating interracially because it is not "traditional" or not their "personal preference," they were drawing on norms and rules of race relations that they were socialized into by their family and group; however, they did not see it that way. The white college students did not believe that they *chose* not to interact with blacks, but that it occurred naturally or as a result of the black students' actions. The students' belief that they would have nothing in common with a black individual conveys the idea that whites and blacks are inherently different. The issue of physical attraction was also raised, but the color component was ignored, as if a preference for blondes was the same as an aversion to African Americans and possibly black skin in general. These statements reflect a color-blind discourse that is dominant in American society, where it is considered polite to "ignore" color or racial differences. White students often expressed support for interracial dating and marriage in general, but they chose to associate exclusively with other whites, making it necessary to question their "endorsement of color blindness in romantic relationships."[10] There is an "apparent contradiction between the students' stated preference for a color-blind approach to life and their (white) color-coded reality."[11]

The white students' responses are similar to those of the interracial couples who described the college campus as supportive while simultaneously explaining the ways whites and blacks were separated. David was around white students only because he was in theater, band, and water polo. Similarly, Victor noticed a lack of black students in his classes and in his social circles but attributed it to nonracial factors, such as the individual choices of blacks not to be involved or to take those classes. These interracial couples (and the white students) adopted a color-blind approach that allowed them to view the college (and themselves) as accepting of interracial relationships. Since the white students did not state directly that they had a problem with interracial relationships, the black-white couples interpreted their words as supportive, even though their actions pointed to an avoidance of interracial interaction. The white students emphasized the "self-segregation" of black students, making the separation of the races the black students' problem, not theirs. Therefore, they can maintain that they are not opposed to interracial dating. Like manifestations of contemporary racism, the opposition to interracial unions is subtle and often not readily apparent because it is articulated in individual terms; for example, individuals will say, "I do not have a problem with interracial couples, but *I* wouldn't date outside my race." The opposition is usually expressed in color-blind terms, emphasizing problems interracial couples face in society.

Black Students Speak: What Interracial Symbolizes?

Black students stated that interracial friendships do occur, but they expressed reservations about how close these friendships really are. A male student from Central State University said, "Like my man Rodney [King] said, we get along for the most part, but there's not a lot of hanging out." Interracial friendships were repeatedly characterized as "superficial" and that "real friends who you hang out with all the time, it is more with your own race." However, as one student observed, since the number of black students is "small compared to whites . . . you have to interact."

Unlike the white students, the black students viewed interracial dating as relatively common, especially black males with white females. These relationships, however, were characterized as secretive or discrete and not necessarily considered acceptable for a number of reasons. At all three schools, interracial relationships were not seen as acceptable. As one of the male students at Collegiate University stated, "It's not accepted. I'm not feeling the vibe for interracial couples on campus." Students at one of the schools even mentioned that an "interracial dating forum" was held once a year on campus to discuss students' issues, which came about as a result of "an incident where a list of people who dated interracially was put out there and there was an outlash of the black community." In general, black-white relationships are viewed as unacceptable based on the problems that these couples face and the looks they get "all the time from everybody." Like the white student who compared campus views to the larger society, one woman stated, "It's not accepted, so I think the campus just mirrors the rest of society." The black students stated that both black and white students would have a problem with interracial couples, pointing to the opposition of the larger society as an influence.

Interracial relationships were seen as problematic by the black students for different reasons than the white students discussed, primarily because the motives of those involved and the sincerity of the relationship is questioned. The black students, particularly the black women, repeatedly brought up the idea that black men seek out white women for very specific reasons, including sex, money, and assistance (similar to the stereotypes Chris and Victoria said they dealt with in college).

> FEMALE 1: Unfortunately, most interracial relationships aren't for good reasons, just not genuine on their motivation . . .

> FEMALE 2 [*Interrupting*]: It's even worse than not being genuine. It's dating outside your race for a purpose. . . . black guys want their laundry done, homework done, food cooked. Black guys tell black girls off because they won't do their shit.

> FEMALE 3: No, it's so bad that I've heard seniors tell freshmen when they say they can't do their homework, "Haven't you found yourself a white girl yet?"

> FEMALE 4: When I see a black man with a white woman on campus, *especially* if he's an athlete, I just know she is buying him things and doing things for him. That's what it's about.

White women were also perceived as available for "sex without commitment," or as one student said, "it's just sex . . . and the white girls don't care." The assumption is that blacks and whites date for different reasons than same-race couples. In particular, the black female students interviewed believed that a relationship between a black man and a white woman is based on what the man can get from the relationship, whether it be sex, status, money, or services such as laundry and homework.

Based on the meanings attached to interracial dating and what it symbolized to these students, it is not surprising that most of the students did not feel interracial dating was an option for them. There was a general consensus among the black students that they would not choose to date interracially, citing certain issues such as white racism, commitment to the black community, and personal preference. As one Collegiate University black male student said, "Me personally, I got no time for white people. I don't know how or *why* someone could ever get over the racism . . . to date a white person." Other students said they did not date interracially because of their commitment to the black community. One female student said interracial dating was "not an option, it's important to preserve your race, the cultural and racial preservation of our community." Another female student echoed the black community respondents' discussion of becoming more cynical about interracial dating as one grows older: "I did date white guys when I was young, but I grew up around a whole bunch of white folks. . . . I wouldn't do it anymore. I want someone to complement me, and I don't think a white person could. No white person can understand, you just want to be with someone who knows what prejudice feels like without having to explain how it feels."

Like the white students, the black students' general consensus was that the views of their friends and the black community on campus influenced their decision not to date interracially, particularly because of the meanings attached to dating white. The black students agreed that if they dated interracially they would be "talked about." As one Collegiate University woman explained, "Blacks just like to see other blacks, especially black men who are successful, to stay black, be with a black woman . . . it's just about respecting and applauding those who don't go interracial." Another black female student from Central State University offered a similar perspective: "Blacks have a problem with it. I'd be uncomfortable knowing someone who dated a white person, because whites just don't understand [*shaking her head*], don't understand how anyone would make that choice."

Black male students in particular discussed the pressure to find a black mate, implying that there were opportunities to date interracially. At Central State University, one male "admitted" to dating a white woman on campus for a few weeks but stated that "the social perception just got to me. I didn't want to be known as *that guy who dates the white girl*." Another male student said, "I had a black girl come right and tell me, 'You better not date a white girl,' because she wouldn't be my friend anymore. I think there is a worry about what black girls would say if you dated a white girl." The black students also discussed the idea that black individuals who engage in interracial relationships are "selling out," stating that "viewing someone as a sellout is not ignorant." They described it as "actually [coming] from education about your past." One woman said she believed that "education doesn't bring a more open outlook." According to her, when blacks become "more knowledgeable about the history of racism and learn what whites have done," interracial marriage is viewed more negatively.

However, the students acknowledged that when it came to black women dating white men, the prevailing attitude was different. At Collegiate University, one woman stated, "A black woman with a white man can go further and there's not the same idea that she's going to desert the black community," adding that "the white man may see her as a liability to his success." At St. Stephen's, one of the women explained that "some black women would date a white guy or not have a problem with other black girls doing it, because you see so many black guys running around with white girls that it's almost like, 'See, this is what you get.'" At Central State University, another woman stated, "When I see a black girl with a white guy, I think it must be love. He must be doing something right for her to cross over like that, or maybe he has money."

Based on these responses, it seems that the opposition to interracial relationships revolves around the negative perceptions of the black individual, symbolic meanings attached to interracial unions, and anger toward whites because of the racism and prejudice that blacks have experienced; yet the students' responses definitely varied depending on whether the interracial union involved a black man or black woman. Overall, the black students were more vocal than white students about their views and more openly expressed how the issue of interracial relationships is debated within their community.

Does Interracial Dating Mean Marriage?
Interracial Rites of Passage

The prevalence of interracial dating seems to depend on the group and even the university addressed. Even in the celebratory *New York Times* article referred to earlier, one of the authors admits he "was excited to track down interracial couples at Ole Miss, thinking they would be perfect to make my point about this hopeful trend. But none were willing to talk about the issue on record. . . . 'Even if people wanted to marry [interracially], I think they'd keep it kind of quiet,' explained a minister on campus." Increased visibility and engagement in black-white sexual unions does not necessarily signal racial progress or a lasting relationship, but possibly just a temporary trend or fad, similar to the 1920s era of the Harlem Renaissance and the white fascination with "slumming." Among a number of the black-white couples, white students, and black students, interracial dating is also characterized as a trend or fashion statement. Andre and Susan, who are seniors in college, stated that they had not experienced any significant problems on campus, at least within their social circle, and they described their friends as a diverse group accepting of their relationship. But they did raise this important point about interracial dating on college campuses:

> SARA: Andre said that, like, "I don't want us to be trendy." Like sometimes it's the cool thing to do—to be homosexual, or to be a lesbian,

or to be in an interracial relationship. That's cool and that's hip and like that's what comes into play, too. You know people like—"that's so great, you must be so open-minded." That's kind of . . .

ANDRE [*interrupting Sara*]: Acting like that is almost as bad as people saying, "Oh, how disgusting."

Sara's comparison between homosexuality and interracial relationships is interesting because it conjures the image of interracial dating as deviant or different from the norm—same-race heterosexuals.

Labeling interracial unions as inherently sexual and deviant can be understood as a punishment similar to the way individuals were physically punished historically for engaging in interracial sex. Though the public punishment of interracial couples is no longer common, the popular media (newspaper, radio, films, television, and now the Internet) can be seen as offering society "the same kind of entertainment" once supplied by public hangings and lynchings.[12] The images of interracial couples as deviant are now reinforced through the popular culture by depicting interracial relationships as unsuccessful or by not portraying interracial couples at all. Whether it be through laws, discourses, popular media, or informal pressures, the main purpose of labeling interracial marriage as deviant is to keep the white and black races as distinct and separate groups.

The connection between interracial relationships and societal norms of sexuality is illustrated in the ways interracial couples are discussed in comparison to gay and lesbian couples. The discourses against interracial sexuality and homosexuality are often interwoven, since both are seen as straying from the same-race, heterosexual norms of sexuality. As Judith Butler argues, "cultural prohibitions against miscegenation and homosexuality converge in order to produce a normative heterosexuality (with its gender differences) that guarantees the reproduction of racial purity."[13] This is illustrated by couples such as Sara and Andre's discussion of how interracial couples are seen as trendy, along with bisexuality, on the college campus. In addition, a black college student stated that her mother would rather have her be a lesbian than marry a white man. These examples illustrate the ways that both interracial sexuality and homosexuality are produced and reproduced as being outside the realm of "acceptable" or "normal" behavior.

More important, Andre and Sara's narrative depicts interracial dating as a rite of passage, or fad, that some students engage in, not necessarily a reflection of interracial relationships as long-term commitments or a sign that race relations have improved. Based on this differentiation between casual dating and long-term relationships/marriage, the continuing importance of the institution of marriage is emphasized. It seems that despite the increasing reports of a decline in marriage and the sacredness of marriage vows, when it comes to interracial marriage (like gay marriage), preserving the "sanctity" of this institution is given primary importance. Based on the community responses, though, there may be an increasing visibility of interracial couples; especially among young people there is a significant difference between interracial dating versus marriage. While interracial dating may be marginally tolerated or even acceptable on college campuses or in society, the idea of getting *married* to someone outside one's race is still much more problematic. The college students, both black and white, discussed how marriage across racial lines was unacceptable to their parents, even if interracial dating was allowed. This resonates with the opposition of the families—both white and black—to interracial marriage.

Within the long and complex history of "race relations," marriage rules and laws (informal and formal) can be seen as extensions of white political supremacy. Legal interracial marriages and their biracial offspring obviously threaten the white power structure by threatening, among other things, to "mongrelize" white families, communities, and even the white race. Many blacks, however, also object to interracial marriage and white members in their families and communities. Even worse is the idea of losing a black individual to the white community. The couples discussed priests who opposed their marriage, friends or community members who expressed surprise or disgust at their marriage, and appalled strangers who attended their wedding.

This opposition reflects on the meaning of the institution of marriage generated by white society, where marriage serves as a protection against anomie, "a social arrangement that creates for individuals . . . (a) sort of order."[14] The raging political and social controversy over whether gays and lesbians should be allowed to get married speaks to the ways the institution of marriage is used to enforce societal mores. The institution of marriage is part of the broader structural configuration of society and is the main social area for an individual's self-realization.[15] Through marriage, two people can come together and redefine themselves. Therefore, this society, where group membership is all-important and identity is based primarily on one's racial group, would object to individuals from different "racial" groups redefining themselves apart from their racial identities. Since marriage between a black and a white individual has traditionally been seen as a symbol of the full assimilation of blacks into American society, as Robert Park first argued, then their occurrence could result in them becoming more accepted and thus less deviant from society's norms, unless groups and communities respond in a way to discourage the practice. Therefore, groups tend to "monitor" the identity of each member's marriage partner to ensure that it is matched and perceived by others as being conjoined with the identity of the member.[16] One recent study found that people are more likely to live with a partner of a different race than to marry them, "consistent with the [belief] that cohabitation represents a less formal union, and thus [is] often entered into with people who are not suitable for marriage."[17] A mere transgression is tolerated or even hoped for, but a violation of the "sacred institution" of marriage and family is less tolerable. This idea of interracial dating as a college experience and not as a signal of increasing long-term acceptance of interracial couples is further supported by the students' discussions of their families. There may be an increasing visibility of interracial couples among college students, but according to the students interviewed there remains a significant difference between dating and marriage, especially based on consideration of familial views.

Gender Troubles

Gender matters in a number of ways. As mentioned earlier, interracial unions are imagined and responded to differently depending on whether they involve a black man and a white woman or a black woman and a white man. According to the white communities, relationships between white women and black men still are the most problematic. For example, one white college student said her family would never accept it if she married a black man, even though her brother was married to a black woman. Also, among white college students black men were seen as lazy, unfaithful, and even criminal. The only statements made about white men with black women were that white men found black women "unattractive."

The black students discussed the "trend" for black males to date interracially and the perception of the "highly sought after" status black men had among white women. For example, at St. Stephen's, one of the black women stated, "White women just have this idea of it's so great to be with a black guy because he's a big black stud. You can tell the white girl that he's a dog and she still wants him probably even more." At Central State University, one of the black female students also expressed these sentiments, saying "black men are in fashion, call it the resurgence of the black male. It's like interracial dating is a fashion statement, a token, especially when it is a black athlete . . . white girls are always saying, 'oh, black guys are so much cooler, so much cuter,' and always asking to be hooked up with them." But if black-white relationships are trendy, the black students didn't see the trend applying to black women. They described the image of the black male as a sex symbol in contrast to the continued devaluation of black females.

One of the central beliefs involving interracial couples on the college campus is the sexual nature of these relationships. The black students, and some of the black-white couples themselves, discussed the societal perception that white women want black men for sex.

> LEE: With white girls and black guys people think it is about sex . . . and in some situations, let's say, college kids—a black basketball player [with a white girl]—that's just sex.

In college particularly, the black students tended to characterize white women with black men as "easy"—easy to sleep with, easy to use for money or services such as cooking and laundry, and easy to control. Chris and Victoria discussed these stereotypes, drawing from their own experiences and memories of their college days.

> VICTORIA: Oh, God, I think I have heard every negative thing about white women, black men. I understand it more now but in school it was hard because it was like every day someone was saying something about me from all sides—white guys were like, "Why throw it away on a black guy? He's just using you," and black girls would harass me, call me names, and always act like Chris was with me because I had money or did things for him, which I *didn't,* and I think I let it get to me, but he definitely did worse, when all his [black] friends and their girls would tell him, "How could you make her your girl?" or just try to break trust.

> CHRIS: This is a sore subject for her because we did have a lot of problems, and I think when we were younger, it's like you do let what friends say kind of change the way you feel, and just like Victoria said, I think for me another part of it was this perception among the guys I played with [college basketball team] that she would sleep around because that was how a lot of the white girls who liked black guys acted.

This couple's experiences reflect the way others perceive interracial relationships. The images and issues that the couples confront are similar to the ideas expressed by the college students, particularly the black college students' views on black men with white women. Interestingly, one of the black partners, Victor, denied the importance of race, yet in his discussion of why he almost exclusively dated white women in college, these images of white women as "easy" compared to "difficult" black women also surfaced.

> VICTOR: It's not like I would go out and say, well I'll only go out with white women, but I will also confess that with us males, if you don't have to work so hard, why should you? If you sit back, if you went to a party and there were black and white women there it was easier to make conversation and easier to get the white women interested in you than it was with the black women. Because [white women] are already curious to begin with, and it is this curiosity factor that you could play upon. The black women already knew you in a sense. She knew a thousand men like you. It was much easier to know there was this crowd of [white] women who wanted to talk to you. They were coming to talk to you. They were curious. Then you had this crowd of [black] women over here who, well, anyway, why work so hard?"

Victor's comments are strikingly similar to the following dialogue among black students from all three universities. At Collegiate University, a black female student argued, "There's this perception of black women as more confrontational, too much trouble, white girls are easy, easy to control, that's the dynamic you have operating there." Other black female students said that "black guys feel that white girls are easier, sexually loose, and, on the flipside, that black women are too aggressive, too controlling, have an attitude, not confident, but nasty, gold-digger." Another woman said her black male friends tell her that "the guys I know say they are 'just sleeping with the white girl,' and [white women] are more subservient, don't ask where are you going or what are you doing. You don't have to call them your girlfriend; white girls are just easier to have sex with." The only black man to discuss the issue at any of the three schools stated that he thought "black women are naggers, it seems like you're constantly arguing. You don't want to seem like a chump to your boys." Then he quickly added, "That doesn't mean I'd date a white woman."

In white and black communities, the contrasting images of black women as the opposite of white women has a historical basis. White women were put on a pedestal as the symbol of femininity, beauty, and purity for all men, while black women were seen as strong, overpowering, physically unappealing, and sexually promiscuous. The black students stated that white women are still viewed as more desirable but are also seen as sexually loose and sub-servient, which only enhances their desirability. Black women, however, are viewed as undesirable to white and black men because they are too strong and too aggressive. These negative images of black women also imply a lack of femininity, since to be submissive is still characterized as feminine in this male-dominated society.

Considering the different images of those who are involved interracially, it is not surprising that white and black men and women have different views on these relationships. Within the community research, the white women and men had similar views on interracial relationships: most whites stated that they had not and would not date interracially. Among the black respondents, there was a difference between the responses of the men and women, which is at least partly based on negative images of black and white women and how they impact black women differently. Black women seemed to have the strongest views on interracial couples and had the most to say on the issue, even though they were not involved interracially. The particular ways that interracial relationships affect black women (and their responses) was a promi-nent theme. Even in the couples' narratives the issue of opposition of black women was mentioned repeatedly, especially by the black men/white women couples.

Through the focus group responses, the black women discussed how devastating the rise in interracial dating is to them personally as women look-ing for partners, as well as to the collective self-esteem of black women. For example, at Collegiate University, one student discussed how, as a black woman, it is difficult enough to have to deal with whites who treat her as if she is inferior, but it is even harder "to have your own men act like white is better, and systematically choose white women over you. It is hard not to get angry because it feels as if no one values your worth as a woman." One of the men agreed, stating that he viewed "interracial relationships negatively particularly for the way it makes black women feel," mentioning how he has seen what his "sisters have gone through" and he just "respect[s] black women too much." Other women students discussed how they see black men on cam-pus "treating white girls better. They don't treat or respect black women like that." Another woman described feeling abandoned: "You grow up with these men all your life, but then you're not good enough to be a wife. It is disre-spectful and degrading." One of the black women at St. Stephen's offered this advice to the other black women: "I used to let it hurt me, but now I say black women turn that anger on yourselves, and think that guy is missing out on me. Don't show you are mad. Don't settle for someone who doesn't treat you like white girls are treated. Find a man. Stop hating and find a man who treats you well. When a white girl says, 'I got me a black man,' you can say good because you got you the same."

At Collegiate University, the issue became so problematic that it came to the attention of Dr. Cooper, an African American professor and administrator I interviewed. She was "very much involved in" incidents where "black females were angry at black males because of the lack of available men" due to interracial dating. Some of the black men and women had a formal conversation about the issue, and as a result "interracial dating is not a focus anymore [of black students] because there is no longer a significant number of black males interracially dating like there once was." Cooper acknowledged how interracial dating is a special problem for black women on campus because it tends to be black men who date or have dated interracially.

The black students offered various reasons why it is not more common for black women and white men to date. Some argued that black women are not interested in white men, such as one woman at St. Stephen's who argued that "black women are just more attracted to black men." Similarly, at Central State University a man stated, "Black women don't want a white man. That's why you don't see more of it." Yet most of the black women discussed their belief that white men are not attracted to them. One student—who belonged to a women's group that addressed "issues of beauty and how light skin for women is valued, which make black women devalued"—discussed how "black men can be dark-skinned and they are still valued." Another black student explained that "black men tend to like bigger bodies, like black women have, but white guys are used to white girls who don't have a butt." A number of the black women referenced the American standards of beauty, which privilege white skin, long hair, and certain physical features, as responsible for white men not finding black women attractive. Another reason offered was the idea that "white guys are hesitant to approach black women." One of the women stated that she didn't know "what white guys think about black girls," adding that she does wonder what they think, since only one white guy ever tried to talk to her. As one black woman argued, "white guys just aren't as aggressive as white women. That's why they don't get to know black women, but you have white women falling all over black guys." The comments of the white male students interviewed support the idea that many white men do not view interracial dating as desirable or an option.

The emotional narratives of the black women in the student groups reveal how opposition to interracial dating is not about whites being inferior or undesirable, but about how interracial relationships make black women feel about themselves. Interracial dating is seen as a rejection of the black community and, more specifically, a devaluation of black women and black femininity that is learned from white society. Black opposition to interracial relationships can be traced to white racism, which has produced a society where blackness is devalued and constructed as different and inferior to whiteness. Furthermore, black women see intermarriage as a rejection of black sexuality, particularly black femininity and black womanhood, and an embracement of white women and white womanhood.

Cultural Messages

Based on the experiences of the black-white couples, and the views of the college students, there are undoubtedly certain meanings attached to interracial dating and particular views (mainly opposition) of interracial relationships. Considering the dominant role that popular culture, particularly television and film, play among the younger generations, it is noteworthy to consider popular culture's messages about black-white relationships that are geared toward the college-aged generation.

Among those interviewed, the role of popular culture varied. For the white students, the issue of popular culture and interracial depictions was not relevant. Quite possibly since interracial relationships were not something that most of the students were concerned with, they did not have commentary or did not think much about the ways interracial couples were portrayed in film, or even the lack of depictions of black-white couples. Yet among the black students, the role of popular culture and its connection to interracial dating was explicitly discussed.

The black students raised the issue of the role of popular culture and how black celebrities' relationships impact the black community's views on interracial dating. Among the black college students, a number of women gave examples of "sellouts," from television personalities like Bryant Gumbel to film characters from movies such as *Waiting to Exhale* (which featured a black man who left his black wife and children for his white secretary). As one woman explained, "Black celebrities who leave their black wives for white women are a sellout. What kind of message is that? All of a sudden he needs a white woman and leaves his family!" Furthermore, black celebrities who have made statements about their preference to date interracially or who have married interracially were discussed. One of the black male students remarked, "Black people definitely got mad when [Los Angeles Lakers basketball player] Kobe Bryant or Tiger Woods chose white women. On the black radio stations it is discussed like World War III was coming." One woman stated, "There's a lot of black celebrities that degrade black women and that's where the black guys get the idea that it's okay . . . like Wesley Snipes, [former NBA basketball player] Dennis Rodman get on national TV saying they wouldn't date a black woman." There was a sense, particularly among the black women, that the prominence of black male celebrities who date or marry white women, and the tendency to portray black women as sexually promiscuous and only attractive if they are light skinned, encourages young black men to believe that white women are more desirable.

Interracial Images for Generation X

It is widely argued that there is an increasing number of films that feature black-white couples, particularly movies for younger people. However, this growing interest in portraying black-white relationships does not necessarily signal more positive images of these unions. Since the late 1990s there have been a number of widely viewed movies that addressed the issue of black-white relationships among the younger generations. As David Schwartz, chief curator of film at the American Museum of the Moving Image in New York, argues, "One thing I think is great about teen movies is issues of class and race are right there on the surface," such as recent teen movies like *Save the Last Dance*, *O* (a 2001 boarding school remake of Shakespeare's *Othello*), *Cruel Intentions*, and *Romeo Must Die*.[18]

Tackling what was once a cinematic taboo—depicting an intimate relationship between a black-white couple on screen—Hollywood, or at least those producing movies for the younger generations, is increasingly including interracial couples in their story lines. Nonetheless, the underlying beliefs about the interracial relationships depicted in these films are often ambivalent. For example, in the 2000 film *Romeo Must Die* (which is very loosely based on Shakespeare's *Romeo and Juliet*), Han (Jet Li) is a Chinese cop who comes to California to seek revenge for the gang-related murder of his brother. What he finds, though, is a fierce war between his father's syndicate and that of an African American mob family for control of some waterfront land, as both groups are trying to make a deal with a corrupt football team owner to build a new stadium. Han teams up with the African American mob boss's daughter Trish (hip-hop singer Aaliyah), who is also interested in bringing about justice. Despite the implied attraction between the two and the classic Romeo and Juliet romance on which it is based, there is no intimacy or development of a relationship.[19] In *Romeo Must Die*, the possibility of an interracial relationship was as far as the movie would go.

A number of films geared toward the college-aged generation still emphasize stereotypes of difference and opposition even while attempting to celebrate the meshing of different races and cultures. For example, in the 1998 teen blockbuster *Cruel Intentions*, a young white woman schemes to destroy another young white woman by convincing a young black man to seduce her, since having sex with a black man would ruin her and her family's reputation. Even in this film geared toward the "MTV generation," there is an acknowledgment that interracial unions are taboo, or at least scandalous.

The biggest teen film involving an interracial story line is the 2001 *Save the Last Dance*, which grossed over $91 million. The film was produced by MTV Films with Paramount Pictures, and according to MTV President Van Toffler, MTV saturated its audience with information and marketing of the film. The entire plot of the movie revolves around Sara Johnson (Julia Stiles), a white teen who goes to live with her father in a predominantly black inner-city Chicago neighborhood after her mother dies. At the high school in this new neighborhood she becomes friends with Chenille Reynolds, a popular black teen, and develops a relationship with Chenille's brother Derek (Sean Patrick Thomas). The movie highlights all the problems that erupt as the relationship between Sara and Derek intensifies, not unlike those pointed out by the college students I interviewed.

Set in a predominantly black neighborhood, much of the movie focuses on the responses of the black community, using a few key characters to represent the collective opposition. One of Derek's friends, Malakai, has just gotten out of a juvenile detention center and is still very much involved with street life, including dealing drugs. Despite Derek's aspirations for college, he is loyal to Malakai because of something that happened in the past. Malakai is against Derek's relationship with Sara. He clearly expresses his views on interracial dating to Sara at a dance club while Sara watches Derek dance with another girl. Malakai tells her, "You'll never look as good with him as she does. That's oil, you're milk, no point trying to mix." Later in the movie, Derek meets up with Malakai and two other guy friends, and they begin questioning him on why he hasn't been around as much:

> FRIEND 1: I've heard you been traveling in new circles, what's up with that?
>
> MALAKAI: Are you tapping that white girl? [*They all laugh.*] That's

why you don't have no time for your boys no more, too busy fronting
...

FRIEND 1: . . . too busy snowflaking, and if that's the case you best be watching your back, 'cause white women don't bring nothing but trouble!

DEREK: That ain't white women, that's women . . .

The discussion then moves to the issue of Derek's involvement and commitment to his friends, the street, and the neighborhood. Malakai asks Derek to come with them to another part of the city to "handle" some guys who have been messing with Malakai's street dealings, and he shows Derek a gun he has in his pants. When Derek says no, Malakai responds, "You act like you don't know who you are anymore, Derek. What's up out there for anyone who ain't you? I'm still from this neighborhood, but you, guess that's what happens when a white girl goes to your head." The word "sellout" is never used, but Derek's friends imply that he has changed because of his relationship with Sara. Malakai even challenges his behavior and commitment to the neighborhood and in essence tells Derek that he has "sold out" his black friends and black community for this white girl.

Nikki, another high school student and ex-girlfriend of Derek, starts a fight with Sara in gym class, which ends with this exchange of words:

NIKKI: You always in my way. . . . it's about you, white girls like you, creeping up, taking our men, the whole world ain't enough, you got to conquer ours too.

SARA: Whatever, Nikki! You know what? Derek and I like each other, and if you have a problem with that, screw you.

When Derek's sister Chenille asks Sara about the fight, she expresses the same sentiments as Nikki:

CHENILLE: You and Derek act like it don't bother people to see you together, like it don't hurt people to see it.

SARA: We like each other. What is the big damn deal? It's me and him, not us and other people.

CHENILLE: Black people, Sara. Black women. Derek's about something, he's smart, he's motivated, he's for real, he's not just gonna

make some babies and not take care of them . . . he's gonna make
something of himself, and here you come, white, so you gotta be
right, and you take one of the few decent men we have left after
jail, drugs, and drive-by, that is what Nikki meant about you up in
our world . . .

Even Chenille, who likes Sara and originally seemed supportive of Sara and
Derek's relationship, understands how Nikki feels and why she said those
things to Sara. Like the black female college students, she referenced the collective opposition of black women based on the belief that interracial dating
(especially when it involves a "good man") is detrimental to black women
and the black community.

Though the views of whites receive little attention, there are a few
scenes worth noting. For example, after Sara goes out to a dance spot with
Chenille and Derek, she talks to one of her white friends in the suburban
neighborhood in Vermont where she had lived with her mother. She tells her
friend about her night out, and the friend responds, "the ghetto . . . anyone
got shot?" Sara continues to tell her that she has met a guy she likes, and the
friend's immediate response is that she didn't know there were "white guys
in her school." Sara explains that he is black, and the friend is silent. Like
the white students interviewed, Sara's friend lives in a white social world
and doesn't even think of the possibility that Sara would be interested in a
black guy, even though she is at a predominantly black school. Also, the white
friend draws upon racialized views of black communities as ghettos where
people get shot.

The movie also depicts many of the black students at the high school
as underachievers, teen parents, not college bound, promiscuous, and/or involved in illegal activity. In fact, Derek stands out in the high school because
he is smart and awaiting acceptance to Georgetown in preparation for medical school. Furthermore, the movie portrays many of the stereotypical images that the black college students I interviewed expressed concern about.
For example, Sara is depicted as intelligent, sincere, and a gifted ballet dancer
who is innocent and naive, while the two main black female characters, Chenille and Nikki, are depicted much differently. Nikki, Derek's ex-girlfriend,
was unfaithful to Derek, which ended their relationship, and she is portrayed
as tough and streetwise. Chenille, Derek's sister, is a teen parent, and while
much attention is paid to Derek's academic goals, there is no mention of
Chenille's intelligence or plans for college. While Sara and Derek are portrayed positively, the other black characters in the film have more negative

portrayals, reproducing some of the stereotypes discussed by the black college students.

The movie's ending echoes the color-blind discourses of some of the black-white couples interviewed. When Derek and Sara stop talking because of the opposition of others, Chenille tells Derek what she said to Sara:

> CHENILLE: I said something to Sara . . . stuff about how maybe Nikki had a point about black men and white women. . . . I'm sorry. I don't even like Nikki, I was tripping off Kenny [the father of her baby]. You can't help who you love, Derek. You're not supposed to. When you love someone, you love them. Look at me. At least you found someone who loves you back . . .

Derek walks away from his sister, and she fears that he may be getting involved with Malakai's illegal activities. She yells to him, "I know what Malakai wants you to do. Why are you tripping off him, Derek? All you trying to do is get the hell up out of here. Ain't no shame or blame in that." This conversation is important because it is a response to Malakai's and Nikki's opposition, and it also echoes the sentiments of the black college students interviewed. Chenille's words characterize Sara and Derek's relationship in individual terms. She says she does not feel there is a problem with black men dating white women, or more specifically Derek dating Sara. Her comments on his goals to go to college address Malakai's accusations. She tells Derrick that striving to leave the neighborhood (and having a white girlfriend) is not selling out, but rather just trying to succeed. Like the color-blind discourse that dominates American society, the movie concludes with the message that despite any collective opposition of whites and blacks, these two individuals can come together and find happiness. This movie could appeal to a wide group because it addresses the issues that blacks (and whites) as a group have with interracial dating. In particular, it could also appeal to those who do date interracially because it brings the issue back to an individual level of "color-blind love." And as the trailer for the movie promises, "against all odds they overcome the obstacles to their dreams, and discover that ultimately the only person you have to be is . . . yourself." The complexity of interracial relationships and societal responses is illustrated in this movie's depiction of both support and opposition for interracial relationships while ultimately reproducing the negative images of black women and men that the black college students I interviewed identified as part of the problem in the first place.

Conclusion

College students, like the larger society, have an ambivalent relationship with interracial dating. In the college environment, the discourse used around black-white relationships may appear supportive ("I think it's sooo cool when I see an interracial couple"), yet beneath these cursory approvals lie racialized beliefs and a distancing from these relationships ("but I'm just not, I don't know, attracted to other races"). While this subtle opposition is both white and black, there is a significant difference between black and white views, and the issue is reflected upon more by the black students. The white students mainly have not dated interracially, do not plan to, and have limited contact with interracial couples or even black students. For the black students, interracial couples seem more visible, the avoidance of white students is not possible, and interracial dating is questioned based on what it represents to black students about racial identity and racial stereotypes. While college campuses undoubtedly offer a place for different races to socialize and some opportunity for interracial dating, the line between black and white seems to remain.

CHAPTER 6

Black_White.com

SURFING THE INTERRACIAL INTERNET

*T*he Internet is a particularly interesting social arena that symbolizes for many the future of interaction and society. The images and discourses around black-white unions on the Internet can serve as an important data source that—like the transcript of an interview—can be read and analyzed for content and meaning, including the social, cultural, and political interactions that take place online.[1] The meaning and significance of these Internet discourses and images are "social products in their own right, as well as what they claim to represent."[2]

The word "interracial" returns thousands of results with search engines such as MSN, Google, Yahoo, and Excite. Surfing through these sites, one can find individual Web pages of interracial couples, large multiracial support sites such as Interracial Voice or the Multiracial Activist, or even pornographic Web sites for those who want to see interracial sex. Based on an extensive review of Web sites where black-white couples or interracial sexuality figure prominently, interracial Web sites can be grouped into three main categories: multiracial organizations/support sites; pornographic Web sites and dating sites;[3] and hate group sites. Like the community narratives, these very different types of Web sites do not simply represent individual views but are part of the reproduction of certain images and ideas about black-white unions that draw from contemporary societal views.[4] The Internet, like society, has a complicated relationship with black-white unions, accepting them in theory but opposing them in practice.

Interracial Communities Online

There are a significant number of Web sites devoted to the celebration of and support for interracial couples, multiracial families, and multiracial issues.[5] These interracial/multiracial Web sites range in size and exposure from individual Web pages of interracial couples and/or multiracial individuals to the larger multipurpose cyberspace sites such as the Multiracial Activist. There are a number of Internet magazines devoted to interracial issues, such as *Interracial Voice, Mavin,* and *New People Interracial Magazine,* with new ones appearing frequently. Also, the multiracial online community includes the Web pages of multiracial organizations such as Association of Multi-Ethnic Americans, Interracial Family Circle, and Project Race. These sites receive a large number of visitors, yet they are attached to organizations founded and built outside of cyberspace. Smaller and specialized sites address particular interracial issues and sell products geared toward multiracial families (iMeltingPot.com; Blindheart.com). Despite the relatively large number of Web sites, the number of hits (visits) they receive varies greatly. Search engines like MSN, along with many of the Web sites themselves, track how many hits a Web site receives, with some averaging thousands of hits per day and others receiving only a few hundred hits ever. Therefore, based on information from the search engines and my review of the various categories of Web sites, much of this discussion revolves around a large multipurpose cyberspace site, The Multiracial Activist (TMA), edited and published by James Landrith, and an Internet magazine, Interracial Voice (IV), edited and published by Charles Michael Byrd.[6] These sites are two of the largest and most prominently featured on the Internet, and, more important, they are exclusively cyberspace communities. Though both TMA and IV will be the main focus, the discourses and ideologies found in these sites are characteristic of the large cyberspace multipurpose sites and Internet magazines devoted to multiracial issues. Furthermore, these two sites contain extensive links and directories to smaller sites and other online (and offline) resources for interracial couples and families.

TMA, founded in 1997 by James Landrith, represents the largest and most frequently visited multiracial site, averaging 3,000 unique hits a day. TMA is one of the most comprehensive and all-encompassing sites for information, covering a wide range of topics and issues related to multiracialism.[7] IV, founded in 1995 by Charles Michael Byrd, averages 1,300 hits a day and self-identifies as "an independent, information-oriented, networking newsjournal, serving the mixed-race/interracial community in cyberspace." A significant part of both of these Web sites, and the many small ones, is the extensive links to other "multiracial related links," which includes categories such as transracial/intercultural adoption, multiracial celebrities/historical figures, interracial children/youth, multiracial clubs/forums, multiracial organizations, multiracial Web publishers, and interracial personal Web sites. Through its essays and guest editorials, which are the major part of the site, IV advocates for the right to identify as multiracial, opposes the "one-drop rule," and maintains that interracial couples/multiracial people are victimized by both white communities and communities of color. Similarly, TMA argues for the "right to self-identify in any racial category or instead choose NO racial identity and instead shed race as an identity altogether." TMA also takes a stand on various political and social issues, such as supporting transracial adoption and opposing the collection of racial data in financial transactions. The main goal of the Web site, according to TMA, is "to educate our community about the need to be vigilant against the racism that still targets people of mixed heritage and those involved in interracial relationships." These sites identify as racist any individuals or groups of all races who are viewed as oppositional toward interracial and multiracial individuals and families.

Overall, these sites provide valuable information about services and support for multiracial individuals and families struggling with a lack of acceptance and problems in the larger society. The information databases that they have compiled, as well as the extensive links between the various multiracial organizations, events, and groups, provide useful documentation of issues involving or affecting the multiracial community. The sites foster a sense of community by disseminating information, outlining goals, providing services and ideas, and creating a shared history. Sites such as TMA and IV provide a space for interracial couples and multiracial family members to correspond with each other in a virtual community where most of the members may never meet, though "in the minds of each lives the image of their communion."[8] While these multiracial Web sites (like ideologies of multiculturalism) promote a positive image of interracial relationships and celebrate multiracial couples and families, they still point to the fact that opposition exists. Interracial couples are still perceived and treated differently, which is why they need these support networks. By drawing on certain racial ideologies, however, these sites further reproduce the idea of interracial couples as different. For example, TMA argues that "biracial/multiracial people, interracial couples/families, and transracially adopted individuals have unique needs that cannot or will not be met by traditional civil rights groups who tend to brush off our community or denigrate us. We need to handle our own affairs. Join The Multiracial Activist in taking charge of our community!"

TMA and IV link individuals through their common experiences and provide an opportunity for interracial couples to communicate, but this information, encouragement, and support is filtered through a color-blind discourse. The contradictions in the belief systems of these sites are complex. There is an acknowledgment that interracial couples and families are treated differently and therefore need to come together; however, at the same time, race is deemphasized. Like a number of the black-white couples interviewed, these sites shift between race consciousness and color-blindness. For example, Landrith states that one of TMA's functions is "to work to help those stuck in a 'one-drop' or 'racialist' mindset," and he "look[s] forward to the day that we as a people can shed 'racial' identities in favor of individual identities."[9] TMA also outlines its strong belief and support for "the right to self-identify in any racial category or instead choose NO racial identity and instead shed race as an identity together" and the "abolition of all the divisive, unconstitutional racial categories." Byrd's response to a woman's letter to the editor on the IV site illustrates the racialized discourse and color-blind ideology that is used. The woman wrote:

> I am a 29-year-old (black and white) mixed female. My white father wasn't around much at all growing up. My mom raised me. Naturally, I identify more with my black culture. . . . I got into a relationship with a man who is ethnic Mon (sino-tibetan chinese etc) from Myanmar. . . . My family is not happy that I am with . . . what they keep calling him . . . "foreigner." . . . This relationship has gotten to be extremely serious. We have both discovered that we really are in love with each other.

Byrd responded:

> So much I could talk about here. A "mixed" woman who still identifies solely as "black" who lets others influence her because she is involved with a "foreigner." *SIGH!* He's a human, and so are you, and I say to hell with racial/ethnic/cultural identity politics.

His solution to her problem of lack of support is to deny that race matters and ridicule her for allowing herself and her boyfriend to be racially and ethnically identified. While aware that interracial couples and families face opposition from the larger society, these Web sites also advocate that people should be color-blind. But what good is it for black-white couples to deny the role race plays if it still affects how others treat them? These types of statements reflect a denial of the ways that race impacts the lives of members of historically excluded racial groups, African Americans in particular. Remarkably absent is any discussion of institutional racial inequalities that exist against all people of color or an acknowledgment that any opposition is rooted in the systemic racism that permeates America.

These Web sites also further the idea that interracial couples and families are different and not part of the racial communities from which they came. Though there is an acknowledgment of Web sites that more generally address issues of race, the majority of the content on the TMA and IV sites focus on interracial couples and families and issues that directly affect only multiracial families. For example, there are various links to what TMA calls "Race Related Links" (which is separate from "Multiracial Related Links") that are categorized as Aboriginal/Native People; Afrocentric/African American Organizations and Websites; Asian/Asian American Organizations and Websites; Hispanic/Latino Organizations and Websites; and multiculturalism and ethnicity.[10] The broader issues of racism, discrimination, and social justice, however, are shadowed behind discussions of the ways that multiracial individuals and families experience racism and discrimination from monoracial communities. Thus a new multiracial category of "us" is advocated, blacks and whites are lumped together as "they," and racial inequality is ignored.

These sites see as identical white opposition and black opposition to interracial relationships (and multiracial identity for children of these unions). While it was clear from my research that the white and the black community members' were both opposed on some level, the opposition had a different basis. However, within TMA's list of individuals and groups who have expressed "repugnant view(s) of multiracial identity/interracial relationships through their words and deeds," they specifically and repeatedly argue that white and black opposition is the same. The power and privilege of whites inherent in the racial hierarchy of American society is rarely discussed. An example is the criticism on TMA of the African American singer Jill Scott. She was cited for her song "Do You Remember?" The song suggests that African Americans who become involved interracially may be doing so for the wrong reasons. TMA responded that "we are led to believe that Ms. Scott is not against 'interracial' marriages/relationships, but is instead, only questioning the intent of some involved. Do not be deceived, this is the same sorry garbage that is spouted by 'white' racialists. If it is not acceptable coming out of the mouth of a 'white' person, why is it okay for Ms. Scott to espouse it? Ms. Scott should be ashamed and so should [people] who make excuses for her bigotry."

The site's criticism of any questioning or opposition to interracial relationships and/or multiracial identity represents a denial of the politicized nature of multiracial identity and interracial relationships, a lack of awareness and understanding of why others may have opposition, and a refusal to acknowledge that white and black opposition is not the same. This criticism also feeds into the color-blind discourses of whites who argue against interracial relationships. As some of the white community members stated (and I have heard some of my family members say), "blacks don't like interracial dating anymore than whites," which is meant to somehow make it okay to oppose it. This type of argument also corresponds to the white college students who attributed the lack of interracial dating on campus to the self-segregation of blacks rather than their own self-segregating practices.

Tying in to the views of the black community members, there is an element of distancing from the black community within these interracial Web sites. A number of black respondents discussed how interracial relationships symbolized a removal from the black community and self-internalization of racism. While playing into the desires of interracial couples and families to escape discrimination and to live in a society that is "blind" to their racial differences, the attempts to form a multiracial community (which are discussed and encouraged on these Web sites) do not challenge racism, but rather allow those who are in multiracial families to escape from the racism of the larger society. Also, simply seeking out other multiracial individuals and families only reinforces the idea that those of the same race, or in this case "multirace," form distinct groups. These Web sites are primarily if not exclusively geared toward multiracial family members. There is virtually no alignment with other racial communities. They are ignoring the racial hierarchy and the white power structure by claiming that blacks are racist and arguing that there is no difference between white and black opposition to a multiracial category. By pointing fingers at black civil rights organizations and publicly shaming these groups for their "mistreatment" of multiracial individuals and families, these sites support the argument that all people are racist and undermine the argument against white supremacy. There is no acknowledgment of the historical circumstances that have created opposition within black communities or the reasons why some black groups oppose multiracial identity. The emphasis is placed on how multiracial individuals and families are discriminated against, yet there is no acknowledgment of how multiracial individuals and families may occupy a more privileged position due to color stratification and the white privilege of family members. Instead, these sites actually privilege those who are multiracial or are in an interracial family. The rhetoric espoused by IV and TMA, particularly, tends to assume that somehow multiracial individuals and families are the only ones capable of understanding and correctly dealing with race. As Landrith states, "for those who've progressed and reached that level, The Abolitionist Examiner exists to help TMA move these individuals onto the understanding that false belief in 'race' as an entity is paramount to the formation of 'racist' concepts and belief systems." Therefore, while TMA and IV support the view that racial categories should be abolished and should not play a role in redressing racial injustices, there is no problem with constructing multiracial individuals and families as separate and different from groups and communities that identify "monoracially," thereby promoting the creation and maintenance of a multiracial community.

Searching for Interracial Sex: Black-White Pornography and Dating Sites

There are a large number of sites for individuals who want to find a partner of a different race as well as sites that cater to those who want to see interracial couples engaging in sexual acts. While these two types of sites have their obvious differences, I argue that both are motivated by individuals who specifically want an interracial encounter, whether it is to build a relationship or to simply watch others online.

In the billion-dollar Internet porn network, interracial sex is a hot commodity. The majority of so-called interracial sites tend to showcase white/ black sex, with Asian and Latino sex acts being categorized separately or on different sites.[11] Most sites focus on either white men with black women or black men with white women, but the sites do not contain images of both, which may suggest that whoever visits these sites does not want to see both. What is often unclear is the race of those producing the images.

On the Internet, black-white sexuality is fetishized, an erotic spectacle that individuals seek out. As one Web site states, "your interracial prayers have finally been answered." Interracial sex is marketed as a fetish or specialty sex act like shemales, gangbangs, animal sex, foot fetishes, and sadomasochism, among many. Yet the same can be said about racial groups in general, where there are many categories, such as black sex and Latino sex, but there is no mention of white (unless it is a white women having sex with a nonwhite man). The black-white sexuality performed online, like black-white couples in society, are under a dominant gaze, which posits same-race, heterosexual couples as the norm.

Not only is black-white sexuality marketed as a specialty act, but the sex acts and scenarios draw from historical images and beliefs about blacks and interracial relations. One major theme is the "cuckold genre," where the images and stories involve white men's wives having sex with black men. For example, at BlackBachelor.com (subtitled Interracial Slut Central) the feature states, "Meet Amanda a Pregnant bored housewife has been fucking young black stud while hubby is away!" Note how the only raced person is the black man, whereas the wife and hubby, who are presumably white, do not need to be racially marked. This depiction of white women and black men appears in many of the sites dedicated to black-white porn. Another site features the caption, "My wife loves BLACKMEN . . . and she loves to make me WATCH while she has sex with them." Some even play on slavery images, using the language of "slut wife/slave and black master," which distorts the historical realities of white masters raping black women. For example, one site uses cartoon images, with one very graphic and stereotypical depiction of what they call "A Black Breeding Girlfriend," a cartoon image of a pregnant white woman giving a black man oral sex while a white male servant watches with his penis chained.[12] Yet in these sex fantasies (which mainly seemed to be produced by white men for white men), it is the white women who are raped or who willingly submit to sexual acts with black men. Some sites offer private parties for those interested in interracial sex, such as Cynara Fox's First Interracial Gangbang, which features porn star Cynara Fox (a white woman) and Amber, "a regular [white] bored housewife," having sex with multiple black men. The site claims they are so popular that the "Interracial Gangbang crew" has begun booking private parties.

Beyond the white slut wife theme, the imagery of young pure white women being seduced by big black men is prominent. For example, numerous sites feature captions such as "innocent college girls get fucked by massive black cocks." Many of these interracial porn sites focus on white teens engaging in sexual acts with multiple black men, with captions such as "going black." Again, the race of the white girls is not mentioned, while the blackness of the men is emphasized. Many of the sites feature stories to accompany the pictures. In particular, one site promises "black cock sucking sluts," and the webmaster writes stories to accompany graphic pictures: " I know I'm going to hell when I die. . . . But I can't help it. . . . I love to film these cute girls fucking and sucking these fucking huge black cocks. . . . A friend of friend that told me that 'she prefers black guys.'" This site is produced by a white man who says he has an obsession with seeing and filming white women with black men. All of the captions that accompany the pictures are derogatory and often racialized. Tying into the couple and community research, a few of the white college women and white partners interviewed had mentioned that they knew white men who were disgusted by white women who had been with black men. Furthermore, these racialized and sexualized images are similar to the historical incidents where white men argued against racial integration and equality because it would lead to black men having sex with white women. What is apparent on these sites is that black-white sexuality is not the norm. Most important, these sites draw from dominant images of black men as sexual threats with large penises and of white women as weak and unable to resist black men.

There are a smaller number of sites that feature interracial sex between black women and white men. On these sites, the emphasis is on the black women as sexual objects and exotic creatures, using words like "brown sugar," "phat black booties," "pink chocolate," or "ghetto girls who talk nasty." The racialized images of black women as ghetto girls, or as overtly sexual and ready to please white men, are drawn upon. Whereas on the sites that feature white women/black men the black men were depicted as the aggressors, on the black women/white men sites the black women are described as satisfying the white men. Images of black women as sexually promiscuous, sexually insatiable, and desiring of white men have a long history and were routinely drawn upon as a justification for white men raping black women during slavery and after. Overall, these pornographic sites demonstrate how interracial sexuality is still different enough to serve as a fetish for some people (enough to keep these sites profitable).

In addition to interracial pornographic sites, there are also a growing number of interracial dating sites that provide a means for finding a partner or lover of a different race (www.interracialsingles.com, interraciallink.com, mixedfeelings.com, and whitewomenblackmen.com). While they do not display images of interracial sex for pleasure, they do market the idea of cultivating interracial romance. For example, on Yahoo!, the first two results for "interracial couples" were "Become an Interracial Couple—100% Interracial Dating Site" and "Ever Want to Date Outside Your Race?"[13] While race is explicit on the pornographic sites, or at least the racialization of the black individuals, on the dating sites there is a complex contradiction between catering to those who specifically want to date outside their race and maintaining that race does not matter when it comes to love. Many of the dating services use the term "color-blind," such as Salt and Pepper Singles (www.saltandpeppersingles.com), which describes itself as "an interracial Mecca where love is color-blind," or Interracial Singles (www.interracialsingles.com), which states one can "find a love that transcends color."

These sites critique the overwhelming tendency for individuals to date others of the same race, implying that this choice to be in a same-race relationship is racially based. The sites still offer a race-based choice in dating, albeit an interracial choice. A number of the black-white couples I interviewed expressed these same sentiments, arguing that love should be "color-blind," even though they exclusively date outside their race. Just as the white college students stated that their choice not to date blacks was a matter of attraction and preference, with no racial implications, like preferring a certain height, hair color, etc., these sites (and some of the black-white couples) used the same reasoning. The decision to date only interracially was presented as a nonracial personal preference, just as the white college students' decision to date only within their race was articulated as a matter of choice, not race. Yet if racialized and prejudiced thinking underlies the decision not to consider someone of a different race, then what underlies the choice to date only a race different than one's own? For the black community respondents, the choice of black individuals, especially of black men to date only white women, was problematized as an internalization of racism and a distancing of oneself from the black community.

The interracial dating sites (and the multiracial support sites) are "color-blind," and there is no sense of why individuals prefer mates of a different race. Furthermore, the dating sites are not isolated but rather are part of an intricate and extensive link to the multiracial Web sites discussed earlier, which make up an online multiracial community, implying that interracial dating is something to be encouraged or marketed. Yet if race and "color" are insignificant, then why is interracial dating being marketed on the Internet through these dating sites?

Hate Sites: The Fear of a Black (Interracial) Planet

The third category of Web sites where interracial sexuality and marriage figure prominently are white supremacist Web sites. These sites are increasingly found on the Internet and are developed by what is commonly referred to as hate groups, who use the Internet to conduct business and recruit members as well as to maintain contact with existing members. In *White Man Falling,* Abby Ferber identified four different categories of white supremacist thought—the Ku Klux Klan, the neo-Nazis, the Christian Identity church, and the militia—with each of these groups sharing an opposition to the mixing of the races. This opposition to interracial sex and marriage comes out of their views on racial superiority and the need to maintain a white power structure. Most of these Web sites code their white supremacist racist language in ways that allow them to argue that this is not hate speech. For example, on the Stormfront Web site a member posted the following: "I do not believe we must push superiority of our race. I think this is a big stumbling block. . . . [Whites] need to be made proud of their culture, then they will feel the superiority which is spoken of so often. . . . You must make the greater calls more subtle."[14] On these sites the idea of interracial sexuality, especially a black man with a white woman, is widely used to rationalize and justify their ideological positions.[15] A color-blind discourse is not used when discussing the mixing of the races, however. On the contrary, race, whiteness, and racial difference are explicitly discussed. Within the membership requirements of the majority of the Web sites, one not only has to be white—which is defined as "a non-Jewish person of wholly European ancestry"—but one is also ineligible if he or she has a "non-White spouse or a non-White dependent."[16] A white Aryan Web site outlines hundreds of goals and problems and argues that "racial mongrelism is evil—racism good. . . . Racial homogeneity protects good civil societies from disintegration and collapse, and is the very foundation for beginning civilization itself."[17]

A major tenet of the white supremacist movement and their Web sites is the perceived threats to whiteness and, in actuality, white power. As Ferber argues in her research on white supremacist organizations, this threat is almost exclusively articulated as the threat of interracial sexuality.[18] Interracial sexuality threatens whiteness and white identity because through interracial relations, biracial children, who blur the racial boundaries, can be produced. Race mixing is seen as a way "not to 'save' or 'redeem' Whites, but to destroy them completely.[19] One Web sites argues that "the purpose of the South's Jim Crow laws were for keeping black males' natural proclivity for rape, robbery and murder corralled; anti-miscegenation laws were to prevent contamination of the white race by those heritable proclivities."[20]

These sites also advocate that something must be done to stop "race-mixing." The National Alliance clearly states that "after the sickness of 'Multiculturalism' . . . has been swept away, we must again have a racially clean area of the earth for the further development of our people. . . . We must have no non-Whites in our living space. . . . We will do whatever is necessary to achieve this White living space and to keep it White." While these hate groups and white supremacist sites may seem extreme in their portrayal of interracial unions as deviant, unnatural, and undesirable, their views actually derive from mainstream thought and should be understood as an example of racialized discourse.[21] Looking at the white community respondents' views and the views expressed here, there are similarities. For example, a number of the white community respondents discussed how it was natural to date within one's own race, because that is who the person is around and who he or she has more in common with. Similarly, on the National Alliance Web site, a National Vanguard article, "Miscegenation: The Morality of Death," argues "miscegenation is not a natural occurrence." In the essay, the author laments that American society promotes race mixing and that children are bombarded with the messages that "miscegenation is good and morally correct, and that Whiteness is evil and morally wrong," citing movies such as *The Last of the Mohicans*, Disney movies such as *Pocahontas,* and Tom Cruise and Nicole Kidman's decision to adopt a black child. The author sees some hope in the current situation, however, stating that "many Whites . . . seem to be carrying around with them two conflicting value systems in relations to race-mixing: the one they publicly purport to hold and the one they actually live their private lives by."[22] In essence, the author's conclusion is similar to my findings: that though most whites publicly use a color-blind discourse to express their acceptance of interracial relationships (the National Vanguard author calls it "a widespread spiritual sickness and confusion"), whites still overwhelmingly choose to exclusively date and marry other whites (which the Vanguard author says proves how hard it is to "implement widespread biological amalgamation").

The connection of these sites to the pornographic sites are clear. Both draw from the image of black men seducing and having sex with white women, even if the images are used for different purposes or most likely have different meanings for the viewer. This only points to how ingrained the ideas and discourses on black-white sexuality and relationships are, where the images are reproduced in many different ways. The white fear of black men having sex with white women, which began during slavery, continues today and is used to justify the ideas and actions of white supremacist groups and to provide sexual pleasure on pornographic sites.

Conclusion

Looking at the Internet provides another lens through which to see the images and ideas about interracial couples that exist in society. Ebay, the "world's online marketplace," where one can literally buy anything, actually encompasses all of these images. A search for "interracial" on Ebay generally yields about fifteen to twenty items that can be categorized as celebratory, sexual, or racist. The celebratory items—"interracial wedding cake toppers," interracial figurines with a white and black individual embracing, pictures and paintings of interracial couples, and even an occasional copy of Randall Kennedy's *Interracial Intimacies*—serve as reminders of how unusual interracial couples are and how difficult it is to find products that feature an interracial couple in mainstream venues, therefore the need for online sales of items such as interracial wedding cake toppers. Pornographic and sexually explicit movies and books are similar to pornographic interracial Web sites. The movies are commonly described as "interracial hot sexXXX." One such video sold for $20.00 and was listed by the seller as Interracial Diane and Jake, "First Homemade video, Jake is well-built Black man, Diane is white Hottie, they love to perform for others . . . if black + white is your fetish then this is for you." Soft-porn books are classified as "interracial sleaze," like *House of Bondage* or *Sin Smugglers,* both of which listed for $9.99 and featured a black man embracing a white woman on their covers. Other items for sale included racist caricatures of blacks with whites on postcards or other memorabilia that play on the idea of black men desiring white women. For example, one postcard that sold for $9.99 was described by the seller as "another interracial card playing on the unfaithful wife and the black hand scenario . . . postally used New York, NY, August 23, 1905." Ebay, like the rest of the Internet, markets and sells interracial unions in particular ways.

In short, these three types of Web sites and their underlying ideologies paint a picture in which color and race are both everything and nothing. The discourses used on the multiracial/interracial support sites or the interracial dating sites cling to essentialist views of race while simultaneously denying race altogether, even the ways race (as a social construction) shapes everyday experiences. While race and racial difference is explicitly outlined on the white supremacist sites, and to some extent the pornographic sites, the sites promote the idea that interracial couples are deviant. There is no discussion of racial inequality, unless in a distorted and historically inaccurate way. To a large extent, the Web sites reflect the dominant ideologies about black-white couples in the larger society: interracial relationships are not the norm or most people's preference; the couples are overtly sexual or sexually deviant; and the relationships create problems such as children. Furthermore, it is evident that many sites consider interracial couples as deviant—a fetish to be watched, a cause to be celebrated, a problem to be fixed, a quest to be fulfilled. Whatever they may be, interracial unions are not the accepted or expected norm of society.

CHAPTER 7

Listening to the
Interracial Canary

*L*ike the miner's canary that warns of
a poisonous atmosphere, black-white couples expose lingering racism, prejudice, and segregation in society. Interracial couples' experiences are important not for what they tell us about themselves but for what they tell us about
the racial attitudes and practices of the families, groups, and communities
from which they come. The central question is not how these families and
communities respond, but why black-white intimacy evokes such emotional
and complex responses. Why couples come together is less telling than why
more individuals do not come together across racial lines.

Looking at the research as a whole, what emerges is the ways interracial relationships are problematized—how much more "difficult" it is to be
an interracial couple and treated according to that image. Even though the
couples did not describe their lives as difficult, their experiences reveal the
many ways their identities, their relationships, and their lives are challenged
by others. The ways that couples differentiated between the public and private demonstrated the complexities of being perceived as an interracial couple,
even if they did not see (or want to see) themselves as such. A number of
couples said that when they were alone race was not an issue and never even
factored into how they related to one another; however, other couples were
acutely aware of how their race and racial differences figured prominently
in who they were as a couple in the eyes of others. While the opposition they
experienced was often very subtle and easily overlooked, it still existed, which
forced the couples to make choices.

There was a stark contrast between the ways couples described their
relationships and the ways that the communities (mirroring popular cultural

images) described interracial relationships in general. All of the problems that were identified by the community groups were addressed differently by the couples. For example, whites described interracial relationships as unnatural, nontraditional, or plagued by cultural differences, while the couples discussed their relationships as the same as intraracial couples, with race rarely playing a role when they were alone together. Many of the black respondents questioned the motives of those involved interracially and wondered how the white partner treated the black partner, though none of the couples mentioned these issues. The couples had varied backgrounds and experiences, and none displayed an individual characteristic or experience that would explain their decision. For example, some white partners grew up in households where racist language and beliefs were common, but at some point they had interests and experiences that led them to diverse surroundings and associations. Other white partners grew up in families and communities that espoused tolerance and acceptance. Some black partners grew up in families where interracial unions were common, while others had families who explicitly opposed interracial marriage. Beyond their upbringing and neighborhoods, the individuals' experiences and beliefs were also much different. However, the couples were similar in how they were responded to and understood by the communities and groups they encountered. Furthermore, the commonality between the couples was their ability to maintain their relationship through the opposition of family, friends, and "societal others."

Black-white couples exist in a borderland in society at the intersections of race, identity, family, and community. Because the individuals in these relationships are viewed as coming from distinctly different groups in this racialized and segregated society, their experiences and the larger views of communities and popular culture tell us many things about American race relations. Like the miner's canary, black-white couples' experiences reveal problems that otherwise may have gone unnoticed, at least for whites. Interracial dating and, more important, marriage remain a line that many still do not want to see crossed, especially in their own families. In the color-blind ideology that exists, it is unacceptable and in some circumstances even illegal for whites to state that one does not want to work with, live near, or be friends with an African American. There are even the common discursive strategies such as "one of my best friends is black," or "I don't care if you are red, black, blue, or green," statements commonly used by whites to "prove" that they are not racist. Yet in these color-blind ideologies of race, it is acceptable, common, and even seen as the desired norm to state that one would not date interracially and would not want their kids to either. "Whatever the formal legal definition of colorblindness, there is no such thing as race-neutral resegregation as a social matter. So long as we live in segregated neighborhoods, attend segregated schools, and choose same-race marriages and families, race will be a significant social boundary."[1] It is not until we accept race as a social and political construction that affects everyone in society will whites and blacks see themselves as part of the same group. As Guinier and Torres argue, we need to focus on race as "a political project that does not ask who you married, or what your daddy was. At its core it does not ask what you call yourself but with whom do you link your fate."[2]

Race: To See or Not to See

The research also points to the contradictory nature of race where race can be emphasized and/or denied by the couples, the community members, and even within the popular cultural images. Within the racial ideologies of color-blindness and race consciousness, there is tension between individual rights and group recognition that America has struggled with, primarily whether one should be treated and protected as an individual or as a member of a group. Also, the discourse of opposition—whether coded in color-blind language or expressed outright—mirrors the contemporary prejudices and racisms that plague our society. The opposition to interracial unions is based within a social structure that is organized on the idea of separate racial groups, with the accompanying ideology that there are distinct differences between the races: whites have produced this racial hierarchy and maintain it through continued separation, with a collective discourse against interracial unions being part of this. Therefore, interracial couples are a social space where these ideologies are played out and where these relationships are constructed as deviant, unnatural, or merely something to oppose in the name of everything "normal" and "traditional."

While race undoubtedly plays a major role in the structure and interaction of groups in society, it is becoming increasingly popular among the larger society to emphasize the declining significance of race, or to not see it or acknowledge it at all. Whites' and blacks' narratives on interracial unions, and even the ways black-white couples discuss their experiences, illustrate the power of these racialized discourses. For example, most white community members stated they had no problem with interracial relationships, yet their actions did not reflect their words. The unimaginable opposition to interracial marriage may not have disappeared, but it has been coded within a color-blind discourse that allows those who want to ignore the opposition to ignore it. Even the ways black-white couples discussed their experiences differed greatly based on the discursive strategy they used; for example, black-white couples recounted stories of white fathers not coming to weddings, white friends rejecting interracial marriages for their kids, and countless other slights, yet some couples still claimed they had never encountered opposition and that society is color-blind, or at least moving to this "ideal." Responses to interracial relationships are complex and often operate on different levels. Based on the research, opposition is rarely expressed in general terms, such as "I am opposed to interracial relationships." Instead, statements are made on an individual or personal level, such as, "I don't care what others do but I just wouldn't," or they mention problems or reasons why interracial relationships do not work, without saying that they are against them. Therefore, couples can choose to read these types of statements as supportive because the individuals are not stating that they are opposed, or the couples can read them as opposition because of their implied message. More important, individuals and communities like those interviewed can claim not to have a problem with black-white unions and to not be "racist," all the while maintaining the color line and reproducing racialized views and behaviors.

This widespread use of nonracial and coded language masks contemporary racism and prejudice, as illustrated in the contradiction between some couples' experiences and their narratives. Therefore, future research should focus not only on what the couples, individuals, or communities tell us, but also on the importance of how their message is delivered and what is being described. I can not argue enough for the need to emphasize the discursive strategies of groups and individuals and how their words relate to their actions. Simply depending on survey data concerning views on race relations and intermarriage misses the larger picture. For example, most of the community respondents I interviewed said they approve of interracial marriages, reflecting the "I don't have a problem with it" part of their narrative. Behind their outward approval, however, exist myriad reasons why they don't really approve, certainly not enough to intermarry themselves or to support that choice for their families. Eduardo Bonilla-Silva argued "the methodological importance" of developing research projects with a qualitative dimension is crucial, particularly when exploring racial discourses such as color-blindness.[3] Without the qualitative component, it would be possible to conclude that the majority of whites support interracial relationships despite certain beliefs and practices to the contrary.

The Persistence of White Racism and the
Black-White Divide

For the various black and white communities interviewed, most individuals stated they did not have a problem with interracial couples, although it was not a choice they (or those close to them) would make. They presented their views as personal preferences or choices, but I argue their viewpoint has more to do with a sense of community, identity, and investment in the current racial social structure in which whites and blacks virtually exist in separate worlds. These discourses and images about interracial unions, as well as how individuals respond, are based on the existence of racial communities and how strongly tied an individual is to these communities: these are "imagined" but no less real communities of others with whom we identify.[4] Both whites and blacks collectively have a vested interest in their membership in a racial group. The meanings attached to one's racial community and identity is central to how one views interracial relationships.

Based on the common responses throughout the community research, I argue that certain discursive strategies are drawn upon to express opposition to interracial relationships by white and black respondents and are shared among these varied groups, demonstrating a "culturally routine structure of interaction."[5] These strategies speak to the importance of group membership and one's identity as part of a certain community that requires a member to follow certain scripts or guidelines for behavior. In these discourses on interracial relationships, there is a sense of blacks and whites as two distinct groups. An "us versus them" ideology clearly exists.

Underlying the opposition of both whites and blacks is the persistence of white racism. While my research has looked specifically at the issue of interracial dating and marriage, my findings fit in with the recent body of works that argue white racism still exists on a large scale but is often hidden or disguised within a color-blind discourse.[6] Otherwise, whites would not be opposed to black-white relationships. In particular, the idea of having a black person in the family would not be viewed as unnatural or undesirable if the dominant idea that blacks are inferior and different did not exist. Considering the white responses in this research and the low rates of interracial marriage between whites and blacks (even in comparison to white-Latino and white-Asian marriages), whites do not view a relationship with a black person as a norm. Interestingly, white racism also underlies the opposition of blacks to interracial relationships. According to the black community members interviewed in this research, their opposition to black-white relationships is based on the painful history of race relations and contemporary experiences of discrimination, rejection, and isolation. Furthermore, interracial relationships are seen as coming out of a devaluation of black culture and internalization of white racism, which further weakens the black community in a number of ways, such as losing successful black men to white communities and the multiracial identity choice that children of black-white couples must increasingly fight for. Even in opposition, whites and blacks come from distinctly different positions.

The contrast between what people said (discourse) and what people did (practice) is important. Unlike the whites who stressed their acceptance of interracial relationships on a general level, yet were surrounded by all-white social worlds, the blacks interviewed stressed the problems they had with interracial dating in general, although they knew and accepted any number of interracial couples and white people into their lives. The roots of the opposition explain this. Blacks are operating out of a history and knowledge of white racism and object initially to having intimate relations—or, in other words, to allowing the "enemy" (white folks) into one's circle of family and friends. Whites begin with a "deficit" among blacks, which is based on a lack of trust, as evidenced in the views against interracial dating and marriage.[7] Whites who become involved interracially and form what are perceived to be real relationships can overcome this "deficit" and be accepted by the black family or community once trust is established. Among white communities, there is less opportunity for blacks to overcome the "deficit" they begin with, because it has less to do with trust and more to do with whites' beliefs of black inferiority and difference.

Therefore, opposition to interracial relationships and marriage signifies more than a personal decision or familial issue. While whites, in particular, present their choices not to intermarry as nonracial and individual, this collective opposition against interracial marriage is part of the larger structure of institutionalized racism. Though laws banning interracial marriage were struck down by the Supreme Court in 1967, whites (and blacks) still draw upon certain images and ideas about black-white unions to discourage the occurrence of these relationships. The basis for white and black opposition affects not only social interaction between blacks and whites but also the social, economic, and political realms. If an individual finds the idea of a relationship with a person of another race unnatural, undesirable, or unacceptable, can it really be assumed that this does not affect how they view members of that race in other areas, such as the workplace, neighborhood, or in political office.

A Multiracial Future: Dream or Nightmare?

A significant factor in opposition to black-white relationships is the "problem" of the children—biracial children—which is drawn upon to explain why black-white relationships are problematic. It is only through black-white unions that children who are both black and white are produced. These biracial offspring threaten racial boundaries and the racial structure—social, cultural, and political institutions—based on the idea of mutually exclusive racial groupings. As Michael Omi and Howard Winant argue, "the determination of racial categories is thus an intensely political process...the census's racial classification reflects prevailing conceptions of race, establishes boundaries by which one's racial 'identity' can be understood, determines the allocation of resources, and frames diverse political issues and conflicts."[8] Considering that both whites and blacks discussed the issue of children as a central concern and reason to question and/or oppose interracial unions, multiracial individuals and identity play a central role in the discourses on race and interracial marriage. Mary Waters discusses how interethnic and interracial families make different choices on the identity of their children, but she acknowledges that for black-white interracial families the choice is much more socially restricted: "black-white marriages are still relatively rare and are not likely to reach very high levels anytime in the near future."[9]

Racial boundaries are maintained only through mutually exclusive racial categories that reflect and reinforce the all pervasive power of race and its classifying character.[10] Naming the children as a reason to question interracial relationships reveals the complicated and layered meanings attached to these unions, and the ways that opposition is coded within particular arguments. It can be understood as part of the color-blind discourse to express "concern" for the children in an effort to deflect attention from the issue of interracial couples, as well as the *other* racialized reasons why these groups may object.

When the community groups (and a number of the couples, speaking of their families) discussed this concern for the children, they often described biracial children as having "problems," referring to them as confused, maladjusted, or "mixed up." Though both whites and blacks discussed the issue of children as a reason to object to interracial relationships, the underlying arguments were different. Whereas whites seemed to object to the creation of "black" children through interracial unions who may be inferior or "pollute" the white race, black opposition seemed to stem from a concern with maintaining the black community. Whites have always maintained that children from interracial unions are to be considered black rather than white, which comes from social and legal traditions that construct the white race as a biologically pure group. Yet many in the black community also argue that children from interracial unions should identify as black, since they will be treated as "black" by both whites and blacks. Claiming a biracial identity is often seen by the black community as a way to be "less black" and an internalization of white racism.

Individuals also referred to the problems the children would face in "society," excluding themselves from this "society of others" who would make it difficult for the children. This reasoning reveals an unwillingness on the part of the groups to admit that they are *themselves* part of this world that treats biracial children as different. Instead, they used an "alienated discourse," revealing an inability or unwillingness to construe race relations as something that they participate in or can change. There was no discussion or acknowledgment that any "problems" that children may have would clearly be a result of how individuals and communities responded to interracial families and biracial children. This opposition undoubtedly reveals one of the central sociopolitical oppositional responses to intermarriage: the threatened outcome of the mixing of the races is a blurring and confusing of racial groups in society. The 2000 Census was the first to allow the opportunity to check more than one race (which is viewed by some as a "multiracial option"), and these choices involving how interracial families and children choose to identify will undoubtedly have important bearings on the future of intermarriage in both white and black communities. While there are some recent and forthcoming works that address these issues, more research is needed.[11] In particular, in-depth studies of biracial individuals and their experiences, focusing on the discursive practices of groups and communities, would be relevant.

The Social Construction of Racial Identity

Emphasizing the "problem" of biracial children highlights the larger issue of identity and race. Much of the opposition to interracial relationships is based on notions of identity and the idea that interracial relationships can change one's identity. Beyond the racial identity crises proclaimed over biracial children, the individual's identity is also in question. Whites often perceive whites who intermarry as unwhitened, and the argument that interracial marriage is too difficult comes out of a desire to maintain and protect one's white privilege and the benefits that accompany whiteness (which is perceived to be lost through interracial marriage). One's whiteness is lost or at least tainted through interracial sex and marriage. White partners and community respondents described how they knew white men who would not date a white woman who had been with a black man; white supremacist organizations do not see an individual as white if they have a nonwhite spouse or child; and even some white partners stated they no longer felt "white." Blacks, too, question the identity of other blacks who date interracially. Black families and communities accuse those who marry interracially as no longer being black, as "acting white," or as being less committed to the black community. One's blackness is perceived as something that can be lessened or lost simply through intimate interaction with a white person, as in the film *Undercover Brother*, where even the most Afrocentric man can be "whitened" by having sex with a white woman. Some of the black partners even described themselves in nonracial terms, and while this was not necessarily based on the relationship, it may have influenced their decision to date interracially in the first place.

I have often seen how my identity, or more specifically others' perceptions of "who I am," is mediated not only by race and ethnicity but also by my membership in a multiracial family. Among whites, it usually brings forth questions and often can serve as a boundary marking that I am not the same as them (white mothers of white children). Most often, among African Americans my membership in a multiracial family seems to break down barriers. Most notably, I observe the reactions when black students see that my children are biracial (or otherwise hear that I was married to a black man). Their perception of me changes, usually leading them to see me as an ally. In fact, my own choice to identify more strongly with my Portuguese roots came about largely as a result of others' perceptions of me as "not white," based on my appearance, my relationships, my activities, and, more recently, my children.

Regulating Race, Sexuality, and Marriage

Despite the increasing reports of a decline in marriage and the sacredness of marriage vows, when it comes to interracial marriage (like gay marriage), preserving the "sanctity" of this institution is still given primary importance. Though there may be an increasing visibility of interracial couples, especially among young people, based on the community responses there is a significant difference between interracial dating versus marriage. The increased visibility and engagement in black-white sexual relations do not necessarily signal racial progress or a lasting relationship but possibly a temporary trend or fad. While interracial dating may be marginally tolerated or even acceptable on college campuses or in society, the idea of getting *married* to someone outside one's race is still much more problematic for both whites and blacks.

Regulating sexuality by preventing or discouraging marriage through legal means or societal pressure links race and sexual orientation. The similarities between opposition to interracial sexuality and homosexuality is clear—the ban on marriage, the criminalization of sexual acts, and the familial responses. Like gay/lesbian relationships, interracial relationships have historically been constructed as inherently sexual and, more important, as sexually deviant. Beliefs about gender, sexuality, and race not only coexist; they are articulated in relation to and through one another. In this research, the connection between interracial relationships and societal norms of sexuality is illustrated in the ways that interracial couples are discussed in comparison to gay and lesbian couples. Discourses against interracial sexuality and homosexuality, however, are often intertwined, since both deviate from the same-race, heterosexual norms of sexuality that exist. Couples such as Sara and Andre observed that interracial couples were seen, along with bisexuality, as trendy on their college campus. One black college student stated that her mother would rather have her be a lesbian than marry a white man. These examples illustrate the ways that both interracial sexuality and homosexuality are produced and reproduced as outside the realm of "acceptable" or "normal" behavior.

Another avenue for future research is the connection between interracial sexuality and homo/heterosexuality, as well as the responses of communities and groups to these issues. The different ways opposition (and/or support) is expressed for interracial relationships in comparison to gay/lesbian relationships has not yet been addressed through research. When I teach a class each semester on marriage and family, the students' class discussion of these two issues are interesting. In general, when interracial marriage is discussed, no students openly object to the idea of raising children to think it is okay to date outside one's race (yet again one must consider this within the color-blind ideology of what people say and what people do). When discussing gay/lesbian relationships and heterosexual privilege, however, students' reactions were much different. For example, I told a story about how people routinely tell my son how handsome he is and how many women's hearts he will break some day. I explained that I had begun to use the reply, "Oh, how can you tell he is heterosexual?" The class laughed, but they wanted to know if I seriously would raise my young son to think that it was acceptable to like girls or boys. While much of the class maintained that they had no problem with gays and lesbians, they did have a serious problem with the idea of what they saw as "encouraging" their children to be homosexual. Similar to a color-blind discourse, attitudes toward gay/lesbian relationships also seem to involve the practice of individuals saying they do not oppose something while not wanting it for oneself or one's family, which still signifies that there is a problem.

A Multiracial Future II: Working toward the Dream

When Martin Luther King Jr. gave his famous "I Have a Dream" speech, one of the most widely remembered lines included, "I have a dream that my four little children will one day live in a nation where they will not be judged by the color of their skin but by the content of their character." Yet King probably never realized how this dream would be used to justify the rampant color-blind racism that permeates our country. King went on to state, "little black boys and black girls will be able to join hands with little white boys and white girls and walk together as sisters and brothers." From my research it would seem that King's dream is still not nearly achieved, as whites and blacks interviewed certainly did not view each other as family and did not want such close interaction through interracial marriage.

Where do we go from here, and what, if anything, can be done? While the focus of this work is on interracial intimacy and marriage, certainly the goal is not to promote more interracial marriage. Society does, however, need to work toward ending the systematic inequalities and racist hierarchical social structure that allow whites to argue that blacks are not good enough for their children. Gerald Torres, a University of Texas Law professor, said that when he was young he dreamed of a raceless society and that by "mixing the colors together we could eliminate the invidious distinctions drawn solely on the basis of appearance."[12] He felt "the children of mixed unions were clearly the hope for the future, and black people should be prohibited from marrying black people and white people should be prohibited from marrying white people." But as an adult he came to see that changes do not come from "physical attraction or regulation...[but] through political action."[13]

A significant part of this political action and change requires challenging whiteness and white privilege wherever it exists or manifests itself.[14] As a white woman, I come face-to-face with white privilege, color-blind discourse, and racism on a daily basis, especially among other whites who do not know my children are biracial/African American. For me, most times it is easy to challenge racist and prejudiced views of other whites, yet sometimes it is still a challenge. For example, recently I was talking to my children's pediatrician, a white woman in her forties. She asked me about my research and what I had found, always having shown a genuine interest in the book project. When telling her about the typical responses of whites and the small number of black-white interracial marriages, she responded, "Well, I don't think that most whites are prejudiced. I think it has more to do with where you live and the lack of exposure," at least partially agreeing with the responses of the white community members. Then she started talking about her teenage son and his belief that it was "better" to be black, because blacks "had more opportunities" at the things that mattered to him such as sports. A number of thoughts raced through my head on how I should respond or what I should say. Instead, I chose to say nothing, ending the discussion with, "Yeah, race is a difficult topic." Rather than challenging her views, I remained silent when I should have been vocal. Change should begin by interrogating ourselves, and the role each of us plays in the construction and maintenance of racial boundaries. We need to revisit the ideas that have become so customary: that it is natural for white families to marry whites and to live in white neighborhoods and that positions of power are held by whites. Whether it be our family, our coworkers, or our physicians, this colorblind discourse needs to be challenged.

Telling my own stories undoubtedly shapes my retelling of others' stories. In all the talk of language and discourse, where I fit in matters. As I interviewed the couples, their stories all had something in common with each other and with my own story, even if I interpreted the incident differently. With the white and the black communities, most responses I heard reminded me of someone I had met or encountered in my own interracial travels: a friend, in-law, enemy, family member, or stranger. How can interracial couples that are so different from one another have experiences that are so similar? How can whites "not have a problem" and blacks "not care" about interracial relationships, yet these relationships remain infrequent, unexpected, and outside the norm? And if there is no collective opposition to interracial relationships, why do different black and white communities separated by age and geographical location employ the same discursive strategies to describe their views and largely express reasons to question and oppose these relationships?

My research is not a celebration of interracial marriage or even a suggestion that we should work to get others to marry interracially. It is, however, a critique of the opposition against interracial relationships, primarily because it is based in the larger racism and racial inequality that permeates our society. Through the racialized words and actions of others to black-white couples, it is clear that race still divides us. Rather than advocate color-blindness, ignoring race or allowing others to ignore it, and hoping it will go away, there needs to be an effort "to change the framework of the conversations about race by naming relationships to power within the context of our racial and political history."[15] The same ideologies that make whites prefer not to marry interracially and makes blacks view interracial marriage as a self-internalization of racism form the basis of racial inequality, the belief in and experience that whites and blacks are distinct separate groups. While this research explored the intersections of race, black-white intimacy, and discourse, it is just the beginning. There are many more stories to be told and any number of perspectives to be uncovered.

Appendix:
Couples Interviewed

Note: All names are pseudonyms. Racial/ethnic identities are in the participants' own words.

1. Lisa, thirty-three-year-old white woman
    Victor, thirty-five-year-old black man ("Obviously black, but I'm human, not a color")

    Strategy: color-blind
    How they met: work
    > They are married and are trying to have children. They live in a middle-class suburb of Connecticut. Both have bachelor's degrees; Lisa teaches elementary school and Victor teaches middle school. They attend a predominantly white Catholic church.

2. Olivia, forty-eight-year-old white woman (Dutch)
    Frank, fifty-five-year-old black African American man

    Strategy: color-blind
    How they met: community (he came into her workplace)
    > They have been married for over twenty years. Olivia is an office manager and Frank is a retired police officer. They live in a predominantly white suburb of New Jersey. They have two teenage sons: one in high school and one in college. They are Catholic.

3. Sandra, thirty-five-year-old white woman (English, German, and Polish)
    David, thirty-seven-year-old African American man

Strategy: color-blind

How they met: college

> They have been married for thirteen years and have two children, who are three months old and three years old. They live in an upper-middle-class part of upper-state New Jersey. Both have master's degrees. Sandra teaches at a college and David works in a firm in Manhattan. They sporadically attend either a Unitarian or a Catholic church.

4. Nancy, forty-two-year-old woman of African ancestry (Cape Verdean)
   Robert, forty-seven-year-old white man (Italian)

   Strategy: color-blind

   How they met: community

   > They have been married for three years with no children. They live in Rhode Island in a middle-class area. Nancy has a bachelor's degree and works as a financial consultant. Robert was in the navy and now works at a post office. They both attend a Catholic church.

5. Brittney, twenty-six-year-old white woman (Portuguese)
   Mark, thirty-two-year-old black man (he identified as "human")

   Strategy: color-blind/ race conscious

   How they met: friend/sister

   > They have been dating for over three years and recently moved in together. They both lived in New York, but when she moved to Massachusetts to have their baby near her family he followed her. They have an infant son. He has a high school diploma and works with a moving company. She also has a high school diploma and works as a waitress.

6. Chris, twenty-eight-year-old black man
   Victoria, twenty-eight-year-old white woman

   Strategy: race conscious

   How they met: college

   > They met as undergraduates in college in California and got married two years ago. She has a master's in social work, and he has a master's in business administration. He is a business executive and she is a social worker.

7. Danielle, twenty-four-year-old white woman (French, Italian)
   Keith, twenty-five-year-old black man

   Strategy: race conscious
   How they met: community
   > They have been together on and off for four years and recently got married. They live in a predominantly black neighborhood in New Jersey. Danielle is unemployed and Keith is a factory supervisor.

8. Jill, twenty-eight-year-old white woman (Irish)
   Lee, thirty-three-year-old black man

   Strategy: race conscious/color-blind (especially with family)
   How they met: community
   > They have been together for five years and have a three-year-old daughter. They recently moved from New York City to a middle-class area in Massachusetts. Jill has a bachelor's degree and works at a nonprofit agency. Lee works in retail. They sporadically attend a Unitarian Universalist church.

9. Kayla, twenty-eight-year-old white woman
   Hank, thirty-year-old African American man

   Strategy: race conscious/color-blind (especially with family)
   How they met: work (but did not date while there)
   > They have been friends for five years and dating for one year. They live in a middle-class suburb in Maine. Both attended college. Hank owns a clothing shop, and Kayla works as a bar manager, though she used to work with children. Kayla was formerly married to Jay, a black man with whom she had two daughters, ages three and six.

10. Gwen, forty-something African American woman
    Bill, fifty-something white man

    Strategy: race conscious
    How they met: work
    > They are married and have a ten-year-old son. They live in an upper-middle-class area in Connecticut. Both have advanced degrees. Gwen is a university professor, and Bill teaches middle school. They

attend a black Baptist church and sometimes a Unitarian Universalist church.

11. Kim, fifty-five-year-old white woman
    Stanley, sixty-three-year-old black-American man

    Strategy: race conscious
    How they met: work
    They have been together for almost thirty years and have one son in college. While they could be described as middle class with a large, well-kept house, they live in a lower-income, predominantly black urban neighborhood in Massachusetts. They work in the same hospital, where Kim is a nurse and Stanley is an anesthesiologist. They sometimes attend a black Baptist church.

12. Jennifer, twenty-two-year-old white woman
    Lance, twenty-year-old black man

    Strategy: race conscious/color-blind
    How they met: community
    They have been dating for two years and live together, though Jennifer also has a dorm room at the university she attends. Lance attends a junior college. Jennifer is from a predominantly white suburb, and they now live in a racially diverse neighborhood in New York City.

13. Sara, twenty-one-year-old Caucasian (Italian)
    Andre, twenty-two-year-old African American man

    Strategy: race conscious/color-blind (especially Sara at times)
    How they met: college
    They have been dating for two years and met at college in New Jersey. Sara comes from a predominantly white middle-class suburb, and Andre comes from a diverse upbringing. After graduation, they are going to separate graduate schools.

14. Sharon, forty-seven-year-old African American woman
    Kevin, forty-nine-year-old white man (Ukrainian and Finnish)

Strategy: color-blind

How they met: community

> They are married and have an eleven-year-old daughter. They live in a middle-class area of the Bronx. Kevin is in a band and is finishing his bachelor's degree. Sharon works in an office.

15. Aisha, twenty-four-year-old African American woman
     Michael, forty-year-old Caucasian man

Strategy: race conscious

How they met: work (he was the manager at a store where she was a salesperson)

> They are married and do not have children. They live in a middle-class area of Manhattan, and both are attending college while working at different computer/Internet companies. They attend a predominantly black church.

NOTES

Introduction: The Interracial Canary

1. Randall Kennedy, *Interracial Intimacies: Sex, Marriage, Identity, and Adoption* (New York: Pantheon Books, 2003).
2. Tim Padgett and Frank Sikora, "Color-Blind Love," *Time*, May 12, 2003; Lynette Clemetson, "Love without Borders," *Newsweek,* September 18, 2000.
3. Eduardo Bonilla-Silva, *Racism without Racists* (Lanham, MD: Rowman & Littlefield, 2003); Leslie Carr, *"Color-Blind" Racism* (Thousand Oaks, CA: Sage Publications, 1997); Ellis Cose, *Color-Blind: Seeing beyond Race in a Race-Obsessed World* (New York: Harper Collins, 1997); Joe R. Feagin, *Racist America* (New York: Routledge, 2000); Ruth Frankenberg, *White Women, Race Matters: The Social Construction of Whiteness* (Minneapolis: University of Minnesota, 1993); Toni Morrison, *Playing in the Dark: Whiteness and the Literary Imagination* (Cambridge: Harvard University Press, 1992); Michael Omi and Howard Winant, *Racial Formation in the United States from the 1960s to the 1980s* (New York: Routledge, 1994).
4. Lani Guinier and Gerald Torres, *The Miner's Canary: Enlisting Race, Resisting Power, Transforming Power* (Cambridge: Harvard University Press, 2002), 2–3.
5. Frankenberg, *White Women*; Guinier and Torres, *The Miner's Canary.*
6. Padgett and Sikora, "Color-Blind Love."
7. Clemetson, "Love without Borders."
8. Ibid.
9. The latest 2000 census data confirms this difference, with interracial marriages accounting for only 1.9 percent of all marriages. Furthermore, the overwhelming majority of interracial marriages are white-Asian couplings (1.2 percent), while white-black couplings account for significantly less (.06 percent).
10. The issue of sexuality and its relationship with interracial relationships will be discussed throughout various parts of the book; however, I focused only on heterosexual relationships because of the difficulty of locating enough gay/lesbian interracial couples, as well as time and space constraints for exploring how

societal responses to gay/lesbian couples are based on opposition to interracial relationships or same-sex relationships or both.

11. This has been well documented by a number of recent studies: Heather Dalmage, *Tripping on the Color Line: Black-White Multiracial Families in a Racially Divided World* (New Brunswick, NJ: Rutgers University Press, 2000); Philomena Essed, *Understanding Everyday Racism* (Newbury Park, CA: Sage Publications, 1991); Feagin, *Racist America*; Frankenberg, *White Women*; Robert P. McNamara, Maria Tempenis, and Beth Walton, *Crossing the Line: Interracial Couples in the South* (Westport, CT: Praeger, 1999); Paul C. Rosenblatt, Teri Karis, and Richard D. Powell, *Multiracial Couples: Black and White Voices* (Thousand Oaks, CA: Sage Publications, 1995).

12. Feagin, *Racist America*, 209.

13. James F. Davis, *Who Is Black: One Nations' Definition* (University Park: Pennsylvania State University, 1991); Feagin, *Racist America*; Abby Ferber, *White Man Falling: Race, Gender, and White Supremacy* (Maryland: Rowman & Littlefield Publishers, 1998); Frankenberg, *White Women;* Rosenblatt, Karis, and Powell, *Multiracial Couples*.

14. When I was a young child in Rhode Island, ethnicity played an important part in my upbringing, but I didn't realize it until many years later. My family deemphasized our ethnicity and instead brought us up as "American." I remember "passing" as Italian and being encouraged to keep silent about being Portuguese, especially in situations where "portugees" (a derogatory way to pronounce Portuguese) were being referred to in the same group as Cape Verdeans and Puerto Ricans in the Italian-dominated areas where we lived.

15. See Dalmage's *Tripping on the Color Line*, 33–70, and Frankenberg's *White Women*, 11, for a discussion of the ways in which whites can experience "rebound racism" as a result of their interracial relationships.

16. Torres argues that the "borderland" is a rich and complex psychological and social space between black and white. Torres, *The Miner's Canary*, 7–9.

17. Omi and Winant, *Racial Formation*.

18. Ibid., viii.

19. Abby Ferber, "Exploring the Social Construction of Race," in *American Mixed Race: The Culture of Microdiversity*, ed. Naomi Zack (Maryland: Rowman & Littlefield, 1995), 159.

20. In *Racial Formation,* Omi and Winant argue that this assimilationist framework arose as an "ethnicity-based theory" in the early twentieth century as a response to biologically based theories of race. This ethnicity-based paradigm includes the debate between an assimilationist perspective, beginning with Robert Park's race relations cycle in *Race and Culture* (New York: Free Press, 1964) and the concept of cultural pluralism introduced by Horace Kallen in *Culture and Democracy in America* (New York: Boni and Liveright, 1924), which focused on the acceptance of different cultures.

21. Omi and Winant, *Racial Formation*.

22. There is a large and diverse group of works that address the issue of interracial sexuality and marriage using psychological approaches and theories. These studies place primary importance on race, arguing for or against different "racial mo-

tivation" theories that state interracial marriages occur *because of the racial differences* rather than in spite of them: H. G. Biegel, "Problems and Motives in Interracial Relationships," *Journal of Sex Research* 2 (1966); Thomas L. Brayboy, "Interracial Sexuality as an Expression of Neurotic Conflict," *Journal of Sex Research* 2 (1966); Marshall Clinard and Robert Meier, *Sociology of Deviant Behavior* (New York: Harcourt Brace, 1989); Joel Crohn, *Mixed Matches: How to Create Successful Interracial, Interethnic, and Interfaith Relationships* (New York: Fawcett Columbine, 1995); Stanley Gaines, Diana Rios, Cherlyn Granrose, and Katrina Bledsoe, "Romanticism and Interpersonal Resource Exchange among African American–Anglo and Other Interracial Couples," *Journal of Black Psychology* 25 (1999); William H. Grier and Price M. Cobbs, *Black Rage* (New York: Basic Books, 1968); M. K. Ho, *Intermarried Couples in Therapy* (Springfield, IL: Thomas, 1990); F. A. Ibrahim and D. G. Schroeder, "Cross-Cultural Couples Counseling: A Developmental Psychoeducational Intervention," *Journal of Comparative Family Studies* 21 (1990); Kristyan M. Kouri and Marcia Laswell, "Black-White Marriages: Social Change and Intergenerational Mobility," *Marriage and Family Review* 88 (1993): 242; and Ernest Porterfield, *Black and White Mixed Marriages: An Ethnographic Study* (New Jersey: Prentice-Hall, 1978). Remarkably absent from this literature is a discussion of the way the dominant group in society defines what behavior is deviant: deviance is a consequence of the application of rules and sanctions by others to an "offender"—the crucial dimension is the *societal reaction* to an act, not any quality of the act itself. Rather than explore why groups in society consider interracial relationships deviant, the emphasis is placed on the couple as if there is something deviant about the couples themselves. Howard S. Becker, *Outsiders: Studies in the Sociology of Deviance* (New York: The Free Press, 1963).

23. More traditional sociological studies have also focused on why individuals intermarry. These studies look at the individual traits and characteristics of blacks and whites who intermarry, examining the similarity or difference in education, employment, involvement in social activities, recreation, residential area, and socioeconomic status. Milton L. Barron, *People Who Intermarry* (Syracuse, NY: Syracuse University Press, 1946); Jessie Bernard, "Note on Educational Homogamy in Negro-White and White-Negro Marriages," *Journal of Marriage and the Family* 28 (1966); idem, "Marital Stability and Patterns of Status Variables," *Journal of Marriage and the Family* 28 (1966); Gary A. Cretser and Joseph L. Leon, "Intermarriage in the U.S.: An Overview of Theory and Research," *Marriage and Family Review* 5 (1982); James H. Gadberry and Richard A. Dodder, "Educational Homogamy in Interracial Marriages: An Update," *Journal of Social Behavior and Personality* (1993); Joseph Golden, "Facilitating Factors in Negro-White Intermarriage," *Phylon* 20 (1959); Tim Heaton and Cardell Jacobson, "Intergroup Marriage: An Examination of Opportunity Structures," *Sociological Inquiry* 70 (2000); David M. Heer, "Negro-White Marriage in the United States," *Journal of Marriage and the Family* (1966); idem, "The Prevalence of Black-White Marriage in the United States, 1960 and 1970," *Journal of Marriage and the Family* 36 (1974); Judith Todd, "Attitudes Toward Interracial Dating: Effects of Age, Sex, and Race," *Journal of Multicultural Counseling*

and Development (October 1992); Belinda Tucker and Claudia Mitchell-Kernan, "New Trends in Black American Interracial Marriage: The Social Structural Context," *Journal of Marriage and the Family* 52 (1990).

Other sociological studies have compared interracial couples to same-race couples, looking at factors such as age at marriage, whether the marriage is the first, fertility rates, divorce rates, stability of marriage, and level of involvement in social networks. Larry D. Barnett, "Interracial Marriage in California," *Marriage and Family Living* (November 1963); Bernard, "Note on Educational Homogamy"; John H. Burma, "Research Note on the Measurement of Interracial Marriage," *American Journal of Sociology* 57 (1952); Heer, "The Prevalence of Black-White Marriage"; Sophia F. McDowell, "Black-White Intermarriage in the United States," *International Journal of Sociology of the Family* 1 (1971); Thomas P. Monahan, "Are Interracial Marriages Really Less Stable?" *Social Forces* 48 (1970); Thomas P. Monahan, "Interracial Marriage in the United States: Some Data on Upstate New York," *International Journal of Sociology of the Family* 1 (1971); Thomas P. Monahan, "Marriage across Racial Lines in Indiana," *Journal of Marriage and the Family* (November 1973); Todd H. Pavela, "An Exploratory Study of Negro-White Intermarriage in Indiana," *Journal of Marriage and the Family* 26 (1964); Robert Schoen, "The Widening Gap between Black and White Marriage Rates: Context and Implications," in *The Decline in Marriage among African-Americans: Causes, Consequences, and Policy Implications,* ed. M. Belinda Tucker and Claudia Mitchell-Kernan (New York: Russell Sage Foundation, 1995); Biegel, "Problems and Motives"; Peter Blau, Terry Blum, and Joseph Schwartz, "Heterogeneity and Intermarriage," *American Sociological Review* 47 (1982); Brayboy, "Interracial Sexuality"; Jeanette R. Davidson, "Theories about Black-White Interracial Marriage: A Clinical Perspective," *Journal of Multicultural Counseling and Development* (October 1992); Kingsley Davis, "Intermarriage in Caste Societies," *American Anthropologist* 43 (1941); Grier and Cobbs, *Black Rage*; Matthijs Kalmijin, "Trends in Black/White Intermarriage," *Social Forces* 72 (1993); Robert K. Merton, "Intermarriage and Social Structure: Fact and Theory," *Psychiatry* 4 (1941).

24. Bernard, "Note on Educational Homogamy" and "Marital Stability and Patterns of Status Variables"; Gadberry and Dodder, "Educational Homogamy in Interracial Marriages"; David A. MacPherson and James B. Stewart, "Racial Differences in Married Female Labor Force Participation Behavior: An Analysis Using Interracial Marriages," *Review of Black Political Economy* (summer 1992); McDowell, "Black-White Intermarriage"; Monahan, "Are Interracial Marriages Really Less Stable?" idem, "Interracial Marriage in the United States"; idem, "Marriage across Racial Lines in Indiana"; Thomas P. Monahan, "An Overview of Statistics on Interracial Marriage in the United States, with Data on Its Extent from 1963–1970," *Journal of Marriage and the Family* (May 1976); idem, "The Occupational Class of Couples Entering into Interracial Marriages," *Journal of Comparative Family Studies* 7 (1976); idem, "Interracial Parentage as Revealed by Birth Records in the United States," *Journal of Comparative Family Studies* 8 (1977); idem, "Interracial Marriage in a Southern Area: Maryland, Virginia, and the District of Columbia," *Journal of Comparative Family Studies* 8

(1977); Porterfield, *Black and White Mixed Marriages*; Tucker and Mitchell-Kernan, "New Trends in Black American Interracial Marriage."

25. Using qualitative interviews with interracial couples in the South, Robert P. McNamara, Maria Tempenis, and Beth Walton's *Crossing the Line* furthers the image of these couples as deviant. The couples are described in great detail, including their lives and experiences, though much of the way the data is reported reproduces stereotypes. For example, with a number of the couples that consist of a black man and white woman, the image of the black man as dominant is conveyed. The researcher describes one black man as "the dominant personality in this relationship. . . . quick to take exception to insults or threats of any kind" (48). Another couple is described as "an example of a couple in which the African American husband clearly dominates the relationship. . . . She dutifully waits for him to come home from work or the gym and appears to dote on his every wish" (50). This is reported with no discussion of the historical relevance of the image of black men dominating submissive white women. Similar to the studies that focus on couples' motives, the researchers seem to expect that interracial couples will be "different" than other couples, as evidenced in the following quotation: "All told, were it not for the fact that the parents were born into different races, this would be a typical American household" (55). This statement follows a lengthy description of their household—wood paneling, family photos, "A" papers on the refrigerator, children playing in the backyard—which surprises the researchers because of its normalcy. When reviewed by Milton Vickerman in *Contemporary Sociology* (March 2000), the reviewer's critique does not touch upon these issues and argues instead that the book puts forth important findings of what it is like to be involved in an interracial relationship and that interracial families "resemble" noninterracial families. Once again, rather than challenge the idea of interracial couples as deviant, the work reproduces the negative images associated with interracial unions: these sociologists see as a *finding* the idea that interracial couples are similar to same-race couples.

26. The value of these studies is questionable on several counts. Underlying the research is an assumption that these couples come together for different reasons than same-race couples and that race or racial factors play a primary role in the couples coming together. This type of research gives validity to the belief that interracial couples are not the same as other couples, or at least considers the idea valid enough to be tested. Once again, same-race couples are used as the norm by which all others are judged. In these types of studies, the socially constructed nature of racial categories remains unchallenged, rarely acknowledging that in a race-conscious society like America, even when whites and blacks are similar in terms of education, employment, recreation, socioeconomic status, and other factors, the perceived and ascribed racial differences still remain as a deterrent to intermarriage, as evidenced in the low rates of intermarriage. Furthermore, since most blacks and whites do not inhabit the same areas or acquire similar education, employment, and involvement in social activities, the focus of these studies should be on the structural constraints such as segregation in residential areas and schools as well as racial discrimination in schools, the workplace, and other institutions that prevent or discourage black-white proximity and

intermarriage, rather than focusing on those individuals who do engage in inter-racial relationships.

27. Rosenblatt, Karis, and Powell's *Multiracial Couples* is one of the most widely cited works on interracial couples and includes in-depth interviews. Emphasis is placed on the couples' relationships, their parenting experiences, what the part-ners have learned from each other, the role of race in the relationships, and the "special blessings" of being an interracial couple. This study discusses the couples' narratives on familial and societal responses, yet it does not address them in great detail. Instead, the couples' relationships are emphasized, and the work often reads as a celebratory look at interracial couples, as evidenced in a con-cluding chapter on the rewards of interracial relationships. Other recent works on interracial couples have taken a qualitative approach and/or have offered au-tobiographical accounts of people's experiences in an interracial relationship or family: Hettie Jones, *How I Became Hettie Jones* (New York: Dutton, 1990); Lisa Jones, *Bulletproof Diva: Tales of Race, Sex, and Hair* (New York: Anchor Books, 1995); Jane Lazarre, *Beyond the Whiteness of Whiteness: Memoirs of a White Mother of Black Sons* (Durham, NC: Duke University Press, 1996); James McBride, *The Color of Water: A Black Man's Tribute to His White Mother* (New York: Riverhead, 1996); Maureen Reddy, *Crossing the Color Line: Race, Parenting and Culture* (New Brunswick, NJ: Rutgers University Press, 1994). Though these approaches move beyond biological or ethnicity-based assimilationist frameworks, some of the works appear to have been written to simply support and promote a multicultural understanding of the interracial couple.

28. Dalmage, *Tripping on the Color Line*, 32.

29. Kennedy, *Interracial Intimacies*, 36.

30. Ibid., 37. This premise is problematic because it seems to overlook how access and opportunity to this flowering of multiracial intimacy is not available to ev-eryone. For example, while stating that he is not implying that we should be blind to racial realities, the reality is that black women have less opportunities to date and marry interracially due to racialized notions of beauty, a smaller percentage of white men who date and marry interracially, and the lower status of black women in the racial hierarchy of America. This message is not likely to change these racial realities.

31. Ian F. Haney-Lopez, "The Social Construction of Race," in *Critical Race Theory,* ed. Richard Delgado (Philadelphia: Temple University, 1995), 196.

32. Throughout the work, individuals and communities will be referred to as white and black and couples will be referred to as interracial. When used in this re-search, these terms are understood as "social groups, not genetically distinct branches of humankind" (Haney-Lopez, "The Social Construction of Race," 193).

33. Using Emile Durkheim's concept, interracial unions are a *social fact* and need to be studied as such, since "these specific facts reside in the society itself that produces them and not in its parts—namely its members." Emile Durkheim, *The Rules of Sociological Method* (New York: Free Press, 1982), 39–40.

34. A number of contemporary works powerfully "localize" racial identities and be-liefs "examining [race] in spaces as small as a college or neighborhood yet ex-plicating also how the small space is linked temporally and territorially to far

larger expanses . . . [providing] a tracing of how, in a given setting, race makes and is made by relations of sex and sexuality, class and culture." Frankenberg, *White Women,* 28.

35. Laurel Richardson, "Postmodern Social Theory: Representational Practices," *Sociological Theory* 9 (1991).

36. Adalberto Aguirre Jr., "Academic Storytelling: A Critical Race Theory Story of Affirmative Action," *Sociological Perspectives* 43 (2000); David Maines and Jeffrey Bridger, "Narratives, Community and Land Use Decisions," *Social Science Journal* 29 (1992).

37. Richard Delgado, *Critical Race Theory* (Philadelphia: Temple University, 1995), xiv.

38. Bonilla-Silva, *Racism without Racists,* 53.

39. Michel Foucault, *The History of Sexuality: An Introduction* (New York: Vintage Books, 1990), 102.

40. Interesting to note is that many studies on interracial couples locate the couples through flyers, advertisements, or Internet postings that require the couples to contact the researcher. Gaines et al., "Romanticism and Interpersonal Resource Exchange"; Miriam Hill and Volker Thomas, "Strategies for Racial Identity Development: Narratives of Black and White Women in Interracial Partner Relationships," *Family Relations* 49 (2000); McNamara, Tempenis, and Walton, *Crossing the Line.*

   At least seven of the couples I interviewed would not have responded to any of these, simply because they did not believe that they had anything interesting to say and did not see their experiences as anything but ordinary. I also attempted to interview couples with different socioeconomic backgrounds.

41. I realize the effect of interviewing the partners together. There may be beliefs, occurrences, and issues that one partner may not have wanted to discuss in front of the other partner. Also, the dynamic of the relationships may have affected who spoke most during the interview. While there was not much I could do about individuals not wanting to share information in front of their partners, I did make sure to ask each partner to speak on any issue even if the partner had already answered. For example, when Lee, who is black, told me that his family was supportive, I asked Jill, Lee's white partner, to describe Lee's family. I would follow this up by asking if she could think of times when she felt his family was supportive and times when they were not.

42. The interviews were tape recorded and transcribed, along with my postinterview thoughts. I have more than four hundred pages of transcripts and field notes that were reviewed and coded into categories of responses. When I began the interviews, I had no idea that I would find differences in the ways couples discussed their experiences. It was only after I had conducted about half of the interviews and had begun to review my field notes and transcribed interviews that I recognized the patterns.

43. Susan Chase, "Taking Narrative Seriously: Consequences for Method and Theory in Interview Studies," in *Interpreting Experience: The Narrative Study of Lives,* ed. Ruth Josselson and Amia Lieblich (Thousand Oaks, CA: Sage Publications, 1995).

44. Essed, *Understanding Everyday Racism*, 54.
45. It is within these spaces that we find the world of everyday life, which, as Berger and Luckmann argue, is important to study, since "everyday life presents itself as a reality interpreted by [wo]men and subjectively meaningful to them as a coherent world. . . . a world that originates in their thoughts and actions." Peter Berger and Thomas Luckmann, *The Social Construction of Reality: A Treatise in the Sociology of Knowledge* (Garden City, NJ: Doubleday, 1966), 20.

    There are a number of recent studies that explore constructions of racial identity and racialized ways of thinking in various realms of society, such as the family, the university, child care centers, neighborhoods, inner cities, upper-class male society, white supremacist organizations, and others. Eduardo Bonilla-Silva and Rogelio Saenz, "'If Two People Are in Love . . .': Color-Blind Dreams, (White) Color-Coded Reality among White College Students in the USA" (unpublished manuscript); Bonilla-Silva, *Racism without Racists*; Phil Cohen, "Laboring under Whiteness," in *Displacing Whiteness: Essays in Social and Cultural Criticism*, ed. Ruth Frankenberg (Durham, NC: Duke University Press, 1997); Deborah Van Ausdale and Joe R. Feagin, "The Use of Racial and Ethnic Concepts by Very Young Children," *American Sociological Review* 61 (1996); Ferber (1998); Charles A. Gallagher, "White Construction in the University," *Socialist Review* 24 (1995); J. Hartigan, "Locating White Detroit," in *Displacing Whiteness: Essays in Social and Cultural Criticism*, ed. Ruth Frankenberg (Durham, NC: Duke University Press, 1997).

46. By choosing churches and colleges, I realize I am targeting certain types of individuals. The college communities are a selective group, only reaching those with the access and resources to begin college. Also, the church communities are undoubtedly different from nightclub or barbershop communities. My decision to use church communities was based not only on the experiences of the couples but also on the feasibility of conducting a focus group rather than individual interviews, which would have been more difficult at many other community sites.

47. St. Matthews is a predominantly white Catholic church in a New England suburb, described by one of its priest as a neighborhood parish that is predominantly Italian and Irish and middle to upper-middle class. Trinity Baptist church is a predominantly black Baptist church in New York City, described by one of its reverends as a three-hundred-member African American congregation with working- to middle-class roots. First Church is a Unitarian place of worship located in a metropolitan Boston area. Its membership was described by one of its reverends as middle- to upper-middle-class professionals from a variety of religious backgrounds, including Catholic, Christian, Jewish, and agnostic. While whites are the majority, a significant proportion (the reverend estimates one-third or one-fourth) are black, Latino, or Asian, as well as a number of interracial families.

48. Collegiate University is an Ivy League university in New England, and the groups included a coed student group that addressed issues of European culture and a coed student group that celebrated the African/African American experience. St. Stephen's is a private Jesuit university in New York, and the student groups included two student organizations that celebrated different European heritages and

a student group based on the celebration of black culture. Central State University is a public state university, and the student groups included the Greek Council for the black fraternities and sororities and a combined group interview with a (white) sorority and fraternity. While the sorority and fraternity that I am identifying as white does not identify itself in racial terms, both groups had only white members.

49. Hill and Thomas, "Strategies for Racial Identity Development," 198. There are a number of works that describe the uses of focus groups and how to conduct this research: Rosaline Barbour and Jenny Kitzinger, *Developing Focus Group Research: Politics, Theory, and Practice* (Thousand Oaks, CA: Sage Publications, 1999); David Morgan, *Focus Groups as Qualitative Research* (Thousand Oaks, CA: Sage Publications, 1997); and Michael Patton, *Qualitative Evaluations and Research Methods* (Thousand Oaks, CA: Sage Publications, 1990).

50. In particular, mainstream contemporary films from the 1990s to 2003 whose storylines involve a black-white couple are analyzed as the most recent examples of film images of interracial unions. Though this analysis does not include all films with a black-white couple, the films that are discussed were chosen because of their high profile and mass marketing (www.cinemedia.com).

51. Popular film is arguably one of the most influential sources of racial ideology, as discussed in Robert Gooding-Williams, *Reading Rodney King, Reading Urban Uprising* (New York: Routledge, 1993); Norman K. Denzin, *Images of Postmodern Society: Social Theory and Contemporary Cinema* (London: Sage Publications, 1991); bell hooks, *Reel to Real: Race Sex and Class at the Movies* (New York: Routledge, 1996); Douglas Kellner, *Media Culture: Cultural Studies, Identity and Politics between the Modern and the Postmodern* (New York: Routledge, 1995); and Hernan Vera and Andrew Gordon, *Screen Savers: Hollywood Fictions of Whiteness* (Lanham, MD: Rowman & Littlefield Publishers, 2003).

52. Kellner, *Media Culture*, 1.

53. David L. Altheide, *Qualitative Media Analysis* (Thousand Oaks, CA: Sage Publications, 1996).

54. As Stuart Hall argues, film creates meaning, but the meanings attached to these images are not "wholly determined by the producer and simply accepted by a passive audience." Stuart Hall, "Encoding/Decoding," in *Culture, Media, Language,* ed. Stuart Hall (London: University of Birmingham, 1980). Films are "sites of constant ideological struggle," where a hegemonic work is produced and then negotiated by the audience. Gina Marchetti, "Ethnicity, the Cinema and Cultural Studies," in *Unspeakable Images: Ethnicity and the American Cinema,* ed. Lester D. Friedman (Urbana: University of Illinois Press, 1991), 283.

55. Margaret M. Russell, "Race and the Dominant Gaze: Narratives of Law and Inequality in Popular Film," in *Critical Race Theory: The Cutting Edge,* ed. Richard Delgado (Philadelphia: Temple University Press, 1995), 57.

56. Denzin, *Images of Postmodern Society;* Jane Gaines, "White Privilege and Looking Relations: Race and Gender in Feminist Film Theory," *Cultural Critique* 4 (1986); hooks, *Reel to Real;* Marchetti, "Ethnicity"; Laura Mulvey, "Visual Pleasure and Narrative Cinema," *Screen* 16 (1975); Russell, "Race and the Dominant

Gaze"; Thomas E. Wartenberg, *Unlikely Couples: Movie Romance as Social Criticism* (Boulder: Westview Press, 1999).

57. Most recently, the "dominant gaze" has been applied to describe "the tendency of American popular cinema to objectify and trivialize the racial identity and experiences of people of color, even when it purports to represent them" (Russell, "Race and the Dominant Gaze," 57; see also, Denzin, *Images of Postmodern Society*, and hooks, *Reel to Real*). Laura Mulvey, in her feminist critique of Hollywood movies, was one of the first to argue that "popular film essentially serves the political function of subjugating female bodies and experiences to the interpretation and control of a heterosexual 'male gaze.'" Mulvey, "Visual Pleasure," in Russell, "Race and the Dominant Gaze," 57. This distinctly male-oriented perspective provides both male and female viewers with gendered (and sexualized) stereotypes, thereby perpetuating gender inequality.

58. Marchetti, "Ethnicity," 278.

59. hooks, *Reel to Real*.

60. Chase, "Taking Narrative Seriously," 14; David Altheide, "Identity and the Definition of the Situation in a Mass-Mediated Context," *Symbolic Interaction* 23 (2000).

61. Within any research it is necessary to address issues of validity and reliability; in particular, much has been written about the problematic nature of interpreting and analyzing narrative research. Carolyn Ellis and Arthur Bochner, *Composing Ethnography: Alternative Forms of Qualitative Writing* (Thousand Oaks, CA: Sage Publications, 1996); Carolyn Ellis and Michael Flaherty, *Investigating Subjectivity: Research on Lived Experience* (Thousand Oaks, CA: Sage Publications, 1992); Essed, *Understanding Everyday Racism*; Ruth Josselson and Amia Lieblich, *Interpreting Experience: The Narrative Study of Lives* (Thousand Oaks, CA: Sage Publications, 1995).

It could be argued that my role as a white female researcher (as well my own involvement in an interracial family) could have resulted in the participants giving answers they believed were appropriate or desirable. I am confident that this is not the case; however, to ensure the validity of the couples' statements, I have included discussions and analyses of their statements in which I compare them to their actual practices, choices, and other statements.

62. Bonilla-Silva and Saenz, "'If Two People Are in Love . . . '"; Essed, *Understanding Everyday Racism*; Gallagher, "White Construction in the University."

63. Altheide, "Identity," 22.

64. Essed, *Understanding Everyday Racism*, 63–64.

65. Herbert Blumer, *Symbolic Interaction: Perspective and Method* (Englewood Cliffs, NJ: Prentice Hall, 1969).

CHAPTER 1   *Loving across the Border*

1. Ruth Josselson and Amia Lieblich, *Interpreting Experience: The Narrative Study of Lives* (Thousand Oaks, CA: Sage Publications, 1995).

2. Philomena Essed, *Understanding Everyday Racism* (Newbury Park, CA: Sage Publications, 1991).

3. The Appendix details the demographic information for each couple. The couples were interviewed together.

4. I use the couples' terms for identifying themselves, providing additional statements when relevant.

5. Michael Thornton, Robert J. Taylor, and Tony N. Brown, "Correlates of Label Use among Americans of African Descent: Colored, Negro, Black, and African American," *Race and Society* 2 (1999): 150.

6. Three couples met in college: Sandra/David, at an Ivy League university, where both hung out in predominantly white social circles; Chris/Victoria, at a public state university in California, where their friends were diverse; and Sara/Andre, at a private Catholic university, where her friends were white and his friends were diverse. Five couples met at work: Victor/Lisa, as schoolteachers; Stanley/Kim, at a hospital; Aisha/Michael, at a store where Michael was the manager; Gwen/Bill, at a high school, where he was teaching and she was doing research; and Kayla/Hank, at a nonprofit organization (although they didn't start dating until both were no longer working there). The other seven couples met in the "community." Danielle/Keith met "out" in a predominantly black inner-city neighborhood; Nancy/Robert met at a predominantly white function for a neighborhood church; Jill/Lee met at a predominantly black club; Sharon/Kevin met through a diverse group of friends; Brittney/Mark met through Mark's sister; Jennifer/Lance met through a mutual friend who was black; and Olivia/Frank met at Olivia's workplace.

7. H. G. Biegel, "Problems and Motives in Interracial Relationships," *Journal of Sex Research* 2 (1966); Thomas L. Brayboy, "Interracial Sexuality as an Expression of Neurotic Conflict," *Journal of Sex Research* 2 (1966); William H. Grier and Price M. Cobbs, *Black Rage* (New York: Basic Books, 1968); Calvin C. Hernton, *Sex and Racism in America* (New York: Anchor Books, 1988); Robert Staples, "Interracial Relationships: A Convergence of Desire and Opportunity," in *The Black Family,* ed. Robert Staples (Belmont, CA: Wadsworth, 1999).

   Even recent psychological studies still test the psychological motives of black-white couples: Joel Crohn, *Mixed Matches: How to Create Successful Interracial, Interethnic, and Interfaith Relationships* (New York: Fawcett Columbine, 1995); Stanley Gaines, Diana Rios, Cherlyn Granrose, and Katrina Bledsoe, "Romanticism and Interpersonal Resource Exchange among African American–Anglo and Other Interracial Couples," *Journal of Black Psychology* 25 (1999); M. K. Ho, *Intermarried Couples in Therapy* (Springfield, IL: Thomas, 1990); F. A. Ibrahim and D. G. Schroeder, "Cross-Cultural Couples Counseling: A Developmental Psychoeducational Intervention," *Journal of Comparative Family Studies* 21 (1990).

8. Grier and Cobbs, *Black Rage*; Hernton, *Sex and Racism in America.* The idea that blacks who engage in interracial relationships suffer from a self-internalization of racism will be further discussed by the community members in chapter 3.

9. Frantz Fanon, *Black Skin, White Masks* (London: Paladin, 1968), 47.

10. Frank and David, who are black, also dated only white women. Lee stated his preference was for black women, but his previous serious relationships had been with white or Latina women. He said he dated Jill initially out of curiosity. Nancy

and Sharon, who are also black, stated they dated various races and ethnicities. While neither said they did not date black men, they did not cite any specific long-term relationships with black men.

11. Jen and Kayla also described a preference for black men. Other white partners such as Jill, Brittney, and Lisa had dated black men before but did not describe their choice as a preference. The white partners Kevin and Robert also described having had relationships with various women of different ethnicities but did not have a preference.

12. One of the main critiques I make about previous research is that many studies focused only on the couple, trying to explain why they came together and how they compared to same-race couples, always placing primary emphasis on their racial differences. These studies neglected to examine how society constructs couples as interracial and responds to these couples in certain ways. Since this study is sociological, I am concerned with societal views, and my research does not cover the psychological and psychoanalytic components that would enable me to make statements about the couples' reasons for coming together.

13. Patricia Hill Collins, *Black Feminist Thought* (New York: Routledge, 2000).

14. For example, Kobe Bryant, a black Los Angeles Lakers basketball star, was accused of raping a young white woman. In court, Bryant's lawyer mentioned the history of black men being falsely accused of raping white women, and he accused of racism the various individuals involved—such as the rape crisis counselor and the employees of the police station who had derogatory T-shirts printed. The media discussed the lawyer's use of race as "playing the race card," implying that the prosecution made race an issue, but the media rarely talks about the racial implications that exist, whether they are played or not. In classic colorblind fashion, to mention race is the problem.

15. These types also reflect what Charles Taylor described as the fundamental struggle in American society between the concept of the rights of individuals versus the rights of groups based on group membership: deemphasizing the role and impact of one's race or interracial relationship can reflect a focus on the individual, and emphasizing one's race and racial affiliations can represent an emphasis on one's membership in a socially constructed racial group. Charles Taylor, "The Politics of Recognition," in *Multiculturalism and the Politics of Recognition,* ed. Amy Gutmann, Steven C. Rockefeller, Michael Walzer, and Susan Wolf (Princeton, NJ: Princeton University Press, 1994).

16. Lani Guinier and Gerald Torres, *The Miner's Canary: Enlisting Race, Resisting Power, Transforming Power* (Cambridge: Harvard University Press, 2002).

CHAPTER 2   *Constructing Racial Boundaries and White Communities*

1. George Herbert Mead, *Mind, Self, and Society* (Chicago: University of Chicago Press, 1934); E. Doyle McCarthy, "The Interactionist Theory of Mind: A Sociology of Social Objects," *Studies in Symbolic Interaction* (1989).

2. Herbert Blumer, *Symbolic Interaction: Perspective and Method* (Englewood Cliffs, NJ: Prentice Hall, 1969), 2.

3. Charles Horton Cooley, *Human Nature and the Social Order* (New York: C. Scribner's Sons, 1922).

4. W. I. Thomas, "On the Definition of the Situation," in *Sociology: The Classic Statements*, ed. M. Truzzi (New York: Random House, 1971).

5. Peter Berger and Thomas Luckmann, *The Social Construction of Reality: A Treatise in the Sociology of Knowledge* (Garden City, NJ: Doubleday, 1966), 41; Michael Omi and Howard Winant, *Racial Formation in the United States from the 1960s to the 1980s* (New York: Routledge, 1994), 60.

6. I realize it is always problematic to talk of racial communities, especially in terms of who defines what or whom constitutes a community. Is it possible, even useful to talk about the responses and views of white communities when it comes to interracial relationships? While the white category constitutes a diverse group of ethnicities, nationalities, classes, statuses, and so forth, I argue that the responses of whites as a group to interracial relationships can be looked at by incorporating in divergent data sources. Eduardo Bonilla-Silva, *Racism without Racists* (Lanham, MD: Rowman & Littlefield, 2003).

7. See Beverly Daniel Tatum's discussion in *"Why Are All the Black Kids Sitting Together?" and Other Conversations about Race* (New York: Basic Books, 1997); Eduardo Bonilla-Silva and Tyrone A. Forman's "'I Am Not a Racist but . . .': Mapping White College Students' Racial Ideology in the U.S.A.," *Discourse and Society* 11 (2000); Heather Dalmage, *Tripping on the Color Line: Black-White Multiracial Families in a Racially Divided Word* (New Brunswick, NJ: Rutgers University Press, 2001); Joe R. Feagin, *Racist America* (New York: Routledge, 2000).

8. Patricia Williams, *Seeing a Color-Blind Future: The Paradox of Race* (New York: Noonday, 1998).

9. To ease this fear of blacks and the threats blacks represent to whites, racist ideologies are constructed that blacks are "fundamentally Other than white people: different, inferior, less civilized, less human, more animal, than whites." Ruth Frankenberg, *White Women, Race Matters: The Social Construction of Whiteness* (Minneapolis: University of Minnesota, 1993). 61. See also Patricia Hill Collins, *Black Feminist Thought* (New York: Routledge, 2000).

10. Eric C. Lincoln, *Race, Religion, and the Continuing American Dilemma* (New York: Hill and Wang, 1999), 173.

11. Lerone Bennett, *Before the Mayflower: A History of Black America* (New York: Penguin Books, 1984); Abby Ferber, *White Man Falling: Race, Gender and White Supremacy* (Maryland: Rowman & Littlefield, 1998); David Barry Gaspar and Darlene Clark Hine, *More Than Chattel: Black Women in Slavery in the Americas* (Bloomington: Indiana University, 1996); Stanford M. Lyman, *Postmodernism and a Sociology of the Absurd and Other Essays on the "Nouvelle Vague" in American Social Science* (Fayetteville: University of Arkansas Press, 1997); Kevin Mumford, *Interzones: Black/White Sex Districts in Chicago and New York in the Early Twentieth Century* (New York: Harper and Row, 1997); Ronald Takaki, *A Different Mirror: A History of Multicultural America* (Boston: Little, Brown and Co., 1993).

12. Bennett, *Before the Mayflower*; Gaspar and Hine, *More Than Chattel*; Lyman, *Postmodernism*. Mumford, *Interzones*; Takaki, *A Different Mirror*.

13. Max Weber, "Membership of a Race," in *Max Weber: Selections in Translation,* ed. W. G. Runciman (Cambridge: Cambridge University Press, 1977), 360.

14. Frankenberg, *White Women,* 75; Lyman, *Postmodernism,* 99.

15. Ferber, *White Man Falling,* 23–24.

16. Ibid.

17. When blacks were asked to list what they most wanted, they gave the same items but in the exact reverse order. Gunner Myrdal, *An American Dilemma* (New York: Harper and Row, 1965).

18. Theodore Cross, *Black Power Imperative: Racial Inequality and the Politics of Nonviolence* (New York: Faulkner, 1984), 157–158. Joe R. Feagin, *Racist America* (New York: Routledge, 2000), 113–114.

19. James F. Davis, *Who Is Black: One Nation's Definition* (University Park: Pennsylvania State University Press, 1991); Ferber, *White Man Falling.*

20. Aldon D. Morris, *The Origins of the Civil Rights Movement: Black Communities Organizing for Change* (New York: Free Press, 1984); Kwame Ture and Charles V. Hamilton, *Black Power: The Politics of Liberation in America* (New York: Vintage Books, 1992).

21. Arthur Schlesinger, *A Thousand Days* (Boston: Houghton Mifflin, 1965), 935.

22. David Theo Goldberg, *Racial Subjects: Writing on Race in America* (New York: Routledge, 1997), 20–21.

23. Jacqueline Johnson, Sharon Rush, and Joe Feagin, "Doing Antiracism and Making a Nonracist Society," *Contemporary Sociology* 29 (2000): 99.

24. Lawrence Bobo and Ryan Smith, "From Jim Crow to Laissez-faire Racism: The Transformation of Racial Attitudes," in *Beyond Pluralism: The Conception of Group and Group Identities in America,* ed. Wendy Katkin, Ned Landsman, and Andrea Tyree (Urbana: University of Illinois Press, 1998); Feagin, *Racist America.*

25. As Bonilla-Silva argues, expanding on Stuart Hall's work, "whites conduct their accounts with the frames, style, and stories available in color-blind America in a mostly unconscious fashion." Bonilla-Silva, *Racism without Racists,* 54.

26. There are a few works that explicitly address this issue. See Bonilla-Silva, *Racism without Racists,* and Teun A. Van Dijk, *Communicating Racism: Ethnic Prejudice in Thought and Talk* (London: Sage, 1989).

27. I am drawing from the concept of implicit censorship as discussed in Judith Butler's *Excitable Speech: A Politics of the Performative* (New York: Routledge, 1997).

28. This discursive strategy of responding to discussions of multiracialism or working for racial equality with a question about the prospect of whites marrying blacks has a long history. For example, after the Civil War when Congress was debating how to proceed after slavery: "whenever anyone proposed measures for the protection of Negro rights, the cry 'Do you want your daughter to marry a Negro?' was raised." Alfred Avins, "Anti-Miscegenation Laws and the Fourteenth Amendment: The Original Intent," *Virginia Law Review* 52 (1966): 1224, as cited in Randall Kennedy, *Interracial Intimacies: Sex, Marriage, Identity, and Adoption* (New York: Pantheon Books, 2003), 22.

29. Cooley, *Human Nature and the Social Order.*

30. Nina Eliasoph, "'Everyday Racism' in a Culture of Political Avoidance: Civil Society, Speech, and Taboo," *Social Problems* 46 (1999): 489.

31. Bonilla-Silva, *Racism without Racists*; Leslie Carr, *"Color-Blind" Racism* (Thousand Oaks, CA: Sage Publications, 1997); Ellis Cose, *Color-Blind: Seeing beyond Race in a Race-Obsessed World* (New York: Harper Collins Publishers, 1997).

32. Other studies on the racial views of whites have also found that whites often articulate a color-blind ideology, particularly when answering questions on interracial marriage. Collectively, whites from all backgrounds participate in white supremacist discourse, yet they code it in color-blind terms, especially on an ideological level. Bonilla-Silva, *Racism without Racists*; Eliasoph, "'Everyday Racism'"; Feagin, *Racist America*; Joe R. Feagin and Hernan Vera, *White Racism: The Basics* (New York: Routledge, 1995); Amanda Lewis, *Race in the Schoolyard* (New Brunswick, NJ: Rutgers University Press, 2003); Janelle Wilson, "Lost in the Fifties: A Study of Collected Memories," in *The Narrative Study of Lives,* ed. A. Lieblich and Ruth Josselson (Thousand Oaks, CA: Sage Publications, 1997).

33. "Racial attitudes capture preferred group positions and those patterns and feelings that undergird, justify, and make understandable a preference for relatively little group differentiation and inequality under some social conditions and for a great deal of differentiation and inequality under others." Bobo and Smith, "From Jim Crow to Laissez-faire Racism," 193–194.

34. Ibid.; Eliasoph, "'Everyday Racism'"; Howard Schuman, Charlotte Steeth, and Lawrence Bobo, *Racial Attitudes in America: Trends and Interpretations* (Cambridge: Harvard University Press, 1988); David Sears, "Symbolic Racism," in *Eliminating Racism,* ed. Phyllis Katz and Dalmas Taylor (New York: Plenum Press, 1988).

35. Analyzing the couples' experiences within their families and other social institutions is complicated because I have access to it only through the couples' recollections and not through the accounts of those individuals to whom the couples refer.

36. The older woman Ellen who had made the statement, "Yeah but would you marry one of them?" never said she had black friends or accepted the idea of black friends. Based on her facial expressions when others mentioned interracial friendships, I interpreted her response as less supportive of even being friends.

37. The narratives of these couples led me to conduct some of the focus groups at churches.

38. "Pastor Bans Interracial Marriage," *Washington Post,* July 10, 2000.

39. I had contacted numerous Catholic churches in areas identified as predominantly, if not exclusively, white and where I had contacts through personal or professional references. Two churches turned me down despite these references, with one of the priests telling me he "didn't feel comfortable discussing this issue" and that it would only "cause problems." Another church referred to a special office in the Catholic archdiocese that dealt with family counseling and problems, signaling the individual's connection between interracial couples and family

problems. I contacted the office, which could not offer any help in my research but did give me the name of Father Carcieri at St. Mathews. After contacting Father Carcieri, he enthusiastically welcomed me to come interview the parishioners, a response that was significantly different than the other priests'.

40. Sandra and David used the term "baptize," yet the Unitarian Universalist Association actually performs a naming ceremony, not a Christian baptism.

41. Regardless of the level of racial awareness of the film, I argue that black-white couples are overwhelmingly depicted as deviant, albeit in subtle ways. The meanings attached to black-white couples with society are mirrored in the couples' experiences, the community's responses, and the film images discussed: the relationship is not based on love, but rather lust, curiosity, or deception (*Cruel Intentions,* 1998; *Jungle Fever,* 1992; *Living Large,* 1991; *One Night Stand,* 1997; *Ricochet,* 1991); there are significant appositional responses and negative consequences as a result of the relationship (*Bulworth,* 1998; *Guess Who's Coming to Dinner,* 1967; *Jungle Fever,* 1992; *Save the Last Dance,* 2002; *Waiting to Exhale,* 1995; *Zebrahead,* 1992); and/or these relationships exist in an alternative or deviant lifestyle, which has already been established as outside of the norm (*Bulworth,* 1998; *Made in America,* 1993; *Monster's Ball,* 2001; *Object of My Affection,* 1998; *One Night Stand,* 1997).

42. Kennedy also identifies the movie *Cruel Intentions* as one where an interracial relationship is portrayed with race having little or no significance, yet this is erroneous. In fact, the premise surrounding the interracial relationships in the film is that a white woman wants to discredit another young white woman, so she encourages her to have a sexual relationship with a black man and then lets her mother know, stating that the interracial affair would ruin the family name. Kennedy, *Interracial Intimacies,* 133.

43. The reluctance to show interracial sex scenes may be based on the views of black sexuality as animalistic, immoral, and disgusting; "the prejudice, the fear, the ignorance, and the guilt concerning black sexuality have been so profound and deep-rooted in the crevices of American fantasy that, until very recent times . . . kissing was absolutely forbidden to Blacks performing on television or on the screen." Lincoln, *Race, Religion,* 241.

44. Michael Eric Dyson, *Between God and Gangsta Rap* (New York: Oxford University Press, 1996).

45. Daniel R. Nicholson, "Developing a Media Literacy of Whiteness in Advertising," in *White Reign: Deploying Whiteness in America,* ed. Joe L. Kincheloe, Shirley Steinberg, Nelson Rodriguez, and Ronald Chennault (New York: St. Martin's Press, 1998), 196.

46. Paul C. Rosenblatt, Teri Caris, and Richard D. Powell, *Multiracial Couples: Black and White Voices* (Thousand Oaks, CA: Sage Publications, 1995), 146–148.

47. There are a number of historical accounts that document the treatment of white and black men and women in regard to interracial sex during slavery and throughout American history. James C. Ballagh, *A History of Slavery in Virginia* (Baltimore, MD: Johns Hopkins Press, 1968); Bennett, *Before the Mayflower*; Lyman, *Postmodernism*; Angela Y. Davis, *Women, Race, and Class* (New York: Vintage Books, 1981); Davis, *Who Is Black: One Nation's Definition*; Ferber, *White Man*

Falling; Paula Giddings, *When and Where I Enter: The Impact of Black Women on Race and Sex in America* (New York: Quill William Morrow, 1984); Takaki, *A Different Mirror*.

48. Davis, *Women, Race, and Class*; Davis, *Who Is Black: One Nation's Definition*; Giddings, *When and Where I Enter*.

49. Judith Butler, "Endangered/Endangering: Schematic Racism and White Paranoia," in *Reading Rodney King, Reading Urban Uprising*, ed. Robert Gooding-Williams (New York: Routledge, 1993), 18, drawing on the work of Frantz Fanon. For a discussion of the ways white men expressed this fear of black men, see Bennett, *Before the Mayflower*, and Takaki, *A Different Mirror*.

50. There are a number of works that document the lynchings and killings of black men for the accusation of sexual relations, real or desired, with white women.

51. There are numerous examples of the destruction of black communities and the physical harm that came to black individuals based on accusations of miscegenation. In the late 1800s, U.S. senator Ben Tillman defended lynching, stating that he would not allow a black man to "gratify his lust on [white] wives and daughters without lynching him." Davis, *Who Is Black: One Nation's Definition*, 190.

In the early 1900s, the black community of Rosewood, Georgia, was virtually wiped out after an alleged incident where a white woman from a neighboring town claimed she was raped by a black man. Since sexual relations between black men and white women were "the ultimate infraction against this system of segregation," black men learned to stare downward when in close proximity to a white woman, so that there would be no reason for him to be accused of desiring her white flesh. Morris, *The Origins of the Civil Rights Movement*, 2.

52. Davis, *Who Is Black: One Nation's Definition*.

53. See Dalmage for an excellent discussion of this issue.

54. "Wild Will Smith on the 'Race Thing,'" *Providence Journal Bulletin*, July 3, 1999.

55. Saad Branker, "Black in White Film," at http://www.iconn.ca/zone451/issue07/verticals/saada.html; Michael Janusonis, "Solid Performance Is Bright Spot in 'Cruel Intentions,'" *Providence Journal Bulletin*, March 5, 1999, E3.

56. *The Pelican Brief* movie was based on a book that involved a romantic relationship between a white woman and a black man. In the movie, however, the relationship between the characters, played by Julia Roberts and Denzel Washington, was platonic. Similarly, in *Kiss the Girls*, the book involved a romance between the two main characters, but when brought to screen, Morgan Freeman played the male lead and a much younger Ashley Judd played the female lead, removing any hint or possibility of an intimate relationship.

57. Ed Guerrero, "Spike Lee and the Fever in the Racial Jungle," in *Film Theory Goes to the Movies*, ed. Jim Collins (New York: Routledge, 1993), 125.

58. Peter Bardaglio, "Midnight Miscegenation: Bulworth Reinforces Rather than Undercuts Certain Racial Stereotypes about White Men and Black Women," *Sun*, June 7, 1998.

59. Halle Berry's choice in these roles (as well as her roles in *Swordfish, The Rich Man's Wife*, and other films) to play opposite a white male lead is relevant because she is a light-skinned biracial black woman (her mother is white and her father is black).

60. Bonilla Silva, *Racism without Racists,* 53–73, outlines this idea extensively in his critique of color-blind discourse.
61. J. L. Austin, *How to Do Things with Words* (Oxford, England: Oxford University Press, 1965).
62. Philomena Essed, *Understanding Everyday Racism* (Newbury Park, CA: Sage Publications, 1991).
63. Erving Goffman, *Forms of Talk* (Philadelphia: University of Pennsylvania Press, 1981).

CHAPTER 3   *Crossing Racial Boundaries and Black Communities*

1. As discussed in the last chapter, using the notion of racial communities can be problematic. While the media often puts forth the idea of a singular or unified black community, this view is not endorsed in the book, but I will argue that we can talk about certain ideas that are prevalent within black communities, despite the socioeconomic, cultural, and other differences that exist. Benedict Anderson, *Imagined Communities: Reflections on the Origin and Spread of Nationalism* (New York: Verso, 1991), 6.
2. Norman K. Denzin, *The Cinematic Society: The Voyeur's Gaze* (Thousand Oaks, CA: Sage Publications, 1995).
3. Philomena Essed, *Understanding Everyday Racism* (Newbury Park, CA: Sage Publications, 1991), 29.
4. Angela Y. Davis, *Women, Race, and Class* (New York: Vintage Books, 1981); Randall Kennedy, *Interracial Intimacies: Sex, Marriage, Identity, and Adoption* (New York: Pantheon Books, 2003); Rachel Moran, *Interracial Intimacy: The Regulation of Race and Romance* (Chicago: University of Chicago Press, 2001); Renee Romano, *Race Mixing: Black-White Marriage in Postwar America* (Cambridge: Harvard University Press, 2003); Ida B. Wells, *On Lynchings: Southern Horrors, A Red Record, Mob Rule in New Orleans* (New York: Arno, 1969).
5. David Barry Gaspar and Darlene Clark Hine, *More than Chattel: Black Women in Slavery in the Americas* (Bloomington: Indiana University, 1996); Paula Giddings, *When and Where I Enter: The Impact of Black Women on Race and Sex in America* (New York: Quill William Morrow, 1984); Kennedy, *Interracial Intimacies*; Moran, *Interracial Intimacy*; Romano, *Race Mixing*; Vron Ware, *Beyond the Pale: White Women, Racism and History* (New York: Verso, 1992); Adrien Katherine Wing and Sylke Merchan, "Rape, Ethnicity and Culture: Spirit Injury from Bosnia to Black America," in *Critical Race Theory,* ed. Richard Delgado (Philadelphia: Temple University, 1995), 516–528.
6. W.E.B. Du Bois, *The Souls of Black Folk* (New York: Bantam, 1903), 9.
7. Wing and Merchan, "Rape, Ethnicity and Culture."
8. Patricia Williams, "Alchemical Notes: Reconstructing Ideals from Deconstructed Rights," in *Critical Race Theory,* ed. Richard Delgado (Philadelphia: Temple University, 1995), 84–94.
9. Davis, *Women, Race, and Class*; Essed, *Understanding Everyday Racism*; Toni Morrison, *The Bluest Eye* (New York: Pocket Books, 1972).
10. In *The Bluest Eye* Toni Morrison wrote about "the devastating effect of perva-

sive European ideals of beauty on the self image of black women." The works of Patricia Hill Collins, bell hooks, and Patricia Williams are also influential to this work, which draws on their theoretical and cultural discussions of these issues from a black feminist standpoint. Collins, *Black Feminist Thought*; bell hooks, *Ain't I a Woman: Black Women and Feminism* (Boston: South End Press, 1981); idem, *Black Looks: Race and Representation* (Boston: South End Press, 1992); idem, *Reel to Real: Race, Sex and Class at the Movies* (New York: Routledge,1996); idem, *Feminist Theory: From Margin to Center* (Boston: South End Press, 2000); Smith, *Not Just Race*; Patricia Williams, *The Alchemy of Race and Rights* (Cambridge: Harvard University Press, 1991); Williams, "Alchemical Notes: Reconstructing Ideals from Deconstructed Rights."

11. Patricia Hill Collins, *Black Feminist Thought* (New York: Routledge, 2000).

12. Ruth Frankenberg, *White Women, Race Matters: The Social Construction of Whiteness* (Minneapolis: University of Minnesota, 1993); Davis, *Women, Race, and Class*. Also relevant is how the *difference* asserted between blacks and whites to maintain racial separation is expressed even through a sociological study that asked whether interracial rape is different—meaning, of course, is the rape of a white women by a black man essentially different? James L. LeBeau, "Is Interracial Rape Different?" *Sociology and Social Research* 73 (1988). Other sociological studies focus on this issue, with the "interracial" rape of white women by black men being attributed to sexual desire among black offenders for white women and/or a general hostility among black offenders toward whites. Larry W. Koch, "Interracial Rape: Examining the Increasing Frequency Argument," *American Sociologist* 26 (1995); Gary D. LaFree, "Male Power and Female Victimization: Toward a Theory of Interracial Rape," *American Journal of Sociology* 88 (1982); and William Wilbanks, "Is Violent Crime Interracial?" *Crime and Delinquency* 31 (1985).

13. Frankenberg, *White Women, Race Matters*.

14. Collins, *Black Feminist Thought*.

15. "Through the Fire," by African American rapper Kanye West, spent weeks on the top music charts in the beginning of 2004. The hip-hop song describes how after a serious car accident West looked like Emmet Till.

16. Davis, *Women, Race, and Class*. James F. Davis, *Who Is Black: One Nation's Definition* (University Park: Pennsylvania State University, 1991); Paul R. Spickard, *Mixed Blood: Intermarriage and Ethnic Identity in Twentieth-Century America* (Madison: University of Wisconsin Press, 1989).

17. Kennedy, *Interracial Intimacies,* 109–112.

18. Heather Dalmage's *Tripping on the Color Line* also provides an excellent discussion of the views of black communities toward interracial relationships.

19. Collins, *Black Feminist Thought,* 262–264.

20. Lawrence Otis Graham, *Member of the Club: Reflections on Life in a Racially Polarized World* (New York: Harper Collins Publishers, 1995); Kwame Ture and Charles V. Hamilton, *Black Power: The Politics of Liberation in America* (New York: Vintage Books, 1992).

21. Cornel West, *Race Matters* (New York: Vintage Books, 1994), 120–122.

22. Spike Lee has openly discussed his views on interracial unions and commented

that the couple in *Jungle Fever* came together only because of sexual beliefs and curiosity. Bert Cardullo, "Law of the Jungle," *Hudson Review* 44 (1992). Annabella Sciorra, the white actress who portrayed Angie, revealed in an interview that she fought with Lee over the character because she wanted to portray her interest in Flipper as more complex than just sexual curiosity. Charles Taylor, "Black and White and Taboo All Over," at http://www.salon.com/ent/feature/2000/02/14/interracial_movies.

23. Ed Guerrero, "Spike Lee and the Fever in the Racial Jungle," in *Film Theory Goes to the Movies,* ed. Jim Collins (New York: Routledge, 1993), 174.

24. Ibid., 177.

25. William A. Harris, "Cultural Engineering and the Films of Spike Lee," in *Mediated Messages and African-American Culture: Contemporary Issues*, ed. Venise T. Berry and Carmen L. Manning-Miller (Thousand Oaks, CA: Sage Publications, 1996), 3–23.

26. Prior to the interracial affair, Miranda had become obsessed with a television program that detailed the beginnings of a romantic encounter between a black man and a white woman in England.

27. Patricia Hill Collins, *Black Sexual Politics: African Americans, Gender, and the New Racism* (New York: Routledge, 2004), 262.

28. Valerie Smith, *Not Just Race, Not Just Gender: Black Feminist Readings* (New York: Routledge, 1998), 65.

29. Frantz Fanon, *Black Skin, White Masks* (London: Paladin, 1968).

30. Graham, *Member of the Club*, 66.

31. Interestingly, couples mentioned that a common image associated with relationships between black women and white men is that the women are after the men's money. For example, Sharon stated, "I think that it is just assumed that the white man has money and that's what the black woman is after."

32. Calvin C. Hernton, *Sex and Racism in America* (New York: Anchor Books, 1988), 66.

33. Ibid.; Paul C. Rosenblatt, Teri Karis, and Richard D. Powell, *Multiracial Couples: Black and White Voices* (Thousand Oaks, CA: Sage Publications, 1995); Smith, *Not Just Race*; West, *Race Matters*; Kennedy, *Interracial Intimacies*.

34. According to Linda Williams's *Playing the Race Card* (Princeton, NJ: Princeton University Press, 2001), during the O.J. Simpson trial, O.J.'s lawyer Johnnie Cochran transformed O.J.'s house before a jury visit: "transformed the playboy mansion into the home of an upstanding black family man. . . . the pictures of white women came down and a silver-framed picture of Simpson and his mother was placed on the bedside table. . . . The transformation of Simpson's Brentwood mansion was an obvious attempt to recapture aspects of a black familial identity Simpson had long ago shed" (286).

35. For a discussion of this issue citing the work of Graham and Jake Lamar, see Randall Kennedy, *Interracial Intimacies: Sex, Marriage, Identity, and Adoption* (New York: Pantheon Books, 2003), 119.

36. Kennedy, *Interracial Intimacies,* 332.

37. Eleven of the partners addressed the idea of selling out and explained why they did not see themselves as selling out: five partners used a color-blind approach,

denying the importance of race, which made it impossible to sell out; two argued that their choice of partner was irrelevant to their race; and four argued they were not sellouts because of their commitment to racial issues. The other four acknowledged they had heard the idea of selling out but did not offer a personal reflection on their own beliefs and thoughts.

38. For an interesting perspective on this story, read the autobiography of Imamu Amiri Baraka's white ex-wife, Hettie Jones, *How I Became Hettie Jones* (New York: Dutton, 1990), and their daughter's book, Lisa Jones, *Bulletproof Diva: Tales of Race, Sex and Hair* (New York: Anchor Books, 1995).

39. This interview was conducted as part of a subsample of the research, where I interviewed black and white individuals who were once involved interracially but now were involved with individuals of the same race. This part of the research is still incomplete and may never be complete due to a number of reasons, including the difficulty of locating interview subjects.

40. Zondra Hughes, "Why Some Brothers Only Date Whites and 'Others,'" *Ebony,* January 2003; Lynn Norment, "Black Men/White Women," *Ebony*, November 1994.

41. Collins, *Black Feminist Thought*; Davis, *Women, Race, and Class*; Essed, *Understanding Everyday Racism*, 93; Williams, *Seeing a Color-Blind Future.*

42. Patricia Hill Collins, *Black Sexual Politics,* 247–278, offers an excellent discussion of this "conundrum" facing black women.

43. Gloria Wade Gayles, *Rooted against the Wind: Personal Essays* (New York: Harper Collins Press, 1996), 110.

44. Collins, *Black Sexual Politics*, 265; discussing Maria Root's *"Love's Revolution": Interracial Marriage* (Philadelphia: Temple University Press, 2001).

45. Collins, *Black Sexual Politics*; Lynda Dickson, "The Future of Marriage and Family in Black America," *Journal of Black Studies* 23 (1993).

46. During the O.J. Simpson trial, eight of the twelve jurors were black women. The collective opposition of black women to interracial relationships has been cited as responsible, at least partly, for the not-guilty verdict. In *Playing the Race Card: Melodramas of Black and White from Uncle Tom to O.J. Simpson* (Princeton, NJ: Princeton University Press, 2001), Linda Williams argues that prosecutor Marcia Clark made a mistake when she allowed so many black women on the jury, because focus groups had shown that "black women resented Nicole Brown and were sympathetic to Simpson. . . . The verdict in the Simpson trial represented the revenge of black women on what they perceived to be the white woman's privileged occupation of the role of victim" (292–293).

47. Heather Dalmage, *Tripping on the Color Line: Black-White Multiracial Families in a Racially Divided World* (New Brunswick, NJ: Rutgers University Press, 2000).

48. Eric C. Lincoln, *Race, Religion, and the Continuing American Dilemma* (New York: Hill and Wang, 1999), 236.

49. I was told by a church board member that Trinity Baptist Church and other churches like it are often included on New York City Tour stops and are frequented by predominantly white tourists hoping to have an "authentic black church experience."

50. Trinity Baptist Church is predominantly African American, with a few white parishioners. The congregation is working middle class, with more female than male
members and a large elderly population. The church, founded in 1795, has about
three hundred members.

51. Caroline A. Streeter, "Ambiguous Bodies: Locating Black/White Women in
Cultural Representations," in *The Multiracial Experience: Racial Borders as the
New Frontier,* ed. M.P.P. Root (Thousand Oaks, CA: Sage Publications, 1996),
312–313.

52. Davis, *Women, Race, and Class*; Collins, *Black Feminist Thought*; hooks, *Ain't I
a Woman*; idem, *Reel to Real*; idem, *Feminist Theory*; Smith, *Not Just Race*; Williams, *The Alchemy of Race and Rights*; Williams, "Alchemical Notes"; Patricia
Williams, *Seeing a Color-Blind Future: The Paradox of Race* (New York: Noonday, 1998); Wing and Merchan, "Rape, Ethnicity and Culture."

53. Collins, *Black Sexualities*; idem, *Black Feminist Thought*.

54. The "loss" no longer involves a lynching or death, but symbolically the black
man is seen as leaving the black community.

55. Dalmage, *Tripping on the Color Line*; Rosenblatt, Karis, and Powell, *Multiracial Couples*.

CHAPTER 4   *Families and the Color Line*

1. J. Hartigan, "Locating White Detroit," in *Displacing Whiteness: Essays in Social and Cultural Criticism,* ed. Ruth Frankenberg (Durham: Duke University
Press, 1997), 184.

2. During the focus group, it was difficult to get the white respondents to discuss
the issues. Based on the group's limited responses and body language, it seemed
that they were either not interested or uncomfortable with the topic of interracial relationships.

3. Nina Eliasoph, "'Everyday Racism' in a Culture of Political Avoidance: Civil
Society, Speech, and Taboo," *Social Problems* 46 (1999).

4. Among the community respondents, only Karen disagreed with what the rest of
the group was saying. She agreed that "kids don't see color unless they are taught
it," mentioning how her daughter finds "all guys" attractive, which is okay with
her.

5. Patricia J. Williams, *Seeing a Color-Blind Future: The Paradox of Race* (New
York: Noonday, 1998).

6. Charles Gallagher, "White Construction in the University," *Socialist Review* 24
(1995). Eduardo Bonilla-Silva, *Racism without Racists* (Lanham, MD: Rowman
& Littlefield, 2003).

7. Heather Dalmage, *Tripping on the Color Line: Black-White Multiracial Families in a Racially Divided World* (New Brunswick, NJ: Rutgers University Press,
2000); Paul C. Rosenblatt, Teri Karis, and Richard D. Powell, *Multiracial
Couples: Black and White Voices* (Thousand Oaks, CA: Sage Publications, 1995).

8. Mary Waters, "Multiple Ethnic Identity Choices," in *Beyond Pluralism: The Conception of Group and Group Identities in America,* ed. Wendy Katkin, Ned
Landsman, and Andrea Tyree (Urbana: University of Illinois Press, 1998), 43.

9. Michael Omi and Howard Winant, *Racial Formation in the United States from the 1960s to the 1980s* (New York: Routledge, 1994), 3.

10. Patricia Hill Collins, *Black Feminist Thought* (New York: Routledge, 2000); James F. Davis, *Who Is Black: One Nation's Definition* (University Park: Pennsylvania State University Press, 1991).

11. Davis, *Who Is Black,* 138–139.

12. Even academic studies on biracial children tend to focus on the problems they encounter, often identifying biracial individuals from psychiatric or counseling centers and focusing on their identity development. Ursula Brown, "Black/White Interracial Young Adult: Quest for a Racial Identity," *American Journal of Orthopsychiatry* 65 (1995); Jewelle Taylor Gibbs, "Identity and Marginality: Issues in the Treatment of Biracial Adolescents," *American Journal of Orthopsychiatry* 57 (1987); M. R. Lyles, A. Yancey, C. Grace, and J. H. Carter, "Racial Identity and Self-esteem: Problems Peculiar to Biracial Children," *Journal of the American Academy of Child and Adolescent Psychiatry* 24 (1985).

13. Davis, *Who Is Black*; Paul R. Spickard, *Mixed Blood: Intermarriage and Ethnic Identity in Twentieth-Century America* (Madison: University of Wisconsin Press, 1989).

14. Ruth Frankenberg, ed., *Displacing Whiteness: Essays in Social and Cultural Criticism* (Durham: Duke University Press, 1997), 126.

15. Collins, *Black Feminist Thought,* 165.

16. For an excellent discussion of this issue, see Kerry Ann Rockquemore's forthcoming book with AltaMira Press.

17. Frankenberg, *Displacing Whiteness*, 97.

18. A number of studies have findings that support the existence of this strong white familial opposition. In a recent study on "white racism" by Joe Feagin and Hernan Vera, a white upper-middle-class businessman was asked how he would feel if his adult child dated a black person: "I'd be sick to my stomach. I would feel like I probably failed as a father, if that was to happen. . . . It would truly be a problem in my family because I could never handle that, and I don't know what would happen, because I couldn't ever handle that, ever." Joe R. Feagin and Hernan Vera, *White Racism: The Basics* (New York: Routledge, 1995), 149. Though his reply is more strongly stated than those of most whites, "his views are in line with the interracial dating and marriage views expressed by many whites." Joe R. Feagin, *Racist America* (New York: Routledge, 2000), 131.

19. Frankenberg, *Displacing Whiteness*.

20. Erving Goffman, *Stigma: Notes on the Management of Spoiled Identity* (Englewood Cliffs, NJ: Prentice-Hall, 1963), 4.

CHAPTER 5   *Racialized Spaces*

1. Today college campuses are more diverse than ever. However, the definition of diversity varies, and what constitutes diversity among the students is not widely agreed upon. Some have even argued that "the rhetoric of diversity (and all the time we spend on it) is avoidance behavior, that it hides the realities of inequities in education and helps us evade the hard work necessary to overcome those

inequities." D. Humphreys, "Campus Diversity and Student Self-Segregation: Separating Myths from Facts," *Leadersguide*, http://www.diversityweb.org/ Leadersguide/SED/studeseg.html (accessed April 7, 2002).

2. "Love and Race," *New York Times*, December 2002, sec. A33. In "Color Blind Love," *Time*, May 12, 2003, Tim Padgett and Frank Sikora report that "young people . . . are even more color-blind than their elders when it comes to matters of the heart."

3. Eduardo Bonilla-Silva and Tyrone A. Forman, " 'I Am Not a Racist, but . . . ': Mapping White College Students' Racial Ideology in the U.S.A.," *Discourse and Society* 11 (2000): 50–85; Charles A. Gallagher, "White Construction in the University," *Socialist Review* 24 (1995): 165–187.

4. There is little agreement about the extent to which colleges and universities have been able to achieve such levels of social diversity. The debate continues regarding the reality of self-segregation on campuses. While some emphasize the success of diversity within racially diverse student bodies, others point to "reports of increasingly tense racial climates and racial self-segregation among students." A. L. Antonio, "Racial Diversity and Friendship Groups in College: What the Research Tells Us," *Diversity Digest,* http://www.diversityweb.org/Leadersguide/ SED/studeseg.html (accessed April 20, 2002). R. Buttny, "Discursive Constructions of Racial Boundaries and Self Segregation on Campus," *Journal of Language and Social Psychology* 18 (1999).

5. Bonilla-Silva and Forman, " 'I Am Not a Racist, but . . . '"; Gallagher, "White Construction in the University"; Beverly Daniel Tatum, *"Why Are All the Black Kids Sitting Together in the Cafeteria?" and Other Conversations about Race* (New York: Basic Books, 1997).

6. At each university, the administrators I spoke to identified themselves as African Americans. The names of the universities and administrators have been changed.

7. "Black Ink," http://www.unc.edu/black_ink (accessed January 22, 2004).

8. Eduardo Bonilla-Silva and Rogelio Saenz, " 'If Two People Are in Love . . . ': Color Blind Dreams, (White) Color-Coded Reality among White College Students in the U.S.A." Unpublished manuscript (2000), 20.

9. Nelson Rodriguez, "Emptying the Content of Whiteness," in *White Reign: Deploying Whiteness in America,* ed. Joel L. Kincheloe, Shirley R. Steinberg, Nelson Rodriguez, and Ronald Chennault (New York: St. Martin's Press, 1998), 31–62.

10. Bonilla-Silva and Saenz, " 'If Two People Are in Love,'" 27.

11. Ibid., 19.

12. Kai Erikson, "Notes on the Sociology of Deviance," in *The Other Side: Perspectives on Deviance,* ed. Howard Becker (New York: Free Press, 1964), 14.

13. Elizabeth Abel, Barbara Christian, and Helen Moglen, *Female Subjects in Black and White: Race, Psychoanalysis, and Feminism* (Berkeley: University of California Press, 1997), 15; Abby Ferber, *White Man Falling: Race, Gender and White Supremacy* (Maryland: Rowman & Littlefield, 1998).

14. Peter L. Berger and Hansfried Kellner, "Marriage and the Construction of Reality," in *Social Interaction: Introductory Readings in Sociology,* ed. H. Robboy, S. Greenblatt, and C. Clark (New York: St. Martin's Press, 1979), 308–322.

15. Ibid.
16. Ibid.
17. Rebecca Gardyn, "Love Is Colorblind . . . or Is It?" *American Demographics* 22 (2000): 11–12.
18. Other movies that appealed to teens, such as *Swordfish, Mission: Impossible 2,* and *Die Another Day,* also featured a storyline that involved an interracial romance.
19. According to the Internet Movie Database (www.imdb.com), the producer, Joel Silver, cut out an onscreen kiss to keep the relationship platonic.

CHAPTER 6   *Black_White.com*

1. David Silver, "Looking Backwards, Looking Forwards: Cyberculture Studies, 1990–2000," in *Web Studies: Rewriting Media Studies for the Digital Age,* ed. D. Gauntlett (London: Arnold, 2000), 19–30.
2. David L. Altheide, *Qualitative Media Analysis* (Thousand Oaks, CA: Sage Publications, 1996).
3. I chose to put pornographic Web sites and dating sites together in one category even though there are obvious differences because both types of sites represent individuals seeking an interracial encounter, whether they want to date interracially or watch explicit interracial sex.
4. Drawing from the methods of ethnographic content analysis that argues the researcher should "interact" with the materials they are studying in order to understand the social context, I have monitored the Web sites for four years and have visited them weekly from September 2001 to March 2003. Also, I sat in on listserv, group e-mail lists, and chat rooms to get an "inside" sense of these sites, including the dating sites. I have spent over fifty hours analyzing the information contained on these Web sites in an effort to critically discuss the meaning or significance of these sites and, more important, the discourses and imagery that are commonly used. Since discourse analysis is interpretative and explanatory, there are always multiple interpretations and explanations depending on the reader (or user); therefore, extensive quotations and examples from the Web sites are used to support the arguments. Altheide, *Qualitative Media Analysis.*
5. Based on information from search engines and my review of various categories of Web sites, I chose to analyze The Multiracial Activist and Interracial Voice, which are among the largest and most prominently featured. More important, they are exclusively cyberspace communities. The Association of Multi-Ethnic Americans (AMEA) and Project Race also receive a large number of visitors, but they are attached to organizations founded and built outside of cyberspace; therefore, I chose not to include them.
6. According to the MSN rating of direct hits to multiracial Web sites, TMA is the most frequently visited "multiracial" site.
7. Currently, TMA identifies itself as "an activist journal covering social and civil liberties issues of interest to individuals who perceive themselves to be 'biracial' or 'multiracial,' 'interracial' couples/families and 'transracial' adoptees." All quotations, unless otherwise identified, are taken directly from the Web site.

8. Benedict Anderson, *Imagined Communities: Reflections on the Origin and Spread of Nationalism* (New York: Verso, 1991), 6.
9. Landrith, personal e-mail to the author, 2002.
10. TMA prominently features certain sites if they link to TMA.
11. A Google search for "interracial sex" generated 618,000 returns; "black-white sex," 34,700. On Yahoo!, "interracial sex" generated 384,000 returns.
12. Midnight X Illustrated Bookstore, http://www.midnightx.com.
13. These search results were received on January 22, 2004; the results and the order in which they are listed can change.
14. Don Black, "White Nationalist Resource Page," http://www.stormfront.org.
15. These sites cannot be found with an Internet search of "interracial," but they can be found with search words like "white power" or "white supremacy."
16. These are the membership rules for the National Alliance, at www.natvan.com, but they are similar to other groups' rules.
17. War on Race, http:// www.resist.com/war_on_race/part3.htm.
18. Abby Ferber, *White Man Falling: Race, Gender, and White Supremacy* (Maryland: Rowman & Littlefield, 1998), 5.
19. The National Alliance.
20. War on Race.
21. Ferber, *White Man Falling*.
22. http://www.natvan.com/national-vanguard/117/racemix.html.

CHAPTER 7   *Listening to the Interracial Canary*

1. Rachel Moran, *Interracial Intimacy: The Regulation of Race and Romance* (Chicago: University of Chicago Press, 2001), 194.
2. Lani Guinier and Gerald Torres, *The Miner's Canary: Enlisting Race, Resisting Power, Transforming Power* (Cambridge: Harvard University Press, 2002), 9–10.
3. Eduardo Bonilla-Silva, *Racism without Racists* (Lanham, MD: Rowman & Littlefield, 2003), 181.
4. Ibid.
5. Nina Eliasoph, "'Everyday Racism' in a Culture of Political Avoidance: Civil Society, Speech, and Taboo," *Social Problems* 46 (1999): 479–502.
6. Bonilla-Silva, *Racism without Racists*; Feagin, *Racist America*; and Guinier and Torres, *The Miner's Canary*.
7. Elijah Anderson discusses the concept of a deficit in a talk he gave at the 2003 University of Pennsylvania conference on ethnography, which will be detailed in his next book.
8. Michael Omi and Howard Winant, *Racial Formation in the United States from the 1960s to the 1980s* (New York: Routledge, 1994).
9. Mary Waters, "Multiple Ethnic Identity Choices," in *Beyond Pluralism: The Conception of Group and Group Identities in America*, ed. Wendy Katkin, Ned Landsman, and Andrea Tyree (Urbana: University of Illinois Press, 1998), 43.
10. Heather Dalmage, *Tripping on the Color Line: Black-White Multiracial Families in a Racially Divided World* (New Brunswick, NJ: Rutgers University Press,

2000); Maureen Reddy, *Crossing the Color Line: Race, Parenting and Culture* (New Brunswick, NJ: Rutgers University Press, 1994).

11. Kerry Ann Rockquemore and David Brunsma, *Beyond Black: Biracial Identity in America* (Thousand Oaks, CA: Sage Publications, 2002); Heather Dalmage, *The Politics of Multiracialism: Challenging Racial Thinking* (Albany: State University of New York Press, 2004).

12. Guinier and Torres, *The Miner's Canary*, 7.

13. Ibid., 9

14. Bonilla-Silva, *Racism without Racists.*

15. Guinier and Torres, *The Miner's Canary*, 15.

BIBLIOGRAPHY

Abel, Elizabeth, Barbara Christian, and Helene Moglen. *Female Subjects in Black and White: Race, Psychoanalysis, and Feminism.* Berkeley: University of California Press, 1997.

Agger, Ben. 1992. *Cultural Studies as Critical Theory.* Bristol, PA: Falmer.

Aguire, Adalberto. "Academic Storytelling: A Critical Race Theory Story of Affirmative Action." *Sociological Perspectives* 43 (2000): 319–339.

Altheide, David. "Identity and the Definition of the Situation in a Mass-Mediated Context." *Symbolic Interaction* 23 (2000): 1–27.

———. *Qualitative Media Analysis.* Thousand Oaks, CA: Sage Publications, 1996.

Ames, Christopher. "Restoring the Black Man's Lethal Weapon: Race and Sexuality in Contemporary Cop Films." *Journal of Popular Film and Television* (1992): 52–60.

Anderson, Benedict. *Imagined Communities: Reflections on the Origin and Spread of Nationalism.* New York: Verso, 1991.

Antonio, A. L. "Racial Diversity and Friendship Groups in College: What Research Tells Us," *Diversity Digest,* http://www.diversityweb.org/Digest/Sm99/research.html.

Ausdale, Deborah Van, and Joe R. Feagin. "The Use of Racial and Ethnic Concepts by Very Young Children." *American Sociological Review* 61 (1996): 779–793.

Austin, J. L. *How to Do Things with Words.* Oxford: Oxford University Press, 1965.

Ballagh, James C. *A History of Slavery in Virginia.* Baltimore, MD: Johns Hopkins University Press, 1968.

Barbour, Rosaline, and Jenny Kitzinger. *Developing Focus Group Research: Politics, Theory, and Practice.* Thousand Oaks, CA: Sage Publications, 1999.

Bardaglio, Peter. "Midnight Miscegenation: Bulworth Reinforces Rather than Undercuts Certain Racial Stereotypes about White Men and Black Women." *Sun* (June 7, 1998).

Barnett, Larry D. "Interracial Marriage in California." *Marriage and Family Living* (1963): 424–427.

Barron, Milton L. *People Who Intermarry.* Syracuse, NY: Syracuse University Press, 1946.

Becker, Howard S. *Outsiders: Studies in the Sociology of Deviance.* New York: Free Press, 1963.

Bennett, Lerone. *Before the Mayflower: A History of Black America.* New York: Penguin Books, 1984.

Berger, Peter L., and Hansfried Kellner. "Marriage and the Construction of Reality." In *Social Interaction: Introductory Readings in Sociology,* ed. H. Robboy, S. Greenblatt, and C. Clark, 308–322. New York: St. Martin's Press, 1979.

Berger, Peter, and Thomas Luckmann. *The Social Construction of Reality: A Treatise in the Sociology of Knowledge.* Garden City, NY: Doubleday, 1966.

Bernard, Jessie. "Marital Stability and Patterns of Status Variables." *Journal of Marriage and the Family* 28 (1996): 421–439.

———. "Note on Educational Homogamy in Negro-White and White-Negro Marriages." *Journal of Marriage and the Family* 28 (1966): 24–27.

Biegel, H. G. "Problems and Motives in Interracial Relationships." *Journal of Sex Research* 2 (1966): 185–205.

Billingsley, Andrew. "Black and White Together: Trends in Interracial Marriage." In *Climbing Jacob's Ladder,* 245–261. New York: Simon and Schuster, 1992.

Blau, Peter, Terry Blum, and Joseph Schwartz. "Heterogeneity and Intermarriage." *American Sociological Review* 47 (1982): 45–62.

Blum, Terry. "Racial Inequality and Salience: An Examination of Blau's Theory of Social Structure." *Social Forces* 62 (1984): 607–617.

Blumer, Herber. "Race Prejudice as a Sense of Group Position." *Pacific Sociological Review* 1 (1958): 3–7.

———. *Symbolic Interaction: Perspective and Method.* Englewood Cliffs, NJ: Prentice-Hall, 1969.

Bobo, Lawrence, and Ryan Smith. "From Jim Crow Racism to Laissez-Faire Racism: The Transformation of Racial Attitudes." In *Beyond Pluralism: The Conception of Group and Group Identities in America,* ed. Wendy Katkin, Ned Landsman, and Andrea Tyree, 182–220. Urbana: University of Illinois Press, 1998.

Bonilla-Silva, Eduardo. *Racism without Racists.* Lanham, MD: Rowman & Littlefield, 2003.

Bonilla-Silva, Eduardo, and Tyrone A. Forman. "'I Am Not a Racist but . . .': Mapping White College Students' Racial Ideology in the U.S.A." *Discourse and Society* 11 (2000): 50–85.

Bonilla-Silva, Eduardo, and Rogelio Saenz. "'If Two People Are in Love . . .': Color-Blind Dreams, (White) Color-Coded Reality among White College Students in the USA." Unpublished manuscript.

Bossard, James H. S. "Nationality and Nativity as Factors in Marriage." *American Sociological Review* 4 (1939): 792–798.

Branker, Saad. "Black in White Film." www.iconn.ca/zone451/issue07/verticals/saada.html.

Bratter, Jennifer. "Where Is the Love? Black-White Couple Residence in Metropolitan Areas in 1980 and 1990." Paper presented at the 95th American Sociological Association Annual Meeting, 2000.

Brayboy, Thomas L. "Interracial Sexuality as an Expression of Neurotic Conflict." *Journal of Sex Research* 2 (1966): 179–184.

Brown, John A. "Casework Contacts with Black-White Couples." *Social Casework* 68 (1987): 24–29.

Brown, Ursula. "Black/White Interracial Young Adult: Quest for a Racial Identity." *American Journal of Orthopsychiatry* 65 (1995): 125–130.

Brown, Yasim A., and Anne Montague. *The Colour of Love: Mixed Race Relationships*. London: Virago, 1992.

Burma, John H. "Research Note on the Measurement of Interracial Marriage." *American Journal of Sociology* 57 (1952): 587–589.

Butler, Judith. "Endangered/Endangering: Schematic Racism and White Paranoia." In *Reading Rodney King, Reading Urban Uprising*, ed. Robert Gooding-Williams, 15–22. New York: Routledge, 1993.

———. *Excitable Speech: A Politics of the Performative*. New York: Routledge, 1997.

———. "Passing, Queering: Nella Larsen's Psychoanalytic Challenge." In *Female Subjects in Black and White: Race, Psychoanalysis, Feminism*, ed. Elizabeth Abel, Barbara Christian, and Helene Moglen, 266–284. Berkeley: University of California Press, 1997.

Buttny, R. "Discursive Constructions of Racial Boundaries and Self-Segregation on Campus." *Journal of Language and Social Psychology* 18 (1999): 247.

Cardullo, Bert. "Law of the Jungle." *Hudson Review* 44 (1992): 639–647.

Carr, Leslie. *"Color-Blind" Racism*. Thousand Oaks, CA: Sage, 1997.

Carter, Stephen. *Reflections of an Affirmative Action Baby*. New York: Basic Books, 1991.

Chase, Susan. "Taking Narrative Seriously: Consequences for Method and Theory in Interview Studies." In *Interpreting Experience: The Narrative Study of Lives*, ed. Ruth Josselson and Amia Lieblich, 1–26. Thousand Oaks, CA: Sage Publications, 1995.

Clemson, Lynette. "Love without Borders." *Newsweek,* September 19, 2000.

Clinard, Marshall, and Robert Meier. *Sociology of Deviant Behavior.* New York: Harcourt Brace, 1989.

Cohen, Phil. "Laboring under Whiteness." In *Displacing Whiteness: Essays in Social and Cultural Criticism,* ed. Ruth Frankenberg, 244–282. Durham, NC: Duke University Press, 1997.

Collins, Patricia Hill. *Black Feminist Thought*. New York: Routledge, 2000.

———. *Politics: African Americans, Gender, and the New Racism*. New York: Routledge, 2004.

Cooley, Charles Horton. *Human Nature and the Social Order.* New York: Charles Scribner's Sons, 1922.

Cose, Ellis. *Color-Blind: Seeing Beyond Race in a Race-Obsessed World.* New York: HarperCollins Publishers, 1997.

Cretser, Gary A., and Joseph J. Leon. "Intermarriage in the U.S.: An Overview of Theory and Research." *Marriage and Family Review* 5 (1982): 3–15.

Crohn, Joel. *Mixed Matches: How to Create Successful Interracial, Interethnic, and Interfaith Relationships*. New York: Fawcett Columbine, 1995.

Cross, Theodore. *Black Power Imperative: Racial Inequality and the Politics of Nonviolence*. New York: Faulkner, 1984.

Dalmage, Heather. *The Politics of Multiracialism: Challenging Racial Thinking*. Albany: State University of New York Press, 2004.

——. *Tripping on the Color Line: Black-White Multiracial Families in a Racially Divided World*. New Brunswick, NJ: Rutgers University Press, 2000.

Davidson, Jeanette R. "Theories about Black-White Interracial Marriage: A Clinical Perspective." *Journal of Multicultural Counseling and Development* (1992): 150–157.

Davis, Angela Y. *Women, Race and Class*. New York: Vintage Books, 1981.

Davis, F. James. *Who Is Black: One Nation's Definition*. University Park: Pennsylvania State University Press, 1991.

Davis, James A., and Tom W. Smith. *General Social Surveys, 1972–1990*. Chicago: National Opinion Research Center, 1991.

Davis, Kingsley. "Intermarriage in Caste Societies." *American Anthropologist* 43 (1941): 376–395.

Delgado, Richard. *Critical Race Theory*. Philadelphia: Temple University Press, 1995.

D'Emilio, John, and Estelle Freedman. *Intimate Matters: A History of Sexuality in America*. New York: Harper & Row, 1998.

Denzin, Norman K. *The Cinematic Society: The Voyeur's Gaze*. Thousand Oaks, CA: Sage Publications, 1995.

——. *Images of Postmodern Society: Social Theory and Contemporary Cinema*. London: Sage Publications, 1991.

Denzin, Norman K., and Yvonne Lincoln. *Handbook of Qualitative Research*. Thousand Oaks, CA: Sage Publications, 2000.

Dickson, Lynda. "The Future of Marriage and Family in Black America." *Journal of Black Studies* 23 (1993): 472–491.

Du Bois, W.E.B. *The Souls of Black Folk*. 1903. New York: Bantam, 1989.

Durkheim, Emile. *The Rules of Sociological Method*. New York: Free Press, 1982.

Dyson, Michael Eric. *Between God and Gangsta Rap*. New York: Oxford University Press, 1996.

——. *Race Rules: Navigating the Color Line*. Reading, MA: Addison-Wesley, 1997.

Eliasoph, Nina. "'Everyday Racism' in a Culture of Political Avoidance: Civil Society, Speech, and Taboo." *Social Problems* 46 (1999): 479–502.

Ellis, Carolyn, and Arthur Bochner. *Composing Ethnography: Alternative Forms of Qualitative Writing*. Thousand Oaks, CA: Sage Publications, 1996.

Ellis, Carolyn, and Michael Flaherty. *Investigating Subjectivity: Research on Lived Experience*. Thousand Oaks, CA: Sage Publications, 1992.

Erikson, Kai. "Notes on the Sociology of Deviance." In *The Other Side: Perspectives on Deviance*, ed. Howard Becker, 9–21. New York: Free Press, 1964.

Essed, Philomena. *Understanding Everyday Racism*. Newbury Park, CA: Sage Publications, 1991.

Fanon, Frantz. *Black Skin, White Masks*. London: Paladin, 1968.

Feagin, Joe R. *Racist America*. New York: Routledge, 2000.

Feagin, Joe R., and Clairece Booher Feagin. "The Continuing Significance of Race: Antiblack Discrimination in Public Places." *American Sociological Review* 56 (1991): 101–116.

Feagin, Joe R., and Hernan Vera. *White Racism: The Basics*. New York: Routledge, 1995.

Ferber, Abby. "Exploring the Social Construction of Race." In *American Mixed Race: The Culture of Microdiversity,* ed. Naomi Zack, 155–168. Maryland: Rowman & Littlefield, 1995.

———. *White Man Falling: Race, Gender and White Supremacy.* Maryland: Rowman & Littlefield, 1998.

Fine, Mary Jane. "Love Is Color-Blind: NYC's Biracial Couples Understand the True Meaning of Diversity." *New York Daily News,* September 29, 2000.

Foucault, Michel. *The History of Sexuality: An Introduction.* New York: Vintage Books, 1990.

Frankenberg, Ruth. *Displacing Whiteness: Essays in Social and Cultural Criticism.* Durham, NC: Duke University Press, 1997.

———. *White Women, Race Matters: The Social Construction of Whiteness.* Minneapolis: University of Minnesota Press, 1993.

Friedman, Lester. *Unspeakable Images: Ethnicity and the American Cinema.* Urbana: University of Illinois Press, 1991.

Gadberry, James H., and Richard A. Dodder. "Educational Homogamy in Interracial Marriages: An Update." *Journal of Social Behavior and Personality* (1993): 155–163.

Gaines, Jane. "White Privilege and Looking Relations: Race and Gender in Feminist Film Theory." *Cultural Critique* 4 (1986): 59–81.

Gaines, Stanley, Diana Rios, Cherlyn Granrose, and Katrina Bledsoe. "Romanticism and Interpersonal Resource Exchange among African American–Anglo and Other Interracial Couples." *Journal of Black Psychology* 25 (1999): 461–489.

Gallagher, Charles A. "White Construction in the University." *Socialist Review* 24 (1995): 165–187.

Gardyn, Rebecca. "Love Is Colorblind . . . or Is It?" *American Demographics* 22 (2000): 11–12.

Gaspar, David Barry, and Darlene Clark Hine. *More Than Chattel: Black Women in Slavery in the Americas.* Bloomington: Indiana University Press, 1996.

Gayles, Gloria Wade. *Rooted against the Wind: Personal Essays.* New York: HarperCollins, 1996.

Gibbs, Jewelle Taylor. "Identity and Marginality: Issues in the Treatment of Biracial Adolescents." *American Journal of Orthopsychiatry* 57 (1987): 265–278.

Giddings, Paula. *When and Where I Enter: The Impact of Black Women on Race and Sex in America.* New York: Quill William Morrow, 1984.

Goffman, Erving. *Forms of Talk.* Philadelphia: University of Pennsylvania Press, 1981.

———. *Stigma: Notes on the Management of Spoiled Identity.* Englewood Cliffs, NJ: Prentice-Hall, 1963.

Goldberg, David Theo. *Racial Subjects: Writing on Race in America.* New York: Routledge, 1997.

Golden, Joseph. "Facilitating Factors in Negro-White Intermarriage." *Phylon* 20 (1959): 273–284.

Gooding-Williams, Robert. *Reading Rodney King, Reading Urban Uprising.* New York: Routledge, 1993.

Gordon, Milton. *Assimilation in American Life: The Role of Race, Religion and National Origins.* New York: Oxford University Press, 1964.

Graham, Lawrence Otis. *Member of the Club: Reflections on Life in a Racially Polarized World.* New York: HarperCollins, 1995.

Grier, William H., and Price M. Cobbs. *Black Rage.* New York: Basic Books, 1968.

Guerrero, Ed. *Framing Blackness: The African-American Image in Film.* Philadelphia: Temple University Press, 1993.

———. "Spike Lee and the Fever in the Racial Jungle." In *Film Theory Goes to the Movies*, ed. Jim Collins, 170–188. New York: Routledge, 1992.

Guinier, Lani, and Gerald Torres. *The Miner's Canary: Enlisting Race, Resisting Power, Transforming Power.* Cambridge: Harvard University Press, 2003.

Gurak, Douglas T., and Mary M. Kritz. "Intermarriage Patterns in the U.S.: Maximizing Information from the U.S. Census Public Use Samples." *Public Data Use* 6 (1978): 33–43.

Hall, Stuart. "Encoding/Decoding." In *Culture, Media, Language*, ed. Stuart Hall, 128–138. London: University of Birmingham, 1980.

———. "Ethnicity, Identity and Difference." *Radical America* 23 (1991): 9–20.

Haney-Lopez, Ian F. "The Social Construction of Race." In *Critical Race Theory*, ed. Richard Delgado, 191–203. Philadelphia: Temple University Press, 1995.

———. *White by Law: The Legal Construction of Race.* New York: New York University Press, 1996.

Harre, R., and G. Gillett. *The Discursive Mind.* Thousand Oaks, CA: Sage Publications, 1994.

Harris, William A. "Cultural Engineering and the Films of Spike Lee." In *Mediated Messages and African-American Culture: Contemporary Issues*, ed. Venise T. Berry and Carmen L. Manning-Miller, 3–23. Thousand Oaks, CA: Sage Publications, 1996.

Hartigan, J. "Locating White Detroit." In *Displacing Whiteness: Essays in Social and Cultural Criticism*, ed. Ruth Frankenberg, 180–213. Durham, NC: Duke University Press, 1997.

Heaton, Tim, and Cardell Jacobson. "Intergroup Marriage: An Examination of Opportunity Structures." *Sociological Inquiry* 70 (2000): 30–41.

Heer, David M. "Negro-White Marriage in the United States." *Journal of Marriage and the Family* (1966): 262–273.

———. "The Prevalence of Black-White Marriage in the United States, 1960 and 1970." *Journal of Marriage and the Family* 36 (1974): 246–258.

Hernton, Calvin C. *Sex and Racism in America.* New York: Anchor Books, 1988.

Hill, Mike. *Whiteness: A Critical Reader.* New York: New York University Press, 1977.

Hill, Miriam, and Volker Thomas. "Strategies for Racial Identity Development: Narratives of Black and White Women in Interracial Partner Relationships." *Family Relations* 49 (2000): 193–200.

Ho, M. K. *Intermarried Couples in Therapy.* Springfield, IL: Thomas, 1990.

Hoberman, John. *Darwin's Athletes: How Sport Has Damaged Black America and Preserved the Myth of Race.* Boston: Houghton Mifflin, 1997.

hooks, bell. *Ain't I a Woman: Black Women and Feminism.* Boston: South End Press, 1981.

———. *Black Looks: Race and Representation.* Boston: South End Press, 1992.

———. *Feminist Theory: From Margin to Center.* Boston: South End Press, 2000.

————. *Reel to Real: Race Sex and Class at the Movies*. New York: Routledge, 1996.

Hughes, Zondra. "Why Some Brothers Only Date Whites and 'Others.'" *Ebony*, January 2003.

Hull, Gloria, Barbara Smith, and Patricia Bell Scott. *All the Women Are White, All the Blacks Are Men, but Some of Us Are Brave: Black Women's Studies*. Old Westbury, NY: Feminist Press, 1982.

Humphreys, D. "Campus Diversity and Self-Segregation: Separating Myths from Facts." *Leadersguide*, http://www.Diversityweb.org/Leadersguide/SED/stueseg.html.

Ibraham, F. A., and D. G. Schroeder. "Cross-Cultural Couples Counseling: A Developmental Psychoeducational Intervention." *Journal of Comparative Family Studies* 21 (1990): 193–205.

Janusonis, Michael. "Solid Performance Is Bright Spot in 'Cruel Intentions.'" *Providence Journal Bulletin,* March 5, 1999, E3.

Johnson, Jacqueline, Sharon Rush, and Joe Feagin. "Doing Antiracism and Making a Nonracist Society." *Contemporary Sociology* 29 (2000).

Johnson, Walter R., and Michael Warren. *Inside the Mixed Marriage: Accounts of Changing Attitudes, Patterns, and Perceptions of Cross-Cultural and Interracial Marriages*. Lanham, MD: University Press of America, 1994.

Jones, Hettie. *How I Became Hettie Jones*. New York: Dutton, 1990.

Jones, Lisa. *Bulletproof Diva: Tales of Race, Sex and Hair*. New York: Anchor Books, 1995.

Josselson, Ruth, and Amia Lieblich. *Interpreting Experience: The Narrative Study of Lives*. Thousand Oaks, CA: Sage Publications, 1995.

Kaeser, Gigi, and Peggy Gillespie. *Of Many Colors: Portraits of Multiracial Families*. Amherst: University of Massachusetts Press, 1997.

Kallen, Horace. *Culture and Democracy in America*. New York: Boni and Liveright, 1924.

Kalmijin, Matthijs. "Trends in Black/White Intermarriage." *Social Forces* 72 (1993): 119–146.

Karis, Teri. "Racial Identity Constructions of White Women in Heterosexual Black-White Interracial Relationships." Ph.D. diss., University of Minnesota, 2000.

Kellner, Douglas. *Media Culture: Cultural Studies, Identity and Politics between the Modern and the Postmodern*. New York: Routledge, 1995.

Kennedy, Randall. *Interracial Intimacies: Sex, Marriage, Identity, and Adoption*. New York: Pantheon Books, 2003.

Kincheloe, Joel L., Nelson Rodriguez, Shirley R. Steinberg, and Ronald Chennault. *White Reign: Deploying Whiteness in America*. New York: St. Martin's Press, 2000.

Koch, Larry W. "Interracial Rape: Examining the Increasing Frequency Argument." *American Sociologist* 26 (1995): 76–86.

Korgen, Kathleen Odell. *From Black to Biracial: Transforming Racial Identity among Americans*. Westport, CT: Praeger, 1998.

Kouri, Kristyan M., and Marcia Lasswell. "Black-White Marriages: Social Change and Intergenerational Mobility." *Marriage and Family Review* 19 (1993): 241–255.

LaFree, Gary D. "Male Power and Female Victimization: Toward a Theory of Inter-racial Rape." *American Journal of Sociology* 88 (1982): 311–328.

Lazarre, Jane. *Beyond the Whiteness of Whiteness: Memoirs of a White Mother of Black Sons.* Durham, NC: Duke University Press, 1996.

LeBeau, James L. "Is Interracial Rape Different?" *Sociology and Social Research* 73 (1988): 43–46.

Lewis, Amanda. *Race in the Schoolyard.* New Brunswick, NJ: Rutgers University Press, 2003.

———. "Some Are More Equal Than Others: Whiteness and Colorblind Ideology at the Dawn of the Twenty-first Century." Paper presented at the 95th American Sociological Association Annual Meetings, 2000.

Lewis, Richard, George Yancey, and Siri Bletzer. "Racial and Nonracial Factors That Influence Spouse Choice in Black-White Marriages." *Journal of Black Studies* 28 (1997): 60–78.

Lincoln, C. Eric. *Race, Religion, and the Continuing American Dilemma.* New York: Hill and Wang, 1999.

Locke, Alain LeRoy. *Race Contacts and Interracial Relations: Lectures on the Theory and Practice of Race.* Washington D.C.: Howard University Press, 1992.

Luke, Carmen. "White Women in Interracial Families: Reflections on Hybridization, Feminine Identities and Racialized Othering." *Feminist Issues* (1994): 49–72.

Luke, Carmen, and A. Luke. "Interracial Families: Difference within Difference." *Ethnic and Racial Studies* 21 (1998): 728–754.

Lyles, M. R., A. Yancey, C. Grace, and J. H. Carter. "Racial Identity and Self-Esteem: Problems Peculiar to Biracial Children." *Journal of the American Academy of Child and Adolescent Psychiatry* 24 (1985): 150–153.

Lyman, Stanford M. *Postmodernism and a Sociology of the Absurd and Other Essays on the "Nouvelle Vague" in American Social Science.* Fayetteville: University of Arkansas Press, 1997.

Macpherson, David A., and James B. Stewart. "Racial Differences in Married Female Labor Force Participation Behavior: An Analysis Using Interracial Marriages." *Review of Black Political Economy* (1992): 59–68.

Mahoney, Dennis. "Pastor Shuts Door on Interracial Couple." *Columbus Dispatch,* July 8, 2000.

Maines, David, and Jeffrey Bridger. "Narratives, Community and Land Use Decisions." *Social Science Journal* 29 (1992): 363–380.

Marchetti, Gina. "Ethnicity, the Cinema, and Cultural Studies." In *Unspeakable Images: Ethnicity and the American Cinema,* ed. Lester D. Friedman, 277–307. Urbana: University of Illinois Press, 1991.

Martin, J. N., T. Nakayama, R. Krizek, and L. Bradford. "What Do White People Want to Be Called? A Study of Self-Labels for White Americans." In *Whiteness: The Communication of Social Identity,* ed. T. Nakayama and J. Martin, 27–50. Thousand Oaks, CA: Sage Publications, 1998.

Mathabane, Mark, and Gail Mathabane. *Love in Black and White: The Triumph of Love Over Prejudice and Taboo.* New York: Harper Collins, 1992.

McBride, James. *The Color of Water: A Black Man's Tribute to His White Mother.* New York: Riverhead, 1996.

McCarthy, E. Doyle. "The Interactionist Theory of Mind: A Sociology of Social Objects." *Studies in Symbolic Interaction* (1989).

———. *Knowledge as Culture: The New Sociology of Knowledge.* London: Routledge, 1996.

McDowell, Sophia F. "Black-White Intermarriage in the United States." *International Journal of Sociology of the Family* 1 (1971): 49–58.

McNamara, Robert P., Maria Tempenis, and Beth Walton. *Crossing the Line: Interracial Couples in the South.* Westport, CT: Praeger, 1999.

Mead, George Herbert. *Mind, Self, and Society.* Chicago: University of Chicago Press, 1934.

Merton, Robert K. "Intermarriage and Social Structure: Fact and Theory." *Psychiatry* 4 (1941): 361–374.

Monahan, Thomas P. "Are Interracial Marriages Really Less Stable?" *Social Forces* 48 (1970): 461–473.

———. "Interracial Marriage in a Southern Area: Maryland, Virginia, and the District of Columbia." *Journal of Comparative Family Studies* 8 (1977): 217–239.

———. "Interracial Marriage in the United States: Some Data on Upstate New York." *International Journal of Sociology of the Family* 1 (1971): 94–105.

———. "Interracial Parentage as Revealed by Birth Records in the United States, 1970." *Journal of Comparative Family Studies* 8 (1977): 65–76.

———. "Marriage Across Racial Lines in Indiana." *Journal of Marriage and the Family* (1973): 632–639.

———. "The Occupational Class of Couples Entering into Interracial Marriages." *Journal of Comparative Family Studies* 7 (1976): 175–189.

———. "An Overview of Statistics on Interracial Marriage in the United States, with Data on Its Extent from 1963–1970." *Journal of Marriage and the Family* (1976): 223–231.

Moran, Rachel. *Interracial Intimacy: The Regulation of Race and Romance.* Chicago: University of Chicago Press, 2001.

Morgan, David. *Focus Groups as Qualitative Research.* Thousand Oaks, CA: Sage Publications, 1997.

Morris, Aldon D. *The Origins of the Civil Rights Movement: Black Communities Organizing for Change.* New York: Free Press, 1984.

Morrison, Toni. *The Bluest Eye.* New York: Pocket Books, 1972.

———. *Playing in the Dark: Whiteness and the Literary Imagination.* Cambridge: Harvard University Press, 1992

Mulvey, Laura. "Visual Pleasure and Narrative Cinema." *Screen* 16 (1975): 6–18.

Mumford, Kevin. *Interzones: Black/White Sex Districts in Chicago and New York in the Early Twentieth Century.* New York: Columbia University Press, 1997.

Myrdal, Gunner. *An American Dilemma.* New York: Harper & Row, 1965.

Nakayama, Thomas K., and Judith N. Martin. *Whiteness: The Communication of Social Identity.* Thousand Oaks, CA: Sage Publications, 1998.

Nicholson, Daniel R. "Developing a Media Literacy of Whiteness in Advertising." In *White Reign: Deploying Whiteness in America*, ed. Joe L. Kincheloe, Shirley Steinberg, Nelson Rodriguez, and Ronald Chennault, 193–212. New York: St. Martin's Press, 1998.

Olick, Jeffrey, and Daniel Levy. "Collective Memory and Cultural Constraint: Holocaust Myth and Rationality in German Politics." *American Sociological Review* 62 (1997): 921–936.

Omi, Michael, and Winant, Howard. *Racial Formation in the United States from the 1960s to the 1980s*. New York: Routledge, 1994.

Padgett, Tim, and Frank Sikora. "Color-Blind Love." *Time Magazine*, May 12, 2003.

Park, Robert E. *Race and Culture*. New York: Free Press, 1964.

Park, Robert E., and E. W. Burgess. *Introduction to the Science of Sociology*. Chicago: University of Chicago Press, 1921.

"Pastor Bans Interracial Marriage." *Washington Post*, July 10, 2000.

Patton, Michael. *Qualitative Evaluations and Research Methods*. Thousand Oaks, CA: Sage, 1990.

Pavela, Todd H. "An Exploratory Study of Negro-White Intermarriage in Indiana." *Journal of Marriage and the Family* 26 (1964): 209–211.

Perinbanayagam, R. S. *Signifying Acts*. Carbondale: Southern Illinois University Press, 1985.

Porterfield, Ernest. "Black-American Intermarriage in the United States." *Marriage and Family Review* 5 (1982): 17–34.

———. *Black and White Mixed Marriages: An Ethnographic Study*. Englewood Cliff, NJ: Prentice-Hall, 1978.

Reddy, Maureen. *Crossing the Color Line: Race, Parenting and Culture*. New Brunswick, NJ: Rutgers University Press, 1994.

———. *Everyday Acts against Racism: Raising Children in a Multicultural World*. Seattle: Seal Press, 1996.

Richardson, Laurel. "Postmodern Social Theory: Representational Practices." *Sociological Theory* 9 (1991): 173–179.

Rockquemore, Kerry Ann, and David Brunsma. *Beyond Black: Biracial Identity in America*. Thousand Oaks, CA: Sage Publications, 2002.

Rodriguez, Nelson. "Emptying the Content of Whiteness." In *White Reign: Deploying Whiteness in America*, ed. Joel L. Kincheloe, Shirley R. Steinberg, Nelson Rodriguez, and Ronald Chennault, 31–62. New York: St. Martin's, 1998.

Roediger, David R. *Black on White: Black Writers on What It Means to Be White*. New York: Schocken, 1998.

Romano, Renee. *Race Mixing: Black-White Marriage in Postwar America*. Cambridge: Harvard University Press, 2003.

Root, Maria P. P. *"Love's Revolution": Interracial Marriage*. Philadelphia: Temple University Press, 2001.

Rosenblatt, Paul C, Teri Karis, and Richard D. Powell. *Multiracial Couples: Black and White Voices*. Thousand Oaks, CA: Sage Publications, 1995.

Russell, Kathy, and Midge Wilson. *Divided Sisters: Bridging the Gap between Black Women and White Women*. New York: Anchor Books/Doubleday, 1996.

Russell, Margaret M. "Race and the Dominant Gaze: Narratives of Law and Inequality in Popular Film." In *Critical Race Theory: The Cutting Edge*, ed. Richard Delgado, 56–63. Philadelphia: Temple University Press, 1995.

Rytina, Steven, Peter Blau, Terry Blum, and Joseph Schwartz. "Inequality and

Intermarriage: A Paradox of Motive and Constraint." *Social Forces* 66 (1998): 645–675.

Schlesinger, Arthur. *A Thousand Days*. Boston: Houghton Mifflin, 1965.

Schoen, Robert. "The Widening Gap between Black and White Marriage Rates: Context and Implications." In *The Decline in Marriage among African-Americans: Causes, Consequences, and Policy Implications*, ed. M. Belinda Tucker and Claudia Mitchell-Kernan, 103–111. New York: Russell Sage Foundation, 1995.

Schulman, G. I. "Race, Sex, and Violence: A Laboratory Test of the Sexual Threat of the Black Male Hypothesis." *American Journal of Sociology* 79 (1974): 1260–1277.

Schuman, Howard, Charlotte Steeth, and Lawrence Bobo. *Racial Attitudes in America: Trends and Interpretations*. Cambridge: Harvard University Press, 1988.

Sears, David. "Symbolic Racism." In *Eliminating Racism*, ed. Phyllis Katz and Dalmas Taylor, 53–84. New York: Plenum Press, 1988.

See, L.A.L. "Tensions between Black Women and White Women: A Study." *Affilia* 4 (1989): 31–45.

Silver, David. "Looking Backwards, Looking Forwards: Cyberculture Studies, 1990–2000." In *Web Studies: Rewiring Media Studies for the Digital Age*, ed. D. Gauntlett, 19–30. London: Arnold, 2000.

Smith, Valerie. *Not Just Race, Not Just Gender: Black Feminist Readings*. New York: Routledge, 1998.

———. *Representing Blackness: Issues in Film and Video*. New Brunswick, NJ: Rutgers University Press, 1997.

Spickard, Paul R. *Mixed Blood: Intermarriage and Ethnic Identity in Twentieth-Century America*. Madison: University of Wisconsin Press, 1989.

"Spike Lee Falls Out with Jazzman Bill Lee over Mixed Marriage." *Jet*, May 16, 1994.

Stam, Robert. "Bakhtin, Polyphony, and Ethnic/Racial Representation." In *Unspeakable Images: Ethnicity and the American Cinema*, ed. Lester D. Friedman, 251–276. Urbana: University of Illinois Press, 1991.

Stanfield, John H., and Rutledge M. Dennis. *Race and Ethnicity in Research Methods*. Thousand Oaks, CA: Sage Publications, 1993.

Staples, Robert. "Interracial Relationships: A Convergence of Desire and Opportunity." In *The Black Family*, ed. Robert Staples, 129–136. Belmont, CA: Wadsworth, 1999.

Stephan, Walter G., and Cookie White Stephan. "Intermarriage: Effects on Personality, Adjustment and Intergroup Relations in Two Samples of Students." *Journal of Marriage and the Family* (1991): 241–250.

Streeter, Caroline A. "Ambiguous Bodies: Locating Black/White Women in Cultural Representations." In *The Multiracial Experience: Racial Borders as the New Frontier*, ed. M.P.P. Root, 305–320. Thousand Oaks, CA: Sage, 1996.

Takaki, Ronald. *A Different Mirror: A History of Multicultural America*. Boston: Little, Brown, 1993.

Tatum, Beverly Daniel. *"Why Are All the Black Kids Sitting Together in the Cafeteria?" and Other Conversations about Race*. New York: Basic Books, 1997.

Taylor, Charles. "The Politics of Recognition." In *Multiculturalism and the Politics of Recognition*, ed. Amy Gutmann, Steven C. Rockefeller, Michael Walzer, and Susan Wolf, 25–74. Princeton, NJ: Princeton University Press, 1994.

———. "Black and White and Taboo All Over." *Salon*, http://www.salon.com/ent/feature/2000/02/14/interracial_movies/.

Thomas, W. I. "On the Definition of the Situation." In *Sociology: The Classic Statements*, ed. M. Truzzi, 274–277. New York: Random House, 1971.

Thornton, Michael, Robert J. Taylor, and Tony N. Brown. "Correlates of Label Use among Americans of African Descent: Colored, Negro, Black, and African American." *Race and Society* 2 (1999): 149–164.

Todd, Judith. "Attitudes toward Interracial Dating: Effects of Age, Sex, and Race." *Journal of Multicultural Counseling and Development* (1992): 202–208.

Tucker, Belinda, and Claudia Mitchell-Kernan. "New Trends in Black American Interracial Marriage: The Social Structural Context." *Journal of Marriage and the Family* 52 (1990): 209–218.

Ture, Kwame, and Charles V. Hamilton. *Black Power: The Politics of Liberation in America*. New York: Vintage Books, 1992.

U.S. House. Committee on Government Reform and Oversight, Subcommittee on Government Management, Information and Technology. *Federal Measures of Race and Ethnicity and the Implications for the 2000 Census: Hearings before the Subcommittee on Government Management Information and Technology of the Committee on Government Reform and Oversight,* House of Representatives, 105th Cong., 1st sess., April 23, May 22, and July 25, 1997. Washington, D.C.: GPO, 1998.

Vera, Hernan, and Andrew Gordon. *Screen Savers: Hollywood Fictions of Whiteness*. Lanham, MD: Rowman & Littlefield, 2003.

Wade-Gayles, Gloria Jean. *Rooted against the Wind: Personal Essays*. Boston: Beacon Press, 1996.

Ware, Vron. *Beyond the Pale: White Women, Racism and History*. New York: Verso, 1992.

Wartenberg, Thomas E. *Unlikely Couples: Movie Romance as Social Criticism*. Boulder, CO: Westview Press, 1999.

Washington, Denzel. Interview in *George*, December/January 2000.

Waters, Mary. "Multiple Ethnic Identity Choices." In *Beyond Pluralism: The Conception of Group and Group Identities in America*, ed. Wendy Katkin, Ned Landsman, and Andrea Tyree, 28–46. Urbana: University of Illinois Press, 1998.

Weber, Max. "Membership of a Race." *Max Weber: Selections in Translation*. Ed. W. G. Runciman. Cambridge: Cambridge University Press, 1977.

Wells, Ida B. *On Lynchings: Southern Horrors, a Red Record, Mob Rule in New Orleans*. New York: Arno, 1969.

———. *Race Matters*. New York: Vintage, 1994.

Wiegman, Robyn. "Black Bodies/American Commodities: Gender, Race and the Bourgeois Ideal in Contemporary Film." In *Unspeakable Images: Ethnicity and the American Cinema*, ed. Lester D. Friedman, 308–328. Urbana: University of Illinois Press, 1991.

Wilbanks, William. "Is Violent Crime Intraracial?" *Crime and Delinquency* 31 (1985): 117–128.

"Wild Will Smith on the 'Race Thing.'" *Providence Journal Bulletin*, July 3, 1999.

Williams, Patricia. "Alchemical Notes: Reconstructing Ideals from Deconstructed Rights." In *Critical Race Theory*, ed. Richard Delgado, 84–94. Philadelphia: Temple University Press, 1995.

———. *The Alchemy of Race and Rights*. Cambridge: Harvard University Press, 1991.

———. *Seeing a Color-Blind Future: The Paradox of Race*. New York: Noonday, 1998.

Wilson, Janelle. "Lost in the Fifties: A Study of Collected Memories." In *The Narrative Study of Lives*, ed. A. Lieblich and Ruth Josselson, 147–181. Thousand Oaks, CA: Sage, 1997.

Wing, Adrien Katherine, and Sylke Merchán. "Rape, Ethnicity and Culture: Spirit Injury from Bosnia to Black America." In *Critical Race Theory*, ed. Richard Delgado, 516–528. Philadelphia: Temple University Press, 1995.

Winokur, Mark. "Black Is White/White Is Black: 'Passing' as a Strategy of Racial Compatibility in Contemporary Hollywood Comedy." In *Unspeakable Images: Ethnicity and the American Cinema*, ed. Lester D. Friedman, 190–211. Urbana: University of Illinois Press, 1991.

Younge, Gary. "Why Love Is Never Blind." *Guardian*, March 29, 1999.

Zack, Naomi. *American Mixed Race: The Culture of Microdiversity*. Lanham, MD: Rowman & Littlefield, 1995.

Zavarzadeh, Mas'ud. *Seeing Film Politically*. Albany: State University of New York Press, 1991.

INDEX

ABOUT THE AUTHOR

Erica Chito Childs is an assistant professor of sociology at Eastern Connecticut State University. She received her Ph.D. in sociology from Fordham University in 2001. Her areas of research are race and ethnic relations, multiracial issues, and media/popular culture images. She currently lives in Rhode Island with her two children, Christopher and Jada.